Lecture Notes in Computer Science 14003

Founding Editors

Gerhard Goos
Juris Hartmanis

Editorial Board Members

The series Lecture Notes in Computer Science (LNCS), including its subseries Lecture Notes in Artificial Intelligence (LNAI) and Lecture Notes in Bioinformatics (LNBI), has established itself as a medium for the publication of new developments in computer science and information technology research, teaching, and education.

LNCS enjoys close cooperation with the computer science R & D community, the series counts many renowned academics among its volume editors and paper authors, and collaborates with prestigious societies. Its mission is to serve this international community by providing an invaluable service, mainly focused on the publication of conference and workshop proceedings and postproceedings. LNCS commenced publication in 1973.

Daniela Genova · Jarkko Kari

Editors

Unconventional Computation and Natural Computation

20th International Conference, UCNC 2023
Jacksonville, FL, USA, March 13–17, 2023
Proceedings

 Springer

Editors
Daniela Genova ⓘD
University of North Florida
Jacksonville, FL, USA

Jarkko Kari ⓘD
University of Turku
Turku, Finland

ISSN 0302-9743   ISSN 1611-3349 (electronic)
Lecture Notes in Computer Science
ISBN 978-3-031-34033-8   ISBN 978-3-031-34034-5 (eBook)
https://doi.org/10.1007/978-3-031-34034-5

Preface

The 20th International Conference on Unconventional Computation and Natural Computation (UCNC 2023) was held at the University of North Florida, Jacksonville, Florida, USA on March 13–17, 2023. This was the second UCNC conference since the beginning of the global covid-19 pandemic. The conference was organized as a hybrid event with some scientists taking part virtually online. (See http://ucnc2023.domains.unf.edu/)

This 20th edition of the conference series is dedicated to Professor Cristian Calude in recognition of his founding and further developing of this conference series. The first conference took place in Auckland, New Zealand in 1998, where he is currently Chair Professor of Computer Science at the University of Auckland. He was also UCNC Steering Committee Chair and Co-chair for a long time, during which time he contributed enormously to shaping and developing the conference series. The UCNC community is deeply grateful to Professor Calude for his guidance and influence through the years.

The UCNC series of international conferences is a forum bringing together scientists from many different backgrounds who are united in their interest in novel forms of computation, human-designed computation inspired by nature, and computational aspects of natural processes. The 20th conference of the series continued the tradition of focusing on current important theoretical and experimental results. Typical, but not exclusive, UCNC topics of interest include amorphous computing, cellular automata, chaos and dynamical systems-based computing, cellular, chemical, evolutionary, bacterial, molecular, neural and optical computing, collision-based computing, quantum computing, DNA computing, membrane computing, material computing and programmable matter, super-Turing computation, swarm intelligence, and other nature-inspired algorithms.

The *G. Rozenberg Natural Computing Award* was established in 2023 to recognize outstanding achievements in the field of natural computing. The award is named after Professor Grzegorz Rozenberg to acknowledge his distinguished scientific achievements in many areas of science, including natural computing, as well as his crucial role in developing the UCNC conference series. Professor Rozenberg also invented the name and defined the scope of the natural computing area and continues to serve as Chair Emeritus of the UCNC Steering Committee.

This annual award will be presented at the Unconventional Computation and Natural Computation conference. The recipient of the award will be invited to give the award lecture in the given year. The UCNC Awards Committee selected Professor Jarkko Kari from the Department of Mathematics and Statistics, the University of Turku, Finland, to be the recipient of the inaugural award in 2023 (UCNC 20). He was recognized for his contributions to cellular automata and dynamical systems.

The program committee of UCNC 2023 reviewed 24 full paper submissions, of which 13 were selected for presentation at the conference and a publication in these proceedings. In addition, the conference program included a poster session, an invited tutorial by Ion Petre (University of Turku, Finland) and five invited plenary talks by Thomas Bäck (Leiden University, The Netherlands), Eric Goles (University of Chile, Chile), Christine

E. Heitsch (Georgia Institute of Technology, USA), Lila Kari (University of Waterloo, Canada), and Yukiko Yamauchi (Kyushu University, Japan).

Co-located workshops are essential elements of UCNC conferences. This time there were three such workshops: *The Fourth International Workshop on Theoretical and Experimental Material Computing (TEMC 2023)*, organized by Susan Stepney (University of York, UK), *The Third International Workshop on Reaction Systems (WRS 2023)*, organized by Daniela Genova (University of North Florida, USA), and *The Workshop on Quantum Computing*, organized by Mika Hirvensalo (University of Turku, Finland).

We warmly thank the invited speakers and the workshop organizers, all the authors of the contributed papers and posters, as well as the speakers of the workshops. We are also grateful to the members of the program committee and the external reviewers for their invaluable help in reviewing the submissions and selecting the papers to be presented at the conference. We thank the organizing committee of UCNC 2023 for their tireless help in taking care of all the numerous details in organizing the event. The conference would not have happened without the active support of the University of North Florida and Provost and Vice President for Academic and Student Affairs Karen B. Patterson; The College of Computing, Engineering, and Construction Management and Dean William Klostermeyer; The College of Arts and Sciences and Dean Kaveri Sabrahmanyam; The Department of Mathematics and Statistics and Chair Richard F. Patterson; the School of Computing and Director Sherif Elfayoumy, and IEEE. Finally, we thank the EasyChair conference system, and the LNCS team at Springer for helping in the process of making these proceedings.

March 2023   Daniela Genova
                                                                                      Jarkko Kari

Organization

Steering Committee

Thomas Bäck	Leiden University, The Netherlands
Cristian S. Calude (Founding Chair)	University of Auckland, New Zealand
Enrico Formenti (Co-chair)	Université Côte d'Azur, France
Lov K. Grover	Bell Labs, USA
Mika Hirvensalo (Co-chair)	University of Turku, Finland
Natasha Jonoska	University of South Florida, USA
Jarkko Kari	University of Turku, Finland
Lila Kari	University of Waterloo, Canada
Seth Lloyd	Massachusetts Institute of Technology, USA
Giancarlo Mauri	Università degli Studi di Milano-Bicocca, Italy
Gheorghe Păun	Institute of Mathematics of the Romanian Academy, Romania
Grzegorz Rozenberg (Emeritus Chair)	Leiden University, The Netherlands
Arto Salomaa	University of Turku, Finland
Shinnosuke Seki (Co-chair)	University of Electro-Communications, Japan
Tommaso Toffoli	Boston University, USA
Carme Torras	Institute of Robotics and Industrial Informatics, Spain
Jan van Leeuwen	Utrecht University, The Netherlands

Program Committee

Selim Akl	Queens University, Canada
Cristian S. Calude	The University of Auckland, New Zealand
Matteo Cavaliere	Manchester Metropolitan University, UK
Ho-Lin Chen	National Taiwan University, Taiwan
Jérôme Durand-Lose	Université d'Orléans, France
Enrico Formenti	Université Côte d'Azur, France
Giuditta Franco	University of Verona, Italy
Daniela Genova (Co-chair)	University of North Florida, USA
Yo-Sub Han	Yonsei University, South Korea
Mika Hirvensalo	University of Turku, Finland

Hendrik Jan Hoogeboom — Leiden University, The Netherlands
Jarkko Kari (Co-chair) — University of Turku, Finland
Jongmin Kim — Harvard University, USA
Jetty Kleijn — Leiden University, The Netherlands
Kalpana Mahalingam — Indian Institute of Technology Madras, India
Ian McQuillan — University of Saskatchewan, Canada
Pekka Orponen — Aalto University, Finland
Matthew Patitz — University of Arkansas, USA
Zornitza Prodanoff — University of North Florida, USA
Christian Scheideler — University of Paderborn, Germany
Shinnosuke Seki — University of Electro-Communications, Japan
Susan Stepney — University of York, UK
Gunnart Tufte — Norwegian University of Science and Technology, Norway
Giovanni Viglietta — Japan Advanced Institute of Science and Technology, Japan

Organizing Committee

Brendan Chamberlain
Donn Christy
Ryan Farrell
Daniela Genova (Co-chair)
Furio Gerwitz
Hemani Kaushal

Nazmul Kazi
Rhys Jones
Troy Kidd
Zornitza Prodanoff (Co-chair)
Dylan Strickley

Additional Reviewers

Alastair Abbott
Olivier Bournez
Douglas Cenzer
Hyunjoon Cheon
Penn Faulkner Rainford
David Griffin
Daniel Hader

Adam Kohan
David Liedtke
Luca Manzoni
Andreas Padalkin
Sara Riva
Daniel Warner

Abstracts of Invited Talks

On the Automatic Optimization of Problem-Specific Optimization Heuristics Gleaned from Nature

Thomas Bäck

Leiden Institute of Advanced Computer Science (LIACS),
Leiden University, The Netherlands

Abstract. For decades, researchers have been looking at paradigms gleaned from nature as inspiration for problem solving approaches, for example in the domain of optimization. There are many classes of such algorithms, including for example evolutionary algorithms, particle swarms, differential evolution, ant colony optimization, and the number of proposed variants of them is quite large. This makes it hard to keep track of the variants and their respective strengths, and even more so it creates a difficult situation for non-experts who are interested in selecting the best algorithm for their real-world application problem.

In this presentation, I propose the idea to automatically optimize the optimization heuristic. This task can be approached as an algorithm configuration problem, for which I will present some examples illustrating that this task can be handled by direct global optimization algorithms – in other words, by "automatically optimizing the optimization algorithm". I will give an example how a combinatorial design space of 4608 configuration variants of evolution strategies can be searched, and how the results can be analyzed using data mining. This approach provides an opportunity for discovering the unexplored areas of the optimization algorithm design space. Extensions towards other algorithm design spaces such as particle swarm optimization and differential evolution are then outlined, too.

In the second part of the presentation, I will discuss a range of real-world engineering design applications, for which such an approach could truly provide a competitive advantage. In such cases, optimizing the optimization algorithm requires a proper definition of the problem class, for which the optimization is executed. For the example of automotive crash optimization problems, I will present first results demonstrating that these problems differ a lot from the classical benchmark test function sets used by the academic community, and present an automated approach to find test functions that properly represent the real-world problem. First results on the performance gain that can be achieved by optimizing the optimization algorithm on such real-world problems are also presented.

Unconventional Cellular Automata Models

Eric Goles

Facultad de Ingeniería y Ciencias, Universidad Adolfo Ibáñez, Chile
eric.chacc@uai.cl

Abstract. We will present two unconventional models related to automata networks. The fungal automaton (inspired by the exchange of information in a species of fungi) and a majority consensus algorithm (MCA) based on the majority function over bidimensional lattices. A fungal automaton consists of a d-dimensional cellular automaton such that, according to a certain protocol, at each update the state information of some neighbors may or not be considered. As an example of the complexity of these dynamics, we will study the computational complexity of the classical chip firing game (if the number of tokens in a site is bigger than the neighborhood cardinality, one token is given to each neighbor) on a two-dimensional lattice. We prove that there exists a vicinity such that by opening or closing the connection with some neighbors it is possible to simulate any Boolean circuit (P-completeness) and therefore, this model is capable of simulating a computer (Turing universality). Regarding the consensus search algorithm, we will consider the procedure on a two-dimensional network with Moore's neighborhood (the eight nearest neighbors) and binary opinions $\{0, 1\}$ over each node. The MCA algorithm is as follows: consider an arbitrary node and k neighbors, $2 \leq k \leq 8$, inside the Moore neighborhood. Over those sites, apply the majority operator (the new state will be the most represented in the neighborhood and in the case of a tie, leave it unchanged). A consensus opinion is one in which a fixed point with all the vertices in the same state is reached. We will characterize Moore sub-neighborhoods such that the MCA algorithm over its associated grid converges to the fixed points 0^* or 1^*.

Keywords: Cellular automata · Chip firing game · Majority networks

References

Goles, E., Tsompanas, M.-A., Adamatzky, A., Tegelaar, M., Wosten, H.A.B., Martínez, G.J.: Computational universality of fungal sandpile automata, Phys. Lett. A 384, 126541 (2020)

Modanese, A., Worsch, T.: Embedding arbitrary Boolean Circuits into fungal automata, Karlsruhe Institute of Technology (KIT), Karlsruhe, Germany (2022). arXiv:2208.08779

Sepúlveda, C., Goles, E., Ríos-Wilson, M., Adamatzky, A.: Exploring the dynamics of fungal cellular Automata, Int. J. Unconventional Comput. **18**(2–3), 15–144 (2023)

Goles, E., Medina, P., Montealegre, P., Santivañez, J.: Majority networks and consensus dynamics, Chaos, Solitons and Fractals, 112697

Distributed Computation by Mobile Robots

Yukiko Yamauchi

Kyushu University, 744 Motooka, Nishi-ku, Fukuoka 819-0395, Japan
yamauchi@inf.kyushu-u.ac.jp

Abstract. As mobile computing entities, such as wheeled robots, legged robots, and modular robots become easily programmable and widely available, distributed computation by mobile computing entities attracts much attention. Its applications include drones, molecular robots, swarm behaviors, and so on. In this talk, we will briefly survey distributed computation models for mobile computing entities. We then present existing results on the computational power of several models.

Distributed computing theory considers how to integrate small computations that collectively form the entire distributed system. Conventional computation models consider a network of computers, where each computing entity is equipped with its local memory and exchanges messages with other computing entities. In the past two decades, a variety of new computation models for mobile computing entities have been proposed; *autonomous mobile robots* [8], *metamorphic robotic systems* [4], *population protocols* [1], and *programmable particles* [2]. New distributed computing problems are introduced for these new models; gathering, shape formation, scattering, exploration, evacuation, and so on. To reveal the relation between the computational power of each computing entity and that of the entire distributed system, most existing results consider very weak mobile computing entities, that is, they are *anonymous* (indistinguishable), *oblivious* (memory-less), *asynchronous*, *uniform* (common computation rule), *silent* (communication-less), and *deterministic*. See the book [5] as a survey of results by 2019.

In this talk, we will first present results on the computational power of autonomous mobile robots, each of which can freely move in 2D (or 3D) continuous space. We will show the effect of obliviousness, synchrony, and symmetry of the robots on the shapes that the mobile robot system can form [6, 8, 10, 11].

Next, we will present computational power of a metamorphic robotic system (MRS) that consists of a set of autonomous modules. An MRS moves in the 2D square grid (or the 3D cubic grid) and each module autonomously performs sliding and rotation with keeping the connectivity of the entire MRS. These local moves generate global movement of the MRS. Each module is oblivious (i.e., state-less), but the shape of an MRS can be used as its memory. We will show that an MRS can use its shape as its memory by a necessary and sufficient number of modules for an MRS to solve the exploration problem and evacuation problem [3, 7, 9].

Keywords: Distributed computing · Mobile robots · Metamorphic robotic system

References

1. Angluin, D., Aspnes, J., Diamadi, Z., Fischer, M.J., Peralta, R.: Computation in networks of passively mobile finite-state sensors. In: Proceedings of the 23rd Annual ACM Symposium on Principles of Distributed Computing (PODC 2004), pp. 290–299 (2004). https://doi.org/10.1145/1011767.1011810
2. Derakhshandeh, Z., Dolev, S., Gmyr, R., Richa, A.W., Scheideler, C., Strothmann, T.: Brief announcement: amoebot – a new model for programmable matter. In: Proceedings of the 26th ACM Symposium on Parallelism in Algorithms and Architectures (SPAA 2014), pp. 220–222 (2014). https://doi.org/10.1145/2612669.2612712
3. Doi, K., Yamauchi, Y., Kijima, S., Yamashita, M.: Exploration of finite 2D square grid by a metamorphic robotic system. In: Proceedings of the 20th International Symposium on Stabilization, Safety, and Security of Distributed Systems (SSS 2018), pp. 96–110 (2018). https://doi.org/10.1007/978-3-030-03232-6_7
4. Dumitrescu, A., Suzuki, I., Yamashita, M.: Formations for fast locomotion of metamorphic robotic systems. Int. J. Robot. Res. **23**(6), 583–593 (2004). https://doi.org/10.1177/0278364904039652
5. Flocchini, P., Prencipe, G., Santoro, N. (eds.): Distributed computing by mobile entities: current research in moving and computing. LNCS, Springer (2019). https://doi.org/10.1007/978-3-030-11072-7
6. Fujinaga, N., Yamauchi, Y., Ono, H., Kijima, S., Yamashita, M.: Pattern formation by oblivious asynchronous mobile robots. SIAM J. Comput. **44**, 740–785 (2015). https://doi.org/10.1137/140958682
7. Nakamura, J., Kamei, S., Yamauchi, Y.: Evacuation from a finite 2D square grid field by a metamorphic robotic system. In: Proceedings of the 8th International Symposium on Computing and Networking (CANDAR 2020), pp. 69–78 (2020). https://doi.org/10.1109/CANDAR51075.2020.00016
8. Suzuki, I., Yamashita, M.: Distributed anonymous mobile robots: formation of geometric patterns. SIAM J. Comput. **28**(4), 1347–1363 (1999). https://doi.org/10.1137/S009753979628292X
9. Yamada, R., Yamauchi, Y.: Search by a metamorphic robotic system in a finite 3D cubic grid. In: Proceedings of the 1st Symposium on Algorithmic Foundations of Dynamic Networks, (SAND 2022), pp. 20:1–20:16 (2022). https://doi.org/10.4230/LIPIcs.SAND.2022.20
10. Yamashita, M., Suzuki, I.: Characterizing geometric patterns formable by oblivious anonymous mobile robots. Theor. Comput. Sci. **411**, 2433–2453 (2010). https://doi.org/10.1016/j.tcs.2010.01.037
11. Yamauchi, Y., Uehara, T., Kijima, S., Yamashita, M.: Plane formation by synchronous mobile robots in the three-dimensional Euclidean space. J. ACM **64**(3), 16:1–16:43 (2017). https://doi.org/10.1145/3060272

Tutorial for UCNC 2023

Reaction Systems: A Model of Computation Inspired by the Functioning of the Living Cell

Ion Petre[1,2]

[1] Department of Mathematics, University of Turku, Finland
ion.petre@utu.fi
[2] National Institute for R&D in Biological Sciences, Romania

Abstract. Reaction systems (RS) is a model of computation inspired by the functioning of the living cell. Its main focus is on reactions and facilitation/inhibition dynamical inter-play between reactions. A reaction is described through its reactants, its inhibitors, and its products. The products of a reaction may introduce inhibitors to another reaction, temporarily blocking its triggering. This leads to a novel way of describing dynamical systems that allows an explicit trace of *WHY* a certain property emerges in the system. It is a flexible model of computation that allows both a qualitative, as well as a quantitative view on a system, a set theoretical framework for computation, and the flexibility to model intricate biological behavior.

This tutorial offers a basic introduction to reaction systems, with no prerequisites needed except computational maturity. It introduces the basic notions of reaction systems and reviews a number of research directions motivated by biological considerations. We discuss some of the unique features of reaction systems: its explicit description of inhibition, its approach to competition for resources, its non-permanency philosophy, and the continuous interplay with the environment. We demonstrate the descriptive power of reaction systems through a number of examples, culminating in an RS-based model of the receptor tyrosine kinase signaling network in breast cancer.

Contents

An Investigation to Test Spectral Segments as Bacterial Biomarkers

Silvia Astorino[1], Vincenzo Bonnici[2], and Giuditta Franco[1(✉)]

[1] University of Verona, Strada le Grazie 15, 37134 Verona, Italy
silvia.astorino@studenti.univr.it, giuditta.franco@univr.it
[2] University of Parma, Parco Area delle Scienze, 7/A, 43124 Parma, Italy
vincenzo.bonnici@unipr.it
https://www.univr.it/, https://www.unipr.it/

Abstract. A dictionary-based bacterial genome analysis is performed, through specific k-long factors (called *res*) and their maximal right elongation along the genome (called *spectral segment*), in order to find discriminating biomarkers at the genus and species level. The aim is pursued through a k-mer-based approach previously introduced, here applied on genomes of different bacterial taxa. Intervals for values of k are identified to obtain meaningful genomic fragments, whose collection is a suitable representation to compare genomes according to informational indexes and Jaccard's similarity matrices. Corresponding dictionaries of k-mers are identified to discriminate bacterial genomes at genus and species level. This approach appears competitive in terms of performance (e.g., species discrimination) and size with respect to traditional barcoding methods.

Keywords: Barcoding · k-mers · right special factors · spectral segments

1 Introduction

Computational methodologies avoiding alignment of biological sequences constitute a relevant field of bioinformatics, including alignment-free methods [13,26], which show a considerable reduced computational cost with respect to alignment-based approaches. Alignment-free analysis is often based on dictionaries composed by relatively small words of the same length k, called k-mers, which are extracted from biological sequences [6,23,30]. Those methods find applicability in multiple contexts, such as genome assembly [7,8], genetic reconstruction [15,27,29] and DNA barcoding [10,12]. In particular, they allow handling large quantities of sequences in metagenomic studies [24], which characterize unknown taxa present in an environmental sample (or in a microbiome [28]).

In this paper we continue the investigation initiated in [4], where some informational concepts derived by the notion of k-spectrum applied to genomic k-mers were analyzed. Starting from the dictionary of the k-mers having the property

D. Genova and J. Kari (Eds.): UCNC 2023, LNCS 14003, pp. 1–16, 2023.
https://doi.org/10.1007/978-3-031-34034-5_1

to be followed by the same nucleotide in all their occurrences on the genome (we call RES_k these *Right-Extendable Sequences*, or simply RES when the role of k is obvious), spectral segments have been defined as the iterated $(k-1)$-long overlap concatenations of RES along the genome, maximally and uniquely right-elongated.

In this work we have extracted dictionaries of RES_k, called U_k, and corresponding dictionaries of spectral segments, called Sp_k, from several bacterial genomes downloaded from NCBI (details on the data set are reported in Sect. 2) in order to identify, if existing, a range of the values of k for which this dictionary-based genome representation is valid to classify biological sequences, according to their species or genus membership. We found out some ranges for values of k such that the knowledge of U_k and/or Sp_k would allow us to discriminate the presence or absence of one species or one genus in an unknown bacterial population of an environmental sample. Experimental results are reported in the following, together with interesting notes both on the overlapping of genes (or coding regions) with spectral segments and on the efficiency of the algorithm employed to extract such segments.

The state of the art for this work ranges in a wide variety of contexts. In combinatorics on words the notion of right special factors of a fixed length k has been investigated [1,9,16], where a substring u of a word w is special if there exist at least two occurrences of u in w followed on the right by two distinct letters (i.e., there exist at least two distinct letters a and b such that the strings va and vb are both factors of w). Such k-mers are exactly the non-RES words, because by definition RES words are followed on the right by one same character, in all their occurrences. In the literature of computational genomics, there are several examples of methods that extract genomic substrings, as unitigs [15,27] and omnitigs [25] already defined as discriminant for taxa, carriers of biological significance, and reliable fragments in the reconstruction of a genome. In this work, U_k and Sp_k dictionaries are tested and proposed to classify bacterial genomes, as an alternative to segments in the literature, and potentially to markers commonly used in the laboratory.

Our method could be a competitive solution for supervised machine learning methods, where the values of k use to range from 1 to 6. In [19,20] for example, authors implemented a machine learning approach for the recognition of specific classes of genomic sequences (mainly retrotransposons) based on 6-mers multiplicity. Our results indicate good performance in terms of the ability to discriminate between species (by not necessarily identifying them) in comparison to the use of short DNA sequences, for the purpose of species discrimination (previously coined as DNA barcoding).

A possible application of our approach is indeed DNA barcoding, where usually a single marker gene located on RNA (the 16S rRNA, that is, the coding gene for 16S ribosomal RNA) is employed to characterize bacteria, particularly in the human microbiota. However, traditional barcoding studies usually fail to reach the discrimination at the species level [28]. Metabarcoding is then a point of application of any technique for characterizing a species inside a sample, namely the representation of genomes by their U_k or Sp_k dictionaries.

This paper seeks for an interval of factor lengths that provides us with a distinctive information in terms of corresponding dictionaries (of spectral segments and of *RES*) of bacterial genomes. Moreover, spectral segments which discriminate species and genera turn out to overlap coding regions of bacterial genomes. We briefly describe the bacterial data set used in our experiments in Sect. 2. The methodology is illustrated in Fig. 1 and reported in Sect. 3 together with the software IGtools [3] employed for the analysis. Section 4 is focused on the discussion of achieved outcomes, while Sect. 5 concludes the paper with final remarks.

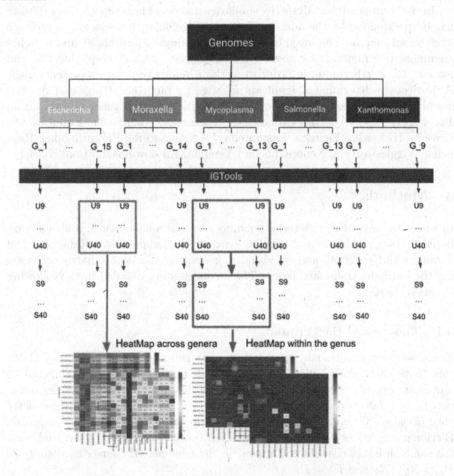

Fig. 1. A sketch of the computational analysis workflow. Dictionaries U_k and Sp_k (in this figure briefly Sk) have been computed by IGtools in the range $9 \leq k \leq 40$ for all the genomes. These are compared by similarity matrices (reported at the bottom), computed on couples of genomes either from two different genera (green square) or representing two different species within the same genus (red square). (Color figure online)

2 Dataset

As we may see in Fig. 1, genera of Escherichia, Moraxella, Mycoplasma, Salmonella and Xanthomonas have been chosen for the work, initially developed in the master thesis of the first author. Each genus collects a number of species, having in turn a few different organisms: in the figure we may distinguish 15 genomes of Escherichia (e.g., with 23 genomes of Escherichia Coli species), 14 genomes of Moraxella, 13 genomes of Mycoplasma and of Salmonella enterica, 9 genomes of Xanthomonas.

In the comparative analysis (by similarity matrices) here reported our dataset has been extended by the additional genus Shigella, with 6 species, in order to work on all genomes employed by the benchmarking *AFproject* [30] and by other alignment-free methods for genetic reconstruction, such as co-phylog [29] and Skmer [23]. Furthermore, in order to work on reference datasets present in the AFproject, to determine a significant k-range for our RES strings and spectral segments, we have extended the dataset with the following genera (having from 1 to 4 species): Citrobacter, Cronobacter, Dickerya, Edwardsiella, Enterobacter, Erwinia, Klebsiella, Pantoea, Pasteurella, Pectobacterium, Photorhabdus, Rahnella, Wigglesworthia, Xenophilus and Yersinia. All downloaded from NCBI.

3 Methods

In order to investigate bacterial genomes, by IGtools software [3,6] we computed statistical indices and specific genomic dictionaries, containing spectral segments and *RES* [4], and we visualize genome similarity by matrices reporting the normalized Jaccard index. These concepts are detailed in the following of this section.

3.1 Theoretical Background

Genomes are formalized by long strings over the alphabet $\Gamma = \{a, c, g, t\}$. In this framework, words, dictionaries and distributions are key instruments to represent genomes. Dictionary D_k collects all distinct k-mers of a string, and it may be split into two disjoint dictionaries: H_k the set of words appearing exactly once (*hapaxes* [6]) and R_k the set of words appearing more than once (*repeats*). Dictionary F_k collects forbidden k-mers, all those k-long words generated from the same alphabet that do not appear in the genome. Of course, by definition, $D_k = H_k \cup R_k$ and $\Gamma^k = D_k \cup F_k$.

A genome G is often represented by the distribution of k-mers within it. Among the others [11,17], here we recall the *k-spectrum distribution*, where each k-mer α of D_k is associated to its multiplicity $multG(\alpha)$ (i.e., the number of times it occurs in the genome). The k-spectrum of a genome G is defined as

$$Spec_k(G) = \{(\alpha, multG(\alpha)) | \alpha \in D_k\}.$$

Two k-mers of a couple (α, β) from $D_k \times D_k$ are k-concatenated if the $(k-1)$-length suffix of α equals the $(k-1)$-length prefix of β. Given $\alpha = x\gamma$ and $\beta = \gamma y$, where x and y belong to Γ, there is a right elongation of α by the symbol y, resulting in αy. If only one k-mer β elongates α along the genome, just one possible symbol y follows α and then the k-mer α is a RES (uniquely right-extendable string).

To assemble spectral segments, RES are iteratively concatenated, until more than one distinct k-mer of the spectrum competes for concatenation. In [4] some procedures were proposed to construct spectral segments, as words whose factors of length k are all RES, *each occurring at most as many times as it does on the genome* G. This constrain naturally reduces the number of different resulting spectral segments. However, it does not guarantee that they occur in the original genome.

A spectral segment is constructed by k-concatenation (that is, along with an overlap long $k - 1$) of RES_k (which are collected in the dictionary U_k). It is elongated to the right until there are no more distinct RES_k capable of doing so or the multiplicity of them runs out. Hence, spectral segments are defined as *maximally uniquely elongated strings from* RES_k. All these spectral segments of variable length are collected in Sp_k.

As final remarks, we may point out that RES is a stronger concept than hapax, and that the concept of k-spectrum is behind the construction of spectral segments. Indeed, an hapax is univocally elongated over the genome since it occurs once, while RES is elongated by the same symbol in its multiple occurrences, and spectral segments are constructed consistently to the multiplicity of each k-mer in the spectrum, by means of k-concatenation.

3.2   IGtool Software

The whole procedure of extraction of spectral segments and RES from a genome G has been executed by IGtools software [3]. Bacterial genomic strings are input to the software in the form of FASTA files. It outputs three different sources of information: statistical indices, RES dictionaries (U_k) and spectral segments dictionaries (Sp_k) for a value of k in the interval defined at the beginning. Namely, it calculates for each sequence eight indices: $|D_k|$, $|H_k|$, $|U_k|$, $|U_k|/|D_k|$, $coverage(U_k, G)$, the *number* of *spectral segments*, the *maximum length*, and the *mean length* among spectral segments.

It implements the procedure of *k-segmentation* explained in [4], which computes the U_k and Sp_k dictionaries through an array that represents the positions of each k-mer in the genome. Formally, a k-mer α from $D_k(G)$ is *univocally elongated* in G if $|\{\beta \in D_k(G) : \alpha[2...k] = \beta[1...k-1]\}| = 1$. The algorithm initializes all positions in the array A of the genome size as false. A position is set as true when the k-mer starting at the position is uniquely elongated to the right in G. As last step, the algorithm searches for consecutive true values in A to construct spectral segments.

Moreover, charts are provided on the *coverage*, that is, the percentage of true positions in the array after the k-segmentation, and the *ratio* $|Uk|/|Dk|$.

The cardinality of dictionaries Sp_k with the average and maximum length of their spectral segments are computed as well (see Table 1). IGtools in comparison with other algorithms for extracting substrings performs the analysis in competitive times. In particular, this observation holds by modifying the software to extract unitigs, being the segments on which most procedures are set. IGtools is here compared with the well-established tool Bifrost [15]. IGtools uses *suffix array SA* and *longest common prefix LCP data structures*, both constructed in linear time, and for this reason it can be set for unitigs extraction without an increase of computational cost. On the other hand, Bifrost constructs a de Bruijn graph to extract segments and relies on *Bloom filter (BF)* [2]. Figure 2 shows an example of unitigs computation by Bifrost and IGtools. Especially for $k < 20$, IGtools is particularly efficient. Considering the range $9 \leq k \leq 40$ on different bacterial genomes, IGtools takes between one-third and one-tenth of the time of Bifrost. Those times suggest that IGtools provides unitigs, and dictionaries in general, in the timeframe proposed for spectral segment extraction without being affected by the output dictionary size. Therefore, it allows to be used on a large number of sequences and for a wide range of k in reduced time and space.

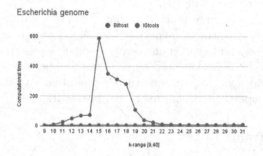

Fig. 2. Computation time on genomes from Escherichia genus. (Color figure online)

The indices computed by IGtools are displayed graphically, while the genome U_k-based and Sp_k-based similarity are retrieved by means of similarity matrices.

3.3 Graphical Tools

A similarity matrix is calculated for each value of k from 9 to 40, thus between specific dictionaries of k-mers. For each couple of genera, 31 similarity matrices exist (one for each value of k), and each matrix represents the U_k-based similarity for a defined k and any genomes pair (see green box in Fig. 1). Each matrix $m x n$ is composed of n rows and m columns, where n and m are the number of species among different genera. If the intersection is computed to compare species inside one genus we have that $m = n$. For example, in Fig 1, matrices on the left side have dimensions 15×14 while matrices on the rigth side are 13×13 squares.

In each cell (i.e., matrix component) the *Jaccard index* is reported, as a measure of the similarity between two sets. It is defined as the intersection size divided by the union size of the dictionaries A and B: $J(A, B) = |A \cap B|/|A \cup B|$. It is a percentage, that is a value between 0 and 1. As it may be deduced from the colour legend, in the matrices red color represents an higher value, while a lower one is identified by the green.

For Sp_k-based similarity within a genus, there are still 31 matrices for each genus (one for each k). Moreover, U_k and Sp_k similarities are calculated for genomes between genera, still through the construction of similarity matrices (see Fig. 1). The similarity matrices have different numbers of rows and columns, as they represent the sequences of two different genera. Since each species has in turn different genomes, for each value of k and any couple of species we have computed 10 matrices, each representing a possible combination of species, either of two genera or within a genus, among the different bacteria.

The purpose has been to demonstrate that RES sequences are significantly present within different genomes in the same species or genus, so that shared segments can identify and characterize sequences of the groups. The analysis starts by searching the similarity between genomes through U_k dictionaries.

Species discriminants identify subtrees of a phylogenetic tree. The phylogenetic trees, constructed by CVtree software [21], employ the distance $D(A, B) = \frac{1-C(A,B)}{2}$, where $C(A, B)$ is the correlation between two species A and B, and often identify genomes from the same family as being the closest. However, these may be not the closest according to the Jaccard coefficient, which is a more demanding string similarity measure.

4   Results

Through a graphical representation of the eight indices calculated by IGtools for k ranging in the interval $9 \leq k \leq 40$, the appropriate k range is defined to extract meaningful spectral segments and specific information on Sp_k and U_k.

4.1   Significant Intervals for Values of k

We studied statistical indices for U_k and Sp_k dictionaries to find a meaningful word length interval, if any, to obtain taxa classification. Indeed, index values and charts have shown likeness over the different bacterial genomes for the k-range equal to $10 \leq k \leq 18$. This information is valid only for bacteria domain. In fact, the study of indices on genomes of eukaryotes, such as Saccharomyces, Ostreococcus and Drosophila, showed that there are no domain-specific k-ranges. Possibly there is a relation of this interval with the genome size, since bacteria in the dataset report common domain genome length (200 000 bp–10 000 000 bp).

In Table 1 we may collect some observed regularities. Even if coverage varies among the organisms in the dataset, for $k = 13$ it reaches its maximum in all cases. The ratio U_k/D_k has been computed to see how different the two dictionaries are.

Only for $k = 17$ the ratio is over 0.90, while for the other values of k the two dictionaries carry different information, according to the (negative) correlation between D_k-based similarity and U_k-based similarity trends. Specifically, Pearson's correlation index has been calculated by a vector containing the U_k-based similarity of a pair of genomes and a vector containing the D_k-based similarity, for the same pair, with respect to the k variation. The two dictionaries lead to negatively correlated similarities for the genomes under investigation, hinting that the sets of RES_k carry more specific information than the sets $D_k(G)$.

We observed that $|Sp_k|$ has a fast increase for $9 \leq k \leq 13$ and an equally rapid decrease for $14 \leq k \leq 20$. It reaches the minimum values for $k > 20$. Mean and Max represent the k from which the values of mean and maximum length of spectral segments begin to increase. Indeed, maximum and average lengths remain low and constant in the interval $9 \leq k \leq 13/15$ (numerous relatively short segments). After $k = 13$ or $k = 15$, both indices increase until $k = 40$. Correspondingly, the cardinality of the Sp dictionary decreases generally under 3000 items, and the mean length of the segments does not grow fast. As a consequence, for $k > 20$, Sp_k dictionaries contain few and long segments, which are less remarkable for analysis.

Table 1. Mean log is the average (on sequences inside the genus) logarithmical genome size. For $k = 13$ a coverage close to 95% reaches its maximum. At $k = 17$ the *ratio* $|U_k|/|D_k|$ is over 0.90. Peak is the value of k at which the number of spectral segments is maximum, while Mean/Max are the values of k at which the mean/maximum length of spectral segments begin to increase.

Relevant values of k length for the informational indexes					
Genera	Mean log	Coverage (> 95%)	Ratio (>0.90)	Peak	Mean/Max
Escherichia	11	13	17	13	13/15
Moraxella	10.50	13	17	12	13/15
Mycoplasma	10	13	17	13	13/15
Salmonella	11	13	17	13	13/15
Shigella	11.10	13	17	13	13/15
Xanthomonas	11	14	17/18	13	13/15
Other bact. genera	10–12	13	17/18	12/13	13/15

4.2 U_k-Based and Sp-Based Analysis

The main quest is to determine whether spectral segments and RES are biomarkers at species and genus levels and for what range of k. We search for biomarkers by means of computing U_k similarity and Sp_k similarity between genomes of the same genus and between genomes of distinct genera. These values were displayed through similarity matrices, within each genus or by pairing two different genera, along with different dictionaries, and k-values.

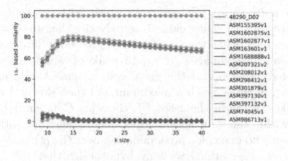

(a)

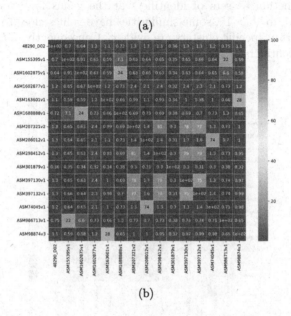

(b)

Fig. 3. The U_{20}-based similarity within the genus Moraxella is shown. Section (a): example of comparison between one species from the genus Moraxella with each of all the others. The legend on the right represents the species inside the genus, and each line shows the values of similarity between one species and another one along with the value of k. No pair of genomes has zero similarity and there are clusters according to Jaccard coefficients. Section (b): of the figure highlights the clustering of genomes according to similarity. Cells that are identified by pairs of genomes of the same species are those that are not dark green and have similarity values greater than 10%, often 30%, upwards to 99%. (Color figure online)

U_k**-Based Similarity.** Computational experiments are reported where the similarity is calculated as the Jaccard index (a value between 0 and 1) on the sets U_k, for $9 \le k \le 40$, taken from a couple of genomes either within one single genus or from different genera. By calculating similarity within one genus, matrices have different configurations depending on the value of k.

For $k = 9$, the matrices are predominantly green, with no significant peaks in the values and no cells with values close to zero. Notice that green cells contain a value ranging from zero (when the color is darker) to about 30%. As k increases, the pattern of the matrices changes. At $k = 15$, peaks of values, in colours ranging from orange to red, emerge and the green cells assume values close to zero. Here, good similarity values reach a maximum and then slowly decrease (while k increasing). Likewise, as in the case of Escherichia Coli, similarity occurs at the strand level within the same species. Specifically, there are both orange/red and green cells, with no one color predominating over the other.

From the above observations we may hypothesize that RES dictionaries potentially function as sets of identifiers at the genus level for $k < 15$. On the other hand, for $k > 15$, some similarities have values close to zero and only similarities within specific clusters are evident. Consequently, RES dictionaries are possible identifiers at the species level.

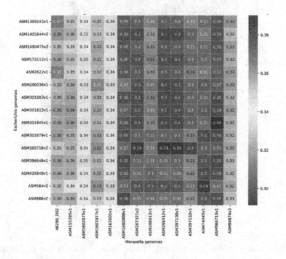

Fig. 4. U_{15}-based similarity between the genera Moraxella and Escherichia is shown. (Color figure online)

We tested if RES can act as genomic markers as well, by computing the U_k-based similarity between the genomes of 10 combinations of pairs of different genera. The coefficient never exceeds 6% (for no value of k), for no pair of genomes and for no combination of genera, as namely seen in Fig. 4. Notice the reference scale: colours vary in a range of 0%–6%. The maximum values are reached for $k \geq 15$. After $k = 15$, all matrix values tend to 0%, without distinction. Genomes of different genera do not have U_k similarities and the heatmaps are basically all homogeneous matrices of zeros.

Sp_k-**Based Similarity.** Computational experiments are reported where the similarity is calculated as the Jaccard index (a value between 0 and 1) on the sets Sp_k, for $9 \leq k \leq 40$, taken from a couple of genomes either within one single genus or from different genera. The optimal k-range for spectral segments is $15 \leq k \leq 25$, since the values have a significant decrease beyond that threshold.

Concerning Sp_k-based similarity within a genus (see Fig. 5 (a) for all values of k), although its values are lower, it shows a division of genomes into clusters corresponding to the same species.

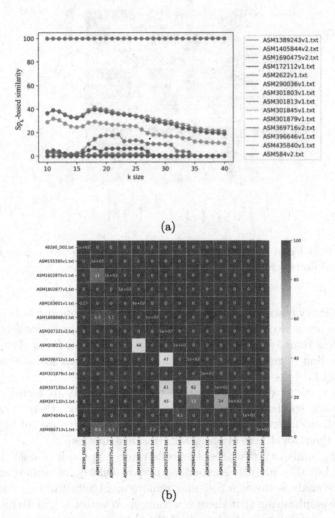

(a)

(b)

Fig. 5. The Sp_{20}-based similarity within the genus Moraxella is shown. Description of details is analogous to the text in caption of Fig. 3. (Color figure online)

As far as Sp_k similarity is concerned, the values are generally lower than those observed with U_k dictionaries, because segments are longer and dictionaries smaller. The similarity matrices have generally low values (lower than those seen for the U_k based similarity). Orange peaks are rare and the green cells are zero from $k = 9$. The heatmaps are homogeneous and clean, and just show a difference between pairs of genomes of the same species from small k. Genomes belonging to the same species have variable coefficients which depend on the species. The range is 10–90%, and values reach a maximum before $k = 20$.

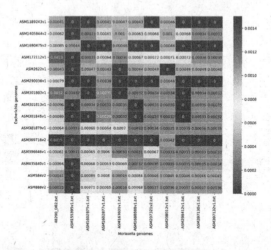

Fig. 6. The Sp_{15}-based similarity between couples of genomes taken from the genera Moraxella and Escherichia is shown. (Color figure online)

The similarity matrices with respect to spectral segments and between genera show values never exceeding 0.5%. In all bacteria organisms, for $k = 9$, there are values less than 1%, decreasing to exactly zero after a few k. For any k, or any combination of genera, the intersection of genomes has size almost zero, as shown in Fig. 6.

The observations above indicate that spectral segments are identifiers within a genus for one species. However, although between genera there is no sharing (of them), all coefficients values within a single genus matrix are not high enough to consider them identifiers of one strain (inside a species).

In the S_p similarity matrices, the cells rarely approach orange, i.e. values above 70%, but they are also surrounded by particularly low values and border on zero. The analysis through Sp_k may remove ambiguity from the intersection study, while emphasising that there is a connection with U_k. The reduced size of the Sp_k, the variability in the length of the segments, and having to deal with segments of increasing size, less prone to repetition, makes the intersection values of greater importance, and means that these results carry new information.

Comparison with the Literature of Barcodes. Barcode of life data system (BOLD) [22] is proposed as a reference for potential barcoding sequences. This database provides identifying sequences for species of the bacterial genera of our dataset. In Table 2, the sequences offered by BOLD are 666 bp long and are single strings. For each species, we average between one and four identification sequences. The only highly represented species is Escherichia Coli. Otherwise, the sequence used for barcoding is 16s RNA, which has range 300–470 bp. On the other hand, dictionaries allow a classification into taxa not related to a single sequence, but to a set of words, having length which range from an average of 2000 bp up to a maximum equal to 200000 bp.

Table 2. Characteristics of possible sets of barcode sequences.

Sequence barcodes comparison		
Source	Segment-length	Set-cardinality
BOLD	666 bp (1000 bp for Escherichia)	1–4
16S RNA	300–470 bp	1
IGTools	Max = 200000 bp (Avg 2000)	3000–100000

4.3 Sp_k-Based Coverage of Genes

It may be relevant to consider the relation between the values of k and the overlapping (or covering) of the spectral segments with the coding portions of genomes.

We say that a spectral segment covers a gene if the two genome portions coincide by at least 95%. We have checked (by means of the Boolean array used by IGtools) the overlap of Sp_k with the genes of each genome, for the interval $10 \leq k \leq 15$. We set $k \leq 15$, to avoid that U_k and D_k dictionaries overlap significantly. Figure 7 shows that in this k-range the spectral segments pass from not covering genes, for $k = 10$ and $k = 11$, to covering them all, for $k = 15$.

Therefore, gene coverage by spectral segments has a very fast growth in the k-range $11 \leq k \leq 13$. Spectral segments cover all coding regions of most genomes already for $k = 13$ or $k = 14$. Either way, for every genome, at $k = 15$ genes are all covered (by keeping in mind that for $k = 13$ the maximum coverage is usually reached, and the dictionaries U_k and D_k are not equal (see Table 1).

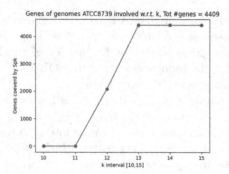

Fig. 7. The picture shows how many genes in a bacterial genome are covered by Sp_k per k-range $10 \leq k \leq 15$. The pattern observed for this specific genome is the same observed for the others.

5   Conclusion

In this paper a k-mer-based method shows to be helpful for determining bacterial species membership, and an accurate set of biomarkers was provided as an alternative to traditional singletons (sets composed by one gene). Main results of this paper may be reported as the identification of two k-parametrized dictionaries, U_k and Sp_k for $15 \leq k \leq 25$, as identifiers of bacterial species. Namely, dictionary U_k for $k < 15$ contains biomarkers at the genus level, while dictionary Sp_k for $15 \leq k \leq 25$, whose spectral segments overlap all the coding regions, discriminates one species within a genus.

The dictionary of a genome traces it back to its taxonomy and characteristics without the sequence itself being known. In fact, comparing dictionaries while following the order of the genetic tree, from leaves to parent, yields a percentage of RES and spectral segments common to the root that is almost zero. Relevantly, there is no set of RES or spectral segments common to all the genomes of a genus. This finding is particularly intriguing and may warrant by itself further investigation thorough a study on other data sets.

The above relationship between a dictionary based similarity and the membership to a phylogenetic tree suggests that spectral segments may be exploited in the phylogenetic domain [14,27,29]. In our experiments, a main difference in the two approaches is emerged with genomes of different species that are located in the same phylogenetic subtree. This observation suggests that dictionaries U_k and Sp_k are more subtle than phylogenetic trees to determine species membership, and that spectral segments distinguish even leaves of a specific subtree.

Future research could focus on a dictionary based method for phylogenetic reconstruction, as a valid alternative to unitigs employed in genome assembly [5, 18]. Indeed, spectral segments are similar but longer than unitigs, so they could be safe and complete solutions for genome assembly. Also potential barcodes could be useful for future applications, such as in the study of the metabiome, overcoming the limitation of distinguishing species in such a large sample.

Biomarker dictionaries are extracted from large amounts of genomes. The method fits with metagenomics, which was developed to handle large quantities of organisms in a less costly and less resource-intensive manner. To generate initial partial tests, we have applied IGtools to the concatenation of 9, 10 and up to 15 sequences. The concatenated sequences representative of a genus show values and peaks that are similar to the individual genomes of that genus, for $10 \leq k \leq 18$. Such a k-range is then pointed out for genomes of the bacterial kingdom, that provides specific information on spectral segments (passing from being many and short to be few and long, and covering all the genes) and RES, which discriminate at the species and genus level, respectively.

References

1. Berstel, J., Karhumäki, J.: Combinatorics on words-a tutorial. current trends in theoretical computer science. Challenge New Century **2**, 415–475 (2004)
2. Bloom, B.H.: Space/time trade-offs in hash coding with allowable errors. Commun. ACM **13**(7), 422–426 (1970)
3. Bonnici, V., Manca, V.: Infogenomics tools: A computational suite for informational analysis of genomes. J. Bioinforma Proteomics Rev. **1**, 8–14 (2015)
4. Bonnici, V., Franco, G., Manca, V.: Spectral concepts in genome informational analysis. Theoret. Comput. Sci. **894**, 23–30 (2021)
5. Cairo, M., Rizzi, R., Tomescu, A.I., Zirondelli, E.C.: Genome assembly, from practice to theory: safe, complete and linear-time. arXiv preprint arXiv:2002.10498 (2020)
6. Castellini, A., Franco, G., Manca, V.: A dictionary based informational genome analysis. BMC Genomics **13**(1), 1–14 (2012)
7. Compeau, P.E.C., Pevzner, P.A., Tesler, G.: How to apply de bruijn graphs to genome assembly. Nat. Biotechnol. **29**(11), 987–991 (2011)
8. Compeau, P.E.C., Pevzner, P.A., Tesler, G.: Why are de bruijn graphs useful for genome assembly? Nat. Biotechnol. **29**(11), 987 (2011)
9. De Luca, A.: On the combinatorics of finite words. Theoret. Comput. Sci. **218**(1), 13–39 (1999)
10. DeSalle, R., Goldstein, P.: Review and interpretation of trends in DNA barcoding. Front. Ecol. Evol. **7**, 302 (2019)
11. Franco, G.: Perspectives in computational genome analysis. In: Jonoska, N., Saito, M. (eds.) Discrete and Topological Models in Molecular Biology. NCS, pp. 3–22. Springer, Heidelberg (2014). https://doi.org/10.1007/978-3-642-40193-0_1
12. Goldstein, P.Z., DeSalle, R.: Integrating DNA barcode data and taxonomic practice: determination, discovery, and description. Bioessays **33**(2), 135–147 (2011)
13. Hao, B., Qi, J.: Prokaryote phylogeny without sequence alignment: from avoidance signature to composition distance. J. Bioinform. Comput. Biol. **2**(01), 1–19 (2004)
14. Haubold, B., Klötzl, F., Pfaffelhuber, P.: andi: fast and accurate estimation of evolutionary distances between closely related genomes. Bioinformatics **31**(8), 1169–1175 (2015)
15. Holley, G., Melsted, P.: Bifrost: highly parallel construction and indexing of colored and compacted de bruijn graphs. Genome Biol. **21**(1), 1–20 (2020)
16. Lothaire, M.: Combinatorics on Words, vol. 17. Cambridge University Press, Cambridge (1997)

17. Manca, V.: The principles of informational genomics. Theoret. Comput. Sci. **701**, 190–202 (2017)
18. Acosta, N.O., Mäkinen, V., Tomescu, A.I.: A safe and complete algorithm for metagenomic assembly. Algorithms Mol. Biol. **13**(1), 1–12 (2018)
19. Orozco-Arias, S., et al.: K-mer-based machine learning method to classify ltr-retrotransposons in plant genomes. PeerJ, **9**, e11456 (2021)
20. Orozco-Arias, S., S Piña, J., Tabares-Soto, R., Castillo-Ossa, L.F., Guyot, R., Isaza, G.: Measuring performance metrics of machine learning algorithms for detecting and classifying transposable elements. Processes **8**(6), 638 (2020)
21. Qi, J., Luo, H., Hao, B.: Cvtree: a phylogenetic tree reconstruction tool based on whole genomes. Nucleic Acids Res. **32**(suppl-2), W45–W47 (2004)
22. Ratnasingham, S., Hebert, P.D.N.: Bold: the barcode of life data system (http://www.barcodinglife.org). Mol. Ecol. Notes **7**(3), 355–364 (2007)
23. Sarmashghi, S., Bohmann, K., Gilbert, M.T.P., Bafna, V., Mirarab, S.: SKMER: assembly-free and alignment-free sample identification using genome skims. Genome Biol. **20**(1), 1–20 (2019)
24. Thomas, T., Gilbert, J., Meyer, F.: Metagenomics-a guide from sampling to data analysis. Microb. Inf. Exp. **2**(1), 1–12 (2012)
25. Tomescu, A.I., Medvedev, P.: Safe and complete contig assembly through OMNIT-IGS. J. Comput. Biol. **24**(6), 590–602 (2017)
26. Vinga, S., Almeida, J.: Alignment-free sequence comparison-a review. Bioinformatics **19**(4), 513–523 (2003)
27. Wittler, R.: Alignment and reference-free phylogenomics with colored de bruijn graphs. Algorithms Mol. Biol. **15**(1), 1–12 (2020)
28. Yen, S., Johnson, J.S.: Metagenomics: a path to understanding the gut microbiome. Mamm. Genome **32**(4), 282–296 (2021). https://doi.org/10.1007/s00335-021-09889-x
29. Yi, H., Jin, L.: Co-phylog: an assembly-free phylogenomic approach for closely related organisms. Nucleic Acids Res. **41**(7), e75–e75 (2013)
30. Zielezinski, A., et al.: Benchmarking of alignment-free sequence comparison methods. Genome Biol. **20**(1), 1–18 (2019)

Uniform Robot Relocation Is Hard in only Two Directions Even Without Obstacles

David Caballero[1], Angel A. Cantu[2], Timothy Gomez[3], Austin Luchsinger[4], Robert Schweller[1], and Tim Wylie[1(✉)]

[1] University of Texas Rio Grande Valley, Edinburg, TX, USA
{david.caballero01,robert.schweller,timothy.wylie}@utrgv.edu
[2] Southwest Research Institute, San Antonio, TX, USA
acantu@d16.swri.us
[3] Massachusetts Institute of Technology, Cambridge, MA, USA
tagomez7@mit.edu
[4] University of Texas Austin, Austin, TX, USA
amluchsinger@utexas.edu

Abstract. Given n robots contained within a square grid surrounded by four walls, we ask the question of whether it is possible to move a particular robot a to a particular grid location b by performing a sequence of global *step* operations in which all robots move one grid step in the same cardinal direction (if not blocked by a wall or other blocked robots). We show this problem is NP-complete when restricted to just two directions (south and west). This answers the simplest fundamental problem in uniform global unit tilt swarm robotics.

1   Introduction

The advanced development of microbots and nanobots has quickly become a significant frontier. However, power and computation limitations at these scales often make autonomous robots infeasible and individually-controlled robots impractical. Thus, recent attention has focused on controlling large numbers of relatively simple robots. Many examples of large population robot swarms exist, ranging from naturally occurring magnetotactic bacteria [14–16] to manufactured light-driven nanocars [13,17]. These microrobot swarms are manipulated uniformly through the use of external inputs such as light, a magnetic field, or gravity. That is, all of the agents in the system react identically to the same global signal. This type of global manipulation also reflects the mechanics of many types of systems dating back centuries to marble mazes and other games.

First proposed in 2013 [7], the tilt model consists of movable polyominoes (as an abstraction of these nanorobots) that exist on a 2D grid board with "open" and "blocked" spaces. These polyominoes can be manipulated by a global signal,

---

This research was supported in part by National Science Foundation Grant CCF-1817602.

causing all polyominoes to step a unit distance in the specified direction unless stopped by a blocked space or another polyomino.

Within this model, the complexity of different problems related to the manipulation of the set of polyominoes is studied. The *reconfiguration* problem asks whether one specified configuration is reachable from another by way of these uniform signals. The relocation problem asks whether a specific polyomino or tile can be relocated to a given location (Fig. 1).

Restricted variants of the model are also considered. One of these restrictions is where the polyominoes are limited to single tiles, greatly limiting the complexity of interactions between polyominoes. The other notable restrictions are limiting the global signals to only 2 or 3 directions, and limiting the complexity of the board geometry, i.e., the arrangement of the blocked spaces.

One of the simplest variants of the model is square board geometry, in which the blocked spaces are limited to a square border with no internal geometry, global inputs limited to two directions, and only single tiles. In this simple model, we study the *relocation* problem, showing that the problem of whether a tile can be relocated to a given position is still NP-complete.

1.1   Related Work

Previous research has investigated the manipulation of robot swarms with precise uniform movements in a 2D environment containing obstacles [7]. In the "Full Tilt" variant of this model where tiles slide maximally in each specified direction, the complexity of determining the minimum move sequence for reconfiguration [6], as well as the complexity for Relocation and Reconfiguration [3,4], have been shown to be PSPACE-complete. Reconfiguration and Relocation have further been shown to be NP-complete when the number of possible directions is limited to 2 or 3 [5]. The single step model, in which robots move a single unit step during each move, was later defined formally, with work studying the complexity of relocating a specified tile to a specific location on the board, showing that the problem is PSPACE-complete even when limited to single tiles [11]. The problem of building shapes (adjusting the positions of the robots in the system to collectively form a specified shape) and the problem of building specified patterns out of labelled tiles (i.e. moving the robots into locations such that their labels adhere to a specified shape and pattern) has also been studied, showing that there are board configurations which allow construction of general shapes in optimal time [8] and patterned shapes in near-optimal time [9].

Previous work has also studied restrictions on this model. The two main restrictions studied are limiting the number of directions the robots can move in, and limiting the complexity of the board's geometry. A hierarchy of board geometries is described in [3]. It was shown that when limiting the number of available directions to 2 and with "monotone" board geometry the problem of relocation is NP-complete [10].

The simplest variant of the model, in which there are single tiles in a square board with no internal obstacles, has not been studied extensively. When all four directions are allowed, work has shown that the problem of arranging the robots

Table 1. An overview of the complexity results related to the relocation and shape reconfiguration problems in the single step model. The open problems are row relocation in 2 directions in the square and general relocation in the square with four directions. Membership in 4 directions is open for both problems.

Problem	Directions	Tile Size	Geometry	Result	Ref.
1st Row Relocation	2/3	1×1	Square	P	[12]
Row Relocation	2/3	1×1	Square	open	-
Relocation	**2**	**1×1**	**Square**	**NP-complete**	**Thm.1**
	2/3	1×1	Monotone	NP-complete	[10]
	4	1×1	General	PSPACE-complete	[11]
	4	1×1,1×2	Square	PSPACE-complete	[11]
Shape	2/3/4	1×1	Square	NP-hard	[1]
Reconfiguration	4	1×1	General	PSPACE-complete	[11]

into a specific shape is NP-hard [1]. Depending on the starting configuration, the tiles can be compacted in an exponential number of ways. When the tiles get compacted, they form a permutation group that was studied in detail in [2]. However, the complexity for relocation and reconfiguration with four directions is still an open question.

1.2 Contributions

We investigate the relocation problem in the single step model. Table 1 shows what was previously known and how our results relate. We answer an open question about the simplest version of the problem. We show that relocation when limited to single tiles, only two directions, and no blocking geometry is still NP-complete. With this in mind, we have also shown that knowing whether a tile can be relocated to the bottom row is in P [12], however, whether a tile can reach an arbitrary row is still an open problem.

We first overview the unit movement (or single step) tilt model in Sect. 2. In Sect. 3 we show that with two directions in the square, relocation is NP-complete. Finally, several important open problems are outlined in the conclusion (Sect. 4).

2 Preliminaries

We give the model and problem definitions related to single step tilt in an open board.

Board. A *board* (or *workspace*) is a rectangular region of the 2D square lattice in which specific locations are marked as *blocked*. Formally, an $m \times n$ board is a partition $\mathbb{B} = (O, X)$ of $\{(x, y) | x \in \{1, 2, \ldots, m\}, y \in \{1, 2, \ldots, n\}\}$ where O denotes a set of *open* locations, and X denotes a set of *blocked* locations- referred to as "concrete." Here, we use the most restrictive geometry in the hierarchy

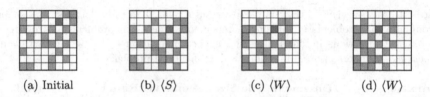

(a) Initial   (b) $\langle S \rangle$ (c) $\langle W \rangle$ (d) $\langle W \rangle$

Fig. 1. An example step sequence. The initial board configuration followed by the resulting configurations after an $\langle S \rangle$ step, $\langle W \rangle$ step, and then final $\langle W \rangle$ step. The red tile is the one to relocate and the red outline square is the target location. (Color figure online)

where O is a square and the only blocked locations are the edges around the board.

Tiles. A tile is a unit square centered on a non-blocked point on a given board. Formally a tile t stores a coordinate on the board c and is said to occupy c.

Configurations. A configuration is an arrangement of tiles on a board such that there are no overlaps among tiles, or with blocked board spaces. Formally, a configuration $C = (\mathbb{B}, \mathbb{T} = \{t_1, \ldots, t_k\})$ consists of a board $\mathbb{B}$ and a set of non-overlapping tiles $\mathbb{T}$. We say two configurations $C = (\mathbb{B}, \mathbb{T} = \{t_1, \ldots, t_k\})$ and $C' = (\mathbb{B}, \mathbb{T}' = \{t'_1, \ldots, t'_k\})$ have the same shape if $\mathbb{T}$ and $\mathbb{T}'$ are translations of each other. The shape of a configuration C is the shape of $\mathbb{T}$.

Step. A *step* is a way to turn one configuration into another by way of a global signal that moves all tiles in a configuration one unit in a direction $d \in \{N, E, S, W\}$ when possible without causing an overlap with a blocked position, or another tile. Formally, for a configuration $C = (\mathbb{B}, \mathbb{T})$, let $\mathbb{T}'$ be the maximal subset of $\mathbb{T}$ such that translation of all tiles in $\mathbb{T}'$ by 1 unit in the direction d induces no overlap with blocked squares or other tiles. A step in direction d is performed by executing the translation of all tiles in $\mathbb{T}'$ by 1 unit in that direction.

We say that a configuration C can be *directly reconfigured* into configuration C' (denoted $C \rightarrow_1 C'$) if applying one step in some direction $d \in \{N, E, S, W\}$ to C results in C'. We define the relation $\rightarrow_*$ to be the transitive closure of $\rightarrow_1$ and say that C can be *reconfigured* into C' if and only if $C \rightarrow_* C'$, i.e., C may be reconfigured into C' by way of a sequence of step transformations.

Step Sequence. A *step sequence* is a series of steps which can be inferred from a series of directions $D = \langle d_1, d_2, \ldots, d_k \rangle$; each $d_i \in D$ implies a step in that direction. For simplicity, when discussing a step sequence, we just refer to the series of directions from which that sequence was derived. Given a starting configuration, a step sequence corresponds to a sequence of configurations based on the step transformation. An example step sequence $\langle S, W, W \rangle$ and the corresponding sequence of configurations can be seen in Fig. 1.

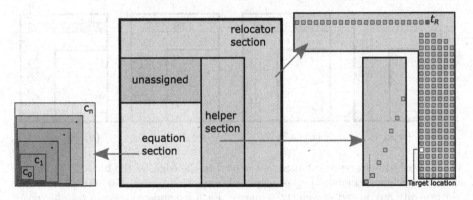

Fig. 2. A high-level view of the layout of the gadgets on the board.

Relocation. Given a tilt system with an $n \times n$ board $\mathbb{B}$, a set of tiles $\mathbb{T} = \{t_1, \ldots, t_m\}$ where each $t_l = (x, y)$ s.t. $1 \le l \le m$, $1 \le x \le n$, and $1 \le y \le n$. Given $t_i, t_j \in \mathbb{T}$, $t_i \ne t_j$ if $i \ne j$. For shorthand, we use $t_{i,j}$ for $t_l = (i, j)$. For the row or column, we use t_{l_r} and t_{l_c}.

Given a specific tile to relocate t_R at location $(r, c) = (t_{R_r}, t_{R_c})$, and a target location $T = (T_r, T_c)$, the relocation problem asks whether a series of steps can translate t_R s.t. $(t_{R_r}, t_{R_c}) = T$.

Definition 1 (Knitting). *The* knitting row *and* knitting column *are the row and column of t_R. Knitting is the act of performing $\langle W \rangle$ movements (or $\langle S \rangle$) when every position of the knitting area (row or column) is occupied by a tile. Thus, t_R maintains its position.*

3   2-Direction NP-Hard Relocation

We design gadgets that encode truth values of literals for a given 3SAT instance equation. We provide two step-sequences for 'assigning' truth values to variables, which reconfigure the gadgets into two distinct configurations. A 'true' value for a literal is interpreted as the presence of an 'output' tile within a target location in a gadget, whereas a 'false' value is simply the absence of that tile. We group three gadgets together to create a clause and check for 3SAT satisfiability by counting the number of output tiles in the gadgets after assigning truth values to all variables. We show that relocation becomes impossible if step-sequences are used beside the ones provided, giving us strict control over the outcome of the system. The move directions considered henceforth are $\langle S, W \rangle$.

Layout. Given a 3SAT instance, we construct a board divided into three regions called the equation section, relocation section, and helper section (Fig. 2). The equation section is composed of multiple subregions called *clause* spaces each containing three gadgets assigned to the three literals for that particular clause. The helper section is the region next to the equation section that contains floating

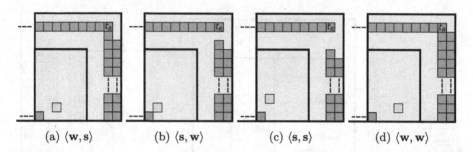

(a) $\langle \mathbf{w}, \mathbf{s} \rangle$ (b) $\langle \mathbf{s}, \mathbf{w} \rangle$ (c) $\langle \mathbf{s}, \mathbf{s} \rangle$ (d) $\langle \mathbf{w}, \mathbf{w} \rangle$

Fig. 3. Dashed lines represent tiles that extend to the edges of the board. The figures show how different combinations of helper tile's position (green tile) and t_R's position can generate any forced movement sequence. Each example represents possible positionings of the helper tile and t_R such that the listed move sequence is forced, given that the helper tile must be placed at the bottom of the board and t_R remain adjacent to the row of tiles. (Color figure online)

tiles used to generate *forced* step-sequences. As detailed in Lemma 1, each helper tile must reside at the bottom of the board in order to geometrically assist the target tile for relocation. The relocator section consists of a row of tiles extending from the left edge of the board along with multiple columns of tiles underneath it that extend from the bottom edge of the board. The target tile $t_R = (t_{R_r}, t_{R_c})$ is defined as the last tile of the row in the relocator section with target location $T = (T_r, T_c)$ such that $T_c = t_{R_c} - 1$ and $T_r = |C| + 2$ for a set of clauses C.

Force Moves. Forcing a step-sequence is achieved by purposely preventing relocation if that sequence is not used. This is done by either trapping the target tile via geometric blocking or preventing the target tile from interacting with other tiles needed for relocation. The columns in the relocator section and helper tiles in the helper section are used together to generate any forced step-sequence (Fig. 3). A $\langle W \rangle$ move is forced when the target tile resides just above a column in the relocator section since a $\langle S \rangle$ move pushes the row of tiles next to the target tile downwards, making the target tile stuck above the column. A $\langle S \rangle$ move is forced when a $\langle W \rangle$ move places a helper tile in the same column as another helper tile, therefore making it impossible to place all helper tiles at the bottom of the board.

Lemma 1. *Every helper tile in the helper section must be placed at the bottom edge of the board in order to make relocation of the target tile possible.*

Proof. The row of tiles adjacent to the target tile prevents it from stepping into the column before it (moving the tile west), blocking the target tile from entering the column of the target location. The target tile must eventually break away from the row by moving on a column of tiles, pushing the row downwards, and moving west into the column before it. We make this scenario available only once when we check if every clause of the 3SAT equation is satisfied and stack as many tiles as there are satisfied clauses beneath the target tile. Similarly, placing every

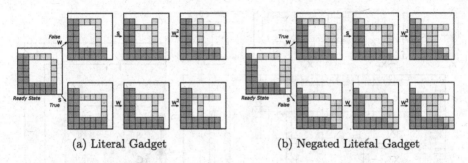

(a) Literal Gadget   (b) Negated Literal Gadget

Fig. 4. The gadgets are in the *ready* state at the beginning of each sequence. Both gadgets are depicted along with how each 'assign' step-sequences affect them. We can track a gadget's truth value by observing the length of the horizontal pillar such that it is assigned true if the pillar is lengthened by a single tile after a step-sequence.

helper tile at the bottom of the board creates a row of tiles just long enough to occupy a position in the same column as the target tile. By positioning the target location $|C| + 2$ above the bottom of the board, every clause must be satisfied along with every single helper tile in the helper section placed at the bottom of the board. The additional tile in the equation comes from a tile we initialize on the board for the purpose of functionality. If a single helper tile is not placed at the bottom of the board, the row of helper tiles can not be long enough to occupy a position in the column of the target tile in the disengage part of the reduction, therefore relocation becomes impossible.

Gadgets. Gadgets are composed of 'pillars' of tiles that extend from blocked tiles adjacent to the bottom and left edges of the equation section. We provide two versions of a gadget for normal and negated literals shown in Fig. 4. We define two 'assign' step-sequences: 'assign true' as $\langle s, \mathbf{w}, \mathbf{w}, \mathbf{w} \rangle$ and 'assign false' as $\langle w, \mathbf{s}, \mathbf{w}, \mathbf{w} \rangle$ such that the last three moves are forced. In the reduction, we execute one of the two 'assign' step-sequences for every variable of a given 3SAT equation so that each gadget assigned to a literal encodes the truth value of that literal in the length of the horizontal pillar. That is, a gadget (literal) evaluates to true if the horizontal pillar lengthens by one after a 'assign' step-sequence is used or false if the pillar remains the same length. The *output position* of a gadget is defined as the position on the horizontal pillar that contains, or does not contain, the additional tile after the 'assign' step-sequence. For the gadgets assigned to literals x_i and x_j where $i < j$, we space out the pillars of x_j so that when x_i is in the *ready* state (see Fig. 4), the pillars of x_j are $\langle s^{1 \times j}, w^{3 \times j} \rangle$ spaces away from the *ready* state. This allows us to assign truth values to each variable in order independently of each other.

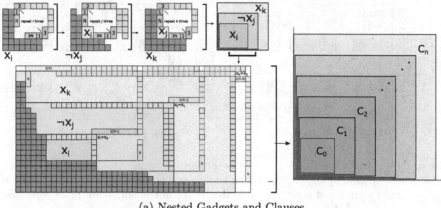

(a) Nested Gadgets and Clauses

Fig. 5. (a) Depiction of clause $c = (x_0 \lor \neg x_1 \lor x_2)$ with $N = 3$ distinct variables. Gadgets and clauses are nested inside each other in order to prevent unwanted intervention of their components.

Clause Spaces. For the set of clauses C of a given 3SAT instance, we define the clause space for clause $c_i \in C$ as the region on the board with three gadgets assigned to each literal in $c_i = (x_i, x_j, x_k)$. The gadgets are allocated consecutively such that the 'next' gadget encompasses the 'previous' gadget by lengthening its pillars with dimensions detailed in Fig. 5. We similarly build each clause space such that the 'next' clause space encompasses the 'previous' clause space as shown in Fig. 6. With this design, each clause space functions independently and in parallel with the other clause spaces.

System Output. Given a sequence of truth assignments for the variables, determining if a clause was satisfied involves placing as many tiles on a single row in the clause space, called the *clause output*, as there are satisfied literals in the clause. To do this, we position floating columns of tiles called *readers* that wrap around each gadget output position after the last variable truth assignment based on the dimensions given in Fig. 5. As shown in Fig. 6, this allows us to step south and lengthen the reader by a single tile if the literal evaluates to true. If at least one reader is lengthened by one, then the clause is said to be satisfied given that the reader occupies a position in the clause output.

To determine satisfiability of the 3SAT equation, we position horizontal readers that extend from the relocator section which wrap around each clause output after using the first readers, seen in Fig. 6d. By repeatedly moving west, these readers are compressed and push out a tile in the relocator section for every satisfied literal in the clause as shown seen Fig. 7d. This way, when the target tile reaches the last column of the relocator section, the amount of tiles underneath

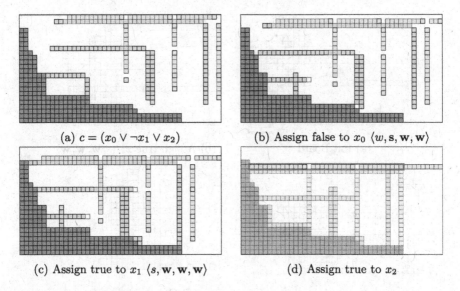

(a) $c = (x_0 \vee \neg x_1 \vee x_2)$

(b) Assign false to x_0 $\langle w, \mathbf{s}, \mathbf{w}, \mathbf{w} \rangle$

(c) Assign true to x_1 $\langle s, \mathbf{w}, \mathbf{w}, \mathbf{w} \rangle$

(d) Assign true to x_2

Fig. 6. Given clause $c = (x_0 \vee \neg x_1 \vee x_2)$ with distinct variables $N = 3$. (a) We first assign 'false' to x_0, which makes literal gadget x_1 move to the *ready* state. (c-d) We then assign false and true to x_1 and x_2, respectively, followed by pushing the output tiles of the gadget to the clause output row.

the target tile is at least the number of satisfied clauses. Similarly, we utilize a reader for the helper tiles in order to join the two rows and occupy a position underneath the target tile given that every helper tile is present in the row. If every clause is satisfied, and every helper tile is placed at the bottom edge of the board, then the target tile can 'disengage' with the row of tiles next to it by stepping downwards until compressing with the tiles beneath it and then relocate to the target location. Similarly, if at least one clause is unsatisfied, or at least one helper tile was not placed at the bottom edge of the board, then the target tile can not 'disengage' with the row of tiles in the same row as the target location, and therefore can not relocate. With this, we define the *get system output* sequence as $\langle s, w, w, w, w \rangle$.

Lemma 2. *Single Step Relocation in a square board with only two directions is NP-hard.*

Proof. We prove this by a reduction from 3SAT. Given a 3SAT instance, we construct a board divided into three sections called the equation section, helper section, and relocator section. From Lemma 1, we can generated any 'forced' step-sequence by utilizing helper tiles in the helper section and columns in the relocator section to create scenarios in which an incorrect step-sequence results in the impossibility of relocation. With this capability, we design two step-sequences

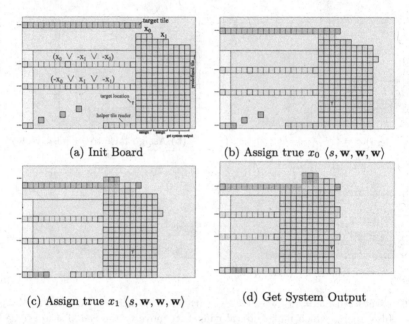

(a) Init Board

(b) Assign true x_0 $\langle s, \mathbf{w}, \mathbf{w}, \mathbf{w} \rangle$

(c) Assign true x_1 $\langle s, \mathbf{w}, \mathbf{w}, \mathbf{w} \rangle$

(d) Get System Output

Fig. 7. The sections are not to size and for demonstrative purposes only. (a) Example of the right side of the board with clauses $(x_0 \lor \neg x_1 \lor \neg x_0)$ and $(\neg x_0 \lor x_1 \lor \neg x_1)$ and variables $N = 2$. The first six columns of tiles in the relocation section, together with the first two helper tiles, generates two assign step-sequences for the variables. (b-c) Assigning true to both variables makes the 3SAT equation evaluate to true. The last helper tile and four columns of tiles in the relocator section forces the user to compress the readers and push out a tile underneath the target tile per satisfied literal.

for assigning truth values to each distinct variable in the 3SAT equation. We force N of any of these two step-sequences at the beginning of the reduction so that each step-sequence reconfigures the appropriate gadgets, where N is the number of distinct variables of the 3SAT instance. Next, we execute the *get system output* step-sequence, which involves moving readers around gadget outputs in order to push out as many tiles as there are satisfied literals to a single row within a clause region. This is followed by a second group of readers that wrap around clause region outputs and push out a tile in the relocation section, underneath the target tile, if a particular clause is satisfied. Afterwards, the satisfiability of the 3SAT equation is evaluated to true if the number of tiles underneath the target tile equals to $|C| + 2$. We get $|C|$ tiles if each clause was satisfied and 1 tile from the helper tiles. The last tile is automatically given since it is pre-initialized on the board. We can see that if any of these conditions are not met, then relocation is impossible. That is, relocation of the target tile is possible if and only if every clause is satisfied and each helper tile is placed at the bottom of the board.

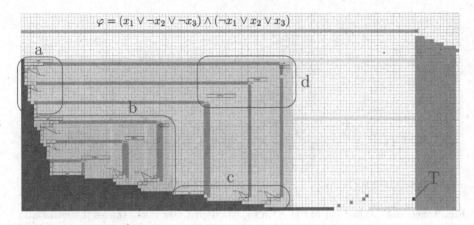

Fig. 8. Initial board example for 3SAT equation $(x_1 \vee \neg x_2 \vee \neg x_3) \wedge (\neg x_1 \vee x_2 \vee x_3)$. Section details are shown in Figs. 9 and 10.

Relocation Membership. Membership in NP for the particular instance we are considering subtly depends on the problem definition and encoding. The single step tilt model, as defined, is a set of open and blocked spaces. Thus, the set of tiles is a subset of those locations, and membership in NP is straightforward. This was shown in [10]. However, given the nature of the square board with all spaces open, an alternate formulation of this specific variant of the problem could take in the dimension of the board, n, encoded in binary, which would imply the board size is exponential in the input size. Each tile can be encoded as only its starting location, which can also be encoded in binary. Such an input would mean the obvious certificate for relocate-ability would no longer be polynomial sized. Membership in NP is still an open question for this version of the problem.

Lemma 3. *Single Step Relocation in a square board with only two directions is in NP [10].*

Theorem 1. *Single Step Relocation in a square board with only two directions is NP-complete.*

Proof. Follows from Lemmas 2 and 3.

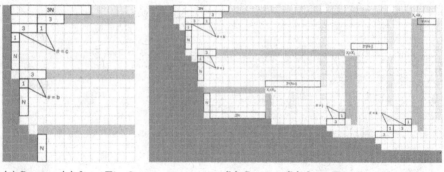

(a) Section (a) from Fig. 8   (b) Section (b) from Fig. 8

Fig. 9. Sections (a) and (b) of Fig. 8. In (a), we depict how many spaces the horizontal pillar of each literal gadget is from the ready state. The horizontal reader is spaced out by $3N$ in order to account for each variable assignment. (b) The dimensions for each gadget in the lowest clause space is depicted.

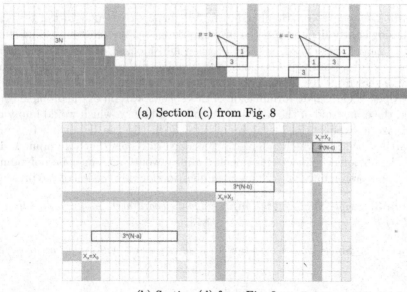

(a) Section (c) from Fig. 8

(b) Section (d) from Fig. 8

Fig. 10. Sections (c) and (d) of Fig. 8. (c) Similarly, each vertical pillar is spaced out given the dimensions depicted. The lower literal gadget in the clause space is provided with enough horizontal space to allow for all variable assignment step-sequences to occur without interference from other tiles on the board. (d) The vertical readers' dimensions for the upper clause space is depicted.

4   Conclusion

In this work we answered an open question by showing that relocation in the single step tilt model, even in the most restrictive case with no fixed geometry except the borders of the space and with only two movement directions, is still NP-complete. As shown in Table 1, there is now a fairly complete characterization of this problem in relation to movement direction, tile size, and board geometry. A few important questions remain, which we overview here.

- Is the relocation problem in the square in NP if the input is specified as the tile locations and a binary encoded integer for the board size? As mentioned, membership is not obvious since the number of steps needed may be exponential in the size of the input.
- In the square with four directions, is single step relocation or shape configuration in NP? Recent work by [2] outlined the basic permutation groups that occur in a polyomino under the single step model, but there is no work addressing the compaction of tiles into different permutation groups. It may be that relocation is not in NP because an exponential number of moves is necessary to move a tile into the correct permutation group, move it to the correct spot in a shape, and then move the shape in the square.
- Following from the previous question, the same reasoning is why membership is still open for reconfiguration (and why all results in Table 1 are only NP-hard). Is shape reconfiguration in the square in NP?
- For the single step tilt model in the square, is general row relocation in P or is it still NP-hard? In [12], they show that knowing whether a tile can relocate to the bottom row (1st Row Relocation) is in P. It is fairly straightforward to modify the 1st Row Relocation algorithm to work for the 2nd row, but every additional row seems to add a higher polynomial. It is clearly bounded by the number of alternations needed between W and S. If only k alternations are needed, then row relocation is possible in $\mathcal{O}(n^k)$, giving a poor FPT algorithm.
- Following from the previous question, is there a configuration requiring $\mathcal{O}(n)$ alternations between W and S?

References

1. Akitaya, H., Aloupis, G., Löffler, M., Rounds, A.: Trash compaction. In: Proceedings of 32nd European Workshop on Computational Geometry, pp. 107–110 (2016)
2. Akitaya, H.A., Löffler, M., Viglietta, G.: Pushing blocks by sweeping lines. In: Proceedings of the 11th International Conference on Fun with Algorithms, FUN 2022 (2022)
3. Balanza-Martinez, J., et al.: Hierarchical shape construction and complexity for slidable polyominoes under uniform external forces. In: Proceedings of the 2020 ACM-SIAM Symposium on Discrete Algorithms, SODA 2020, pp. 2625–2641 (2020). https://doi.org/10.1137/1.9781611975994.160

4. Balanza-Martinez, J., et al.: Full tilt: universal constructors for general shapes with uniform external forces. In: Proceedings of the 2019 ACM-SIAM Symposium on Discrete Algorithms, SODA 2019, pp. 2689–2708 (2019). https://doi.org/10.1137/1.9781611975482.167

5. Becker, A., Demaine, E.D., Fekete, S.P., Habibi, G., McLurkin, J.: Reconfiguring massive particle swarms with limited, global control. In: Flocchini, P., Gao, J., Kranakis, E., Meyer auf der Heide, F. (eds.) ALGOSENSORS 2013. LNCS, vol. 8243, pp. 51–66. Springer, Heidelberg (2014). https://doi.org/10.1007/978-3-642-45346-5_5

6. Becker, A.T., Demaine, E.D., Fekete, S.P., McLurkin, J.: Particle computation: designing worlds to control robot swarms with only global signals. In: sIEEE International Conference on Robotics and Automation, ICRA 2014, pp. 6751–6756 (May 2014). https://doi.org/10.1109/ICRA.2014.6907856

7. Becker, A.T., Habibi, G., Werfel, J., Rubenstein, M., McLurkin, J.: Massive uniform manipulation: controlling large populations of simple robots with a common input signal. In: 2013 IEEE/RSJ International Conference on Intelligent Robots and Systems, pp. 520–527 (Nov 2013). https://doi.org/10.1109/IROS.2013.6696401

8. Caballero, D., Cantu, A.A., Gomez, T., Luchsinger, A., Schweller, R., Wylie, T.: Fast reconfiguration of robot swarms with uniform control signals. Nat. Comput. **20**(4), 659–669 (2021). https://doi.org/10.1007/s11047-021-09864-0

9. Caballero, D., Cantu, A.A., Gomez, T., Luchsinger, A., Schweller, R., Wylie, T.: Building patterned shapes in robot swarms with uniform control signals. In: Proceedings of the 32nd Canadian Conference on Computational Geometry, CCCG 2020, pp. 59–62 (2020)

10. Caballero, D., Cantu, A.A., Gomez, T., Luchsinger, A., Schweller, R., Wylie, T.: Hardness of reconfiguring robot swarms with uniform external control in limited directions. J. Inf. Process. **28**, 782–790 (2020)

11. Caballero, D., Cantu, A.A., Gomez, T., Luchsinger, A., Schweller, R., Wylie, T.: Relocating units in robot swarms with uniform control signals is pspace-complete. In: Proceedings of the 32nd Canadian Conference on Computational Geometry, CCCG 2020, pp. 49–55 (2020)

12. Caballero, D., Cantu, A.A., Gomez, T., Luchsinger, A., Schweller, R., Wylie, T.: Unit tilt row relocation in a square (short abstract). In: Proceedings of the 23rd Thailand-Japan Conference on Discrete and Computational Geometry, Graphs, and Games, TJCDCG3'2020+1, pp. 122–123 (2021)

13. Chiang, P.T., et al.: Toward a light-driven motorized nanocar: Synthesis and initial imaging of single molecules. ACS Nano **6**(1), 592–597 (2012). https://doi.org/10.1021/nn203969b, pMID: 22129498

14. Felfoul, O., Mohammadi, M., Gaboury, L., Martel, S.: Tumor targeting by computer controlled guidance of magnetotactic bacteria acting like autonomous microrobots. In: 2011 IEEE/RSJ International Conference on Intelligent Robots and Systems, pp. 1304–1308 (Sep 2011). https://doi.org/10.1109/IROS.2011.6094991

15. Martel, S.: Bacterial microsystems and microrobots. In: Biomedical Microdevices, vol. 14, pp. 1033–1045 (2012). https://doi.org/10.1007/s10544-012-9696-x

16. Martel, S., Taherkhani, S., Tabrizian, M., Mohammadi, M., de Lanauze, D., Felfoul, O.: Computer 3D controlled bacterial transports and aggregations of microbial adhered nano-components. J. Micro-Bio Robot. (4), 23–28 (2014). https://doi.org/10.1007/s12213-014-0076-x
17. Shirai, Y., Osgood, A.J., Zhao, Y., Kelly, K.F., Tour, J.M.: Directional control in thermally driven single-molecule nanocars. Nano Lett. 5(11), 2330–2334 (2005). https://doi.org/10.1021/nl051915k, pMID: 16277478

Generically Computable Abelian Groups

Wesley Calvert[1], Douglas Cenzer[2](✉), and Valentina Harizanov[3]

[1] Southern Illinois University, Carbondale, IL 62091, USA
wcalvert@siu.edu
[2] University of Florida, Gainesville, FL 32611, USA
cenzer@ufl.edu
[3] George Washington University, Washington, DC 20052, USA
harizanv@gwu.edu

Abstract. Generically computable sets, as introduced by Jockusch and Schupp, have been of great interest in recent years. This idea of approximate computability was motivated by asymptotic density problems studied by Gromov in combinatorial group theory. More recently, we have defined notions of generically computable structures, and studied in particular equivalence structures and injection structures. A structure is said to be generically computable if there is a computable substructure defined on an asymptotically dense set, where the functions are computable and the relations are computably enumerable. It turned out that every equivalence structure has a generically computable copy, whereas there is a non-trivial characterization of the injection structures with generically computable copies.

In this paper, we return to group theory, as we explore the generic computablity of Abelian groups. We show that any Abelian p-group has a generically computable copy and that such a group has a Σ_2-generically computably enumerable copy if and only it has a computable copy. We also give a partial characterization of the Σ_1-generically computably enumerable Abelian p-groups. We also give a non-trivial characterization of the generically computable Abelian groups that are not p-groups.

Keywords: computability · generically computable · Abelian p-group · Σ_n elementary substructure

1 Introduction

Experts in mathematical logic and computability theory show that many interesting problems are undecidable, that is, there is no algorithm for computing a

This research was partially supported by the National Science Foundation SEALS grant DMS-1362273. The work was done partially while the latter two authors were visiting the Institute for Mathematical Sciences, National University of Singapore, in 2017. The visits were supported by the Institute. This material is partially based upon work supported by the National Science Foundation under grant DMS-1928930 while all three authors participated in a program hosted by the Mathematical Sciences Research Institute in Berkeley, California during the Fall 2020 semester. Harizanov was partially supported by the Simons Foundation grant 853762 and NSF grant DMS-2152095.

D. Genova and J. Kari (Eds.): UCNC 2023, LNCS 14003, pp. 32–45, 2023.
https://doi.org/10.1007/978-3-031-34034-5_3

solution to a given problem. Thus it is very important to find unconventional ways in which a solution to the problem may be approximated. The notion of dense computability for sets of natural numbers is that there is an algorithm which computes the solution on an asymptotically dense set. The study of densely computable, generically computable, and coarsely computable sets is now well-established.

The classic motivating example which comes from structure theory is the word problem for finitely generated groups. For many groups with undecidable word problems, including a standard example from [11], the particular words on which it is difficult to decide equality to the identity are very special words (and are even called by this term in some expositions). Thus the problem can be solved on a dense set.

In two recent papers [1,2], the authors have developed the notions of *densely computable* structures and isomorphisms. This builds on the concepts of generically and coarsely computable sets, as studied by Jockusch and Schupp [5,6] and many others, which have been a focus of research in computability. For structures, the question is whether some "large" substructure is computable.

There are, roughly, two extremal possibilities (say, in the case of generic computability):

1. Every countable structure has a generically computable copy, or
2. Any countable structure with a generically computable copy has a computable copy.

It was shown in [1] that each of these can be achieved in certain classes, and that they do not exhaust all possibilities.

The authors also explored these conditions under the added hypothesis that the "large" substructures in question be, in some weak sense, elementary (that is, elements of the substructure satisfy certain formulas which they satisfy in the full structure). Again, we find that there are natural extremal possibilities, and that both they and non-extremal cases are achieved.

Finally, we found that as the elementarity hypotheses are strengthened, all known cases eventually (for Σ_n elementarity at sufficiently large n) trivialize. This demonstrates that these notions of dense computability are structural — they depend fundamentally on the semantics of the structure and not only on the density or algorithmic features of the presentation.

1.1   The Model of Computation

It would be worthwhile to distinguish which results in computable structure theory depend on a "special" (and potentially extremely rare) input, and which are less sensitive. To achieve this goal in the context of word problems on groups, Kapovich, Myasnikov, Schupp, and Shpilrain [8] proposed using notions of asymptotic density to state whether a partial recursive function could solve "almost all" instances of a problem.

Jockusch and Schupp [5] generalized this approach to the broader context of computability theory in the following way. Fix a subset S of $\mathbb{N}$.

1. The density of S up to n, denoted by $\rho_n(S)$, is given by

$$\frac{|S \cap \{0, 1, 2, \ldots, n-1\}|}{n}.$$

2. The asymptotic density of S, denoted by $\rho(S)$, is given by $\lim_{n \to \infty} \rho_n(S)$.

A set A is said to be *generically computable* if and only if there is a partial computable function ϕ such that ϕ agrees with the characteristic function χ_A throughout the domain of ϕ, and such that the domain of ϕ has asymptotic density 1. A set A is said to be *coarsely computable* if and only if there is a *total* computable function ϕ that agrees with χ_A on a set of asymptotic density 1.

The study of generically and coarsely computable sets and some related notions has led to an interesting program of research in recent years; see [6] for a partial survey.

1.2   Densely Computable Structures

A structure $\mathcal{A}$ consists of a set A (the universe or domain of $\mathcal{A}$), together with finitely many functions $\{f_i : i \in I\}$, each f_i of arity p_i, and relations $\{R_j : j \in J\}$, each R_i of arity r_j. The structure $\mathcal{A}$ is said to be computable if the set A and the functions and relations are all computable. A structure $\mathcal{B}$ which is isomorphic to $\mathcal{A}$ is said to be a *copy* of $\mathcal{A}$. Given a structure $\mathcal{A}$, we want to consider what it means to say that $\mathcal{A}$ is generically computable, or "nearly computable" in some other notion related to density. We now present informal versions of the definitions, which will be made precise in Sect. 2. The idea is that $\mathcal{A}$ is generically computable if there is a substructure $\mathcal{D}$ with universe a computably enumerable set D of asymptotic density one which is computable in the following sense: There exist partial computable functions $\{\phi_i : i \in I\}$ and $\{\psi_j : j \in J\}$ such that ϕ_i agrees with f_i on the Cartesian product D^{p_i} and ψ_j agrees with the characteristic function of R_j on D^{r_j}. Similarly, $\mathcal{A}$ is coarsely computable if there is a computable structure $\mathcal{E}$ and a dense set D such that the structure $\mathcal{D}$ with universe D is a substructure of both $\mathcal{A}$ and of $\mathcal{E}$ and all relations and functions agree on D. A more interesting variation requires that $\mathcal{D}$ is a Σ_1 elementary submodel of $\mathcal{A}$, more generally a Σ_n elementary submodel. That is, if we are saying that $\mathcal{A}$ is "nearly computable" when it has a dense substructure $\mathcal{D}$ which is computable (computably enumerable), then the substructure should be similar to $\mathcal{A}$ by some standard.

To be precise, recall that $\mathcal{D}$ is an Σ_n elementary substructure of $\mathcal{A}$ provided that, for any Σ_n formula $\varphi(x_1, \ldots, x_n)$ and any elements $a_1, \ldots, a_n \in D$,

$$\mathcal{A} \models \varphi(a_1, \ldots, a_n) \iff \mathcal{D} \models \varphi(a_1, \ldots, a_n).$$

We will say that the structure $\mathcal{A}$ is Σ_n-*generically computably enumerable* if there is an asymptotically dense set D such that

(a) $\mathcal{D}$ is a Σ_n elementary substructure of $\mathcal{A}$;

(b) there exist partial computable functions $\{\phi_i : i \in I\}$ such that ϕ_i agrees with f_i on D^{p_i};

(c) each R_j restricted to D^{r_j} is a computably enumerable relation.

We remark that generically computable is the same as generically Σ_0, for structures with functions only such as groups since $\mathcal{B}$ is a submodel of $\mathcal{A}$ if and only if it preserves all quantifier-free formulas.

The outline of this paper is as follows. Section 2 contains background on asymptotic density, and gives the generalization of generic computability to structures and isomorphisms. Section 3 presents results on generically computable and Σ_n-generically computably enumerable Abelian groups. We show that every countable Abelian p-group has a generically computable copy. We characterize the class of countable Abelian groups which have generically computable copies. We also characterize Abelian p-groups which have Σ_1-generically computably enumerable copies and those which have generically Σ_2-generically computably enumerable copies.

2   Background

In this section, we provide some background on the notions of asymptotic density and generically computable sets. We define the more general notions of Σ_n-generically computably enumerable structures.

The asymptotic density of a set $A \subseteq \omega$ ($\omega = \mathbb{N}$) is defined as follows.

Definition 1. *The* asymptotic density *of A is* $\lim_n \frac{|A \cap \{0,1\dots,n-1\}|}{n}$*, if this exists.*

In [5], Jockusch and Schupp give the following definition, along with the notion of coarsely computable sets, which we will not discuss here.

Definition 2. *Let $S \subseteq \omega$. We say that S is* generically computable *if there is a partial computable function $\Phi : \omega \to 2$ such that $\Phi = \chi_S$ on the domain of Φ, and such that the domain of Φ has asymptotic density 1.*

The most natural notion for a structure seems to be the requirement that the substructure with domain D resembles the given structure $\mathcal{A}$ by agreeing on certain first-order formulas, existential formulas in particular. Throughout this paper, Σ_n represents the n'th level of the arithmetical hierarchy, as described in Soare [12]. Other background on computability may also be found in [12].

We recall the notion of an elementary substructure.

Definition 3. *A substructure $\mathcal{B}$ of the structure $\mathcal{A}$ is said to be a (fully) elementary substructure ($\mathcal{B} \prec \mathcal{A}$) if for any $b_1, \dots, b_k \in \mathcal{B}$, and any formula $\phi(x_1, \dots, x_k)$,*

$$\mathcal{A} \models \phi(b_1, \dots, b_k) \iff \mathcal{B} \models \phi(b_1, \dots, b_k).$$

The substructure $\mathcal{B}$ is said to be a Σ_n elementary substructure ($\mathcal{B} \prec_n \mathcal{A}$) if for any $b_1, \dots, b_k \in \mathcal{B}$, and any Σ_n formula $\phi(x_1, \dots, x_k)$,

$$\mathcal{A} \models \phi(b_1, \dots, b_k) \iff \mathcal{B} \models \phi(b_1, \dots, b_k).$$

Definition 4. *For any structure* $\mathcal{A}$*:*

1. *A substructure* $\mathcal{B}$ *of* $\mathcal{A}$*, with universe* B*, is a* computable substructure *if the set* B *is c.e and each function and relation is computable on* B*, that is, for any* k*-ary function* f *and any* k*-ary relation* R*, both* $f \upharpoonright B^k$ *and* $\chi_R \upharpoonright B^k$ *are the restrictions to* B^k *of partial computable functions.*
2. *A substructure* $\mathcal{B}$ *of* $\mathcal{A}$*, with universe* B*, is a* computably enumerable (computably enumerable) *structure if the set* B *is computably enumerable, each relation is computably enumerable and the graph of each function is computably enumerable (so that the function is partial computable but also total on* B*).*
3. $\mathcal{A}$ *is* generically computable *if there is a substructure* $\mathcal{D}$ *with universe a computably enumerable set* D *of asymptotic density one such that the substructure* $\mathcal{D}$ *with universe* D *is a computable substructure.*
4. $\mathcal{A}$ *is* Σ_n*-generically computably enumerable if there is a dense computably enumerable set* D *such that the substructure* $\mathcal{D}$ *with universe* D *is a computably enumerable substructure and also a* Σ_n*-elementary substructure of* $\mathcal{A}$*.*

For $n > 0$, any Σ_{n+1}-generically computably enumerable structure Σ_n-generically computably enumerable. For structures with functions but no relations, this also holds for $n = 0$. However, a computably enumerable substructure might not be computable, so a structure $\mathcal{A}$ with relations which is Σ_1-generically computably enumerable is not necessarily generically computable.

Countable Abelian groups have been thoroughly studied by Kaplansky [7], Fuchs [4] and many others. Here is some background from Fuchs [4].

Definition 5. *Let* $\mathcal{A}$ *be an Abelian group and let* p *be a prime number.*

1. $\mathcal{A}$ *is a* p*-group if every element has order a power of* p*.*
2. $A[p]$ *is the subgroup of elements with order a power of* p*.*
3. *The* p*-height* $ht_p^{\mathcal{A}}(x)$ *of an element* $x \in \mathcal{A}$ *is the largest* n *such that* $p^n | x$*, that is, there exists* y *such that* $p^n y = x$*.*
4. *A subgroup* $\mathcal{B}$ *of* $\mathcal{A}$ *is* pure *if, for every prime* q *and every* $b \in B$*,* $ht_q^{\mathcal{B}}(b) = ht_q^{\mathcal{A}}(b)$*. The subscript* q *will be omitted if it is clear from the context.*
5. $\mathcal{A}$ *is* divisible *if every element of* $\mathcal{A}$ *has infinite height, that is, for every* $x \in \mathcal{A}$ *and every* $n \in \mathbb{N}$*, there exists* $y \in \mathcal{A}$ *such that* $x = n \cdot y$*.*
6. *A group is* reduced *if it has no divisible subgroup.*

For any prime p, the group $\mathbb{Z}(p^\infty)$ may be realized as the rational numbers with denominators a power of p, with addition modulo one. These groups are said to be *quasicyclic*.

We need the following results from [4].

Theorem 1 (Baer). *Every Abelian group is a direct sum of a divisible group and a reduced group.*

Theorem 2 (Prüfer). *A countable Abelian* p*-group is a direct sum of cyclic groups if and only if it contains no elements of infinite height.*

Theorem 3 (Szele). *Let $\mathcal{B}$ be a subgroup of the Abelian p-group $\mathcal{A}$ such that $\mathcal{B}$ is the direct sum of cyclic subgroups of the same order p^k, for some finite k. Then $\mathcal{B}$ is a direct summand of $\mathcal{A}$ if and only if $\mathcal{B}$ is a pure subgroup of $\mathcal{A}$.*

The following standard result is Theorem 1 of Kaplansky [7].

Theorem 4. *Any torsion group $\mathcal{A}$ is the direct sum of p-groups $\mathcal{A}[p]$.*

Definition 6. *For an Abelian group $\mathcal{A}$, the Ulm subgroup $U(\mathcal{A})$ is the set of elements of infinite height. This operation may be iterated to obtain the Ulm sequence $\mathcal{A}_0 = \mathcal{A}, \mathcal{A}_1 = U(\mathcal{A}), \mathcal{A}_2 = U(\mathcal{A}_1), \ldots$ and extended to the transfinite ordinals by $\mathcal{A}^{\lambda} = \cap_{\alpha < \lambda} \mathcal{A}_{\alpha}$ and $\mathcal{A}_{\alpha+1} = U(\mathcal{A}_{\alpha})$. The length of a group is the least α such that $\mathcal{A}_{\alpha+1} = \mathcal{A}_{\alpha}$.*

Corollary 1. *Let $\mathcal{A}$ be a countable Abelian p-group and let $\mathcal{A} = \mathcal{C} \oplus \mathcal{D}$, where $\mathcal{C}$ has no elements of infinite height and $\mathcal{D}$ is divisible. Then $\mathcal{A}$ has the form $\bigoplus_{i < \omega} \mathbb{Z}(p^{n_i}) \oplus \bigoplus_{i \leq k} \mathbb{Z}(p^{\infty})$, where $k \leq \omega$.*

In computability theory, the *character* $\chi(\mathcal{A})$ of an Abelian p-group $\mathcal{A}$ is defined to be the set

$$\{(n, k) \in (\omega \setminus \{0\})^2 : \mathcal{A} \text{ has at least } n \text{ factors of the form } \mathbb{Z}(p^k)\}.$$

We say that $K \subseteq (\omega \setminus \{0\})^2$ is a *character* if whenever $(n + 1, k) \in K$, then $(n, k) \in K$. As for injection structures and equivalence structures, it is easy to see that K is a character if and only if $K = \chi(\mathcal{A})$ for some Abelian p-group $\mathcal{A}$.

Computable Abelian p-groups were studied by A. Morozov and the authors in [3]. See Khisamiev [9] for more background.

Proposition 1 (Kulikov). *For any countable Abelian p-group $\mathcal{A}$ and any $n, k \geq 1$, $(n, k) \in \chi(\mathcal{A})$ if and only if $\mathcal{A}$ has a pure subgroup isomorphic to $\bigoplus_{i < n} \mathbb{Z}(p^k)$.*

Proposition 2. *Let $\mathcal{A}$ be an Abelian p-group and let n and k be positive integers. Then*

1. *There is a quantifier-free formula $\phi_{n,k}$ such that, for any Abelian group $\mathcal{A}$ and any $a_1, \ldots, a_n \in \mathcal{A}$, $\phi_{n,k}(a_1, \ldots, a_n)$ if and only if $a_1, \ldots, a_n$ are independent elements each of order p^k, that is, if and only if $\langle a_1 \rangle \oplus \langle a_2 \rangle \oplus \cdots \oplus \langle a_n \rangle$ is isomorphic to $\bigoplus_{i < n} \mathbb{Z}(p^k)$.*
2. *There is a Σ_1 formula $\theta_{n,k}$ such that $\mathcal{A} \models \theta_{n,k}$ if and only if $\mathcal{A}$ has a subgroup of the form $\bigoplus_{i < n} \mathbb{Z}(p^{k_i})$, with each $k_i \geq k$.*
3. *There is a Σ_2 formula $\psi_{n,k}$ such that $\mathcal{A} \models \psi_{n,k}$ if and only if $(n, k) \in \chi(\mathcal{A})$, that is, if and only if $\mathcal{A}$ has a pure subgroup of the form $\bigoplus_{i < n} \mathbb{Z}(p^k)$.*

This was used by Khisamiev [9] to obtain the following.

Theorem 5 (Khisamiev). *For any computable p-group $\mathcal{A}$, $\chi(\mathcal{A})$ is a Σ_2^0 set.*

The following was shown in [3].

Proposition 3. *Let K be a Σ_2^0 character and let p be a prime number. Then there is a computable Abelian p-group $\mathcal{A}$ with character K and with infinitely many divisible components.*

Definition 7. *A function $f : \omega^2 \to \omega$ is said to be an s_1-function if the following hold:*

1. *For every i and s, $f(i,s) \le f(i,s+1)$.*
2. *For every i, the limit $m_i = \lim_{s\to\infty} f(i,s)$ exists.*
3. *For every i, $m_i < m_{i+1}$.*

The character K is said to *possess* the s_1-function f if $(1, m_i) \in K$ for each i. The next lemma is based on Corollary 2.11 and Corollary 2.14 of [3].

Lemma 1. *For any Σ_2^0 character K which is either bounded or possesses a computable s_1-function, there is a computable Abelian p-group $\mathcal{A}$ with character K and no divisible factors.*

3 Σ_n-Generically Computably Enumerable Abelian Groups

This section contains the new results about generically computably enumerable Abelian groups. The following result is immediate from the definition of generically computable structures, and begins to suggest the ubiquity of generically computable copies.

Lemma 2. *Let $\mathcal{A}$ be an Abelian group, and $\mathcal{B}$ an infinite subgroup of $\mathcal{A}$. If $\mathcal{B}$ has a generically computable copy, then $\mathcal{A}$ has a generically computable copy.*

The following phenomenon was unexpected when we first observed the analogous result for equivalence structures.

Proposition 4. *Every countable Abelian p-group $\mathcal{A}$ has a generically computable copy.*

Proof. If the group $\mathcal{A}$ is finite, then of course it is computable. The proof for countably infinite structures is in two steps. First, we show that $\mathcal{A} = (\omega, +_A)$ always has a subgroup $\mathcal{B}$ which is isomorphic to a computable group. Second, we obtain a computable group $\mathcal{D} = (D, +_D)$ isomorphic to $\mathcal{B}$ with universe D a dense co-infinite set, and then extend $\mathcal{D}$ to generically computable $\mathcal{C} = (\omega, +_C)$ isomorphic to $\mathcal{A}$.

The first step is in three cases.

Case 1: $\mathcal{A}$ has a divisible subgroup $\mathcal{B}$. Then it is known that $\mathcal{B}$ has a computable copy.

Case 2: Every element of $\mathcal{A}$ has finite height. Then, by Theorem 2, $\mathcal{A}$ has the form $\bigoplus_{i<\omega} \mathbb{Z}(p^{n_i})$. Let $\{a_i : i < \omega\}$ be a set of generators for $\mathcal{A}$, so that

$A = \oplus_i \langle a_i \rangle$ and a_i has order p^{n_i}. For each i, $p^{n_i-1}a_i$ has order p. Let $B = \oplus_i \langle p^{n_i-1}a_i \rangle$. Then B is a subgroup of A isomorphic to $\oplus_{i<\omega}\mathbb{Z}(p)$, which is known to have a computable copy.

Case 3: A has an element a of infinite height, but no divisible subgroup. Without loss of generaility, we may assume that a has order p. Let $a = a_0$, and for each $n > 0$, choose a_n so that $p^n a_n = a$. For any $m \in \omega$, let $A_m = \{p^{n-m}a_n : n < \omega\}$. In particular, $A_1 = \{p^{n-1}a_n : n > 0\}$, so that every element of A_1 has order p^2. Every element of A_m has order p^{m+1}.

Claim: A has an element b such that $\{x : px = b\}$ is infinite.

Proof of Claim: Suppose not. Then in particular A_1 is finite. We will construct a divisible subgroup of A, contradicting our assumption. This will be done by finding a sequence $(b_i)_{i<\omega} \subseteq \{a_n : n < \omega\}$ of elements of infinite height, beginning with $b_0 = a$, such that $pb_{n+1} = b_n$ for each n. It will then follow that $\{b_0, b_1, \ldots\}$ generates a divisible group. For each element b of A_1, there is some n so that $b = p^{n-1}a_n$. Given that A_1 is finite, there must be some b_1 such that $b_1 = p^{n-1}a_n$ for infinitely many n. It follows that b has infinite height. Let $b_1 = b$ and consider $B_2 = \{p^{n-2}a_n : p^{n-1}a_n = b_1\}$. If B_2 is infinite, then the claim is established. If B_2 is finite, then, as above, there is some $b_2 \in B_2$ such that $b_2 = p^{n-2}a_n$ for infinitely many n. Continuing in this way we reach one of two outcomes.

(1) There will be some n such that $\{x : px = b_n\}$ is infinite.

or

(2) For each n, $pb_{n+1} = b_n$. In this case, $\{b_n : n = 1, 2, \ldots\}$ will generate a divisible subgroup.

This completes the proof of the Claim.

Thus we have found b such that $C = \{x : px = b\}$ is infinite.

Let b have order p^r. Then each element of C has order p^{r+1}. It follows that C generates an infinite subgroup B of A with all elements of order $\leq p^r$. The group B is therefore isomorphic to a computable group, as desired.

Now let $\mathcal{D} = (D, +_D)$ be computable and isomorphic to B, where D is asymptotically dense and co-infinite. Let H be a permutation of ω which maps D to B.

Define the extension $\mathcal{C} = (\omega, +_C)$ of $\mathcal{D}$ by

$$x +_C y = H^{-1}(H(x) +_A H(y)).$$

Then H is an isomorphism from $\mathcal{C}$ to A since $H(x +_C y) = H(x) +_A H(y)$.

In particular, for $x, y \in D$,

$$x +_C y = H^{-1}(H(x) +_A H(y)) = H^{-1}(H(x) +_B H(y)) = x +_D y,$$

since H is a group isomorphism from $\mathcal{D}$ to B.

It follows that $\mathcal{D}$ is a computable subgroup of $\mathcal{C}$. Since D is a dense set, $\mathcal{C}$ is generically computable. So A is isomorphic to a generically computable group, as desired. $\qquad\qquad\square$

Next, we consider countable Abelian groups in general. For each such group $\mathcal{A}$, let $\mathcal{A}[p] = \{x \in \mathcal{A} : p^n x = 0 \text{ for some } n\}$.

Theorem 6. *A countable Abelian group has a generically computable copy if and only if either*

1. $\mathcal{A}[p]$ *is infinite for some prime* p, *or*
2. $\{p : \mathcal{A}[p] \neq 0\}$ *has an infinite computably enumerable subset.*

Proof. Suppose first that $\mathcal{A}$ has a generically computable copy $\mathcal{C}$ and let $\mathcal{D} = (D, +_D)$ be a subgroup of $\mathcal{C}$, where D is a computably enumerable dense set and $+_D$ is computable on D. Suppose that $\mathcal{D}[p]$ is finite for all primes p. Then $\mathcal{D}[p]$ must be nonempty for infinitely many p. Now $\{p : \mathcal{D}[p] \neq 0\}$ is an infinite computably enumerable subset of $\{p : \mathcal{C}[p] \neq 0\} = \{p : \mathcal{A}[p] \neq 0\}$.

Next let p be a prime such that $\mathcal{A}[p]$ is infinite. Then $\mathcal{A}[p]$ has a generically computable copy $\mathcal{B}$. Let $\mathcal{C} = \mathcal{A}[p] \oplus \bigoplus_{q \neq p} \mathcal{A}[q]$. Then $\mathcal{C}$ is isomorphic to $\mathcal{A}$ and $\mathcal{C}[p]$ is generically computable since $\mathcal{C}[p] = \mathcal{B}$ is generically computable.

Finally, suppose that there is an infinite computably enumerable set P of primes p such that $\mathcal{A}[p] \neq 0$. Then $\mathcal{A}$ will have a subgroup isomorphic to $\bigoplus_{p \in P} \mathbb{Z}(p)$, and we proceed as usual. $\square$

Note that Theorem 6 implies that there are countable Abelian groups with no generically computable copy, in contrast to Proposition 4 on primary groups.

We now turn to the topic of Σ_n elementary substructures and Σ_n-generically computably enumerable structures.

Proposition 5. *Let $\mathcal{A}$ be an Abelian group and let $\mathcal{B}$ be a subgroup of $\mathcal{A}$. $\mathcal{B}$ is a Σ_1 elementary subgroup of $\mathcal{A}$ if and only if it satisfies condition*

(*): *For any finite subgroup $\mathcal{C}$ of $\mathcal{A}$, there is a subgroup $\mathcal{D}$ of $\mathcal{B}$ isomorphic to $\mathcal{C}$, such that $\mathcal{B} \cap \mathcal{C} = \mathcal{D} \cap \mathcal{C}$ and the isomorphism is the identity on $\mathcal{B} \cap \mathcal{C}$.*

Proof. Suppose first that $\mathcal{B}$ is a Σ_1 elementary subgroup of $\mathcal{A}$.

Let $C = \{a_1, \ldots, a_m, b_1, \ldots, b_n\}$ be the domain of a finite subgroup of $\mathcal{A}$ with $\mathcal{B} \cap C = \{b_1, \ldots, b_n\}$ and let $\phi(a_1, \ldots, a_m, b_1, \ldots, b_n)$ be a sentence which captures the atomic diagram of $\mathcal{C}$. Then

$$\mathcal{A} \models (\exists x_1)(\exists x_2) \ldots (\exists x_m) \phi(x_1, \ldots, x_m, b_1, \ldots, b_n).$$

Since $\mathcal{B}$ is a Σ_1 elementary submodel, it follows that there are $c_1, \ldots, c_m \in \mathcal{B}$ such that

$$\phi(c_1, \ldots, c_m, b_1, \ldots, b_n).$$

Then the subgroup $\mathcal{D}$ with domain $D = \{c_1, \ldots, c_m, b_1, \ldots, b_n\}$ is isomorphic to $\mathcal{C}$ under the isomorphism mapping each c_i to a_i and mapping each b_j to itself. Furthermore, $\mathcal{B} \cap C = \mathcal{D} \cap C = \{b_1, \ldots, b_n\}$.

For the other direction, suppose that $\mathcal{B}$ satisfies condition (*). Let $b_1, \ldots, b_n \in B$ and consider an arbitrary Σ_1 formula

$$\varphi(b_1, \ldots, b_n) : (\exists x_1, \ldots, \exists x_m)\theta(x_1, \ldots, x_m, b_1, \ldots, b_n),$$

where θ is quantifier-free. By distributing disjunctions in the usual way, we may assume without loss of generality that θ gives a full description of the subgroup generated by $x_1, \ldots, x_m, b_1, \ldots, b_n$. Suppose now that $\mathcal{A} \models \theta(a_1, \ldots, a_m, b_1, \ldots, b_n)$ and consider the subgroup C generated by $\{a_1, \ldots, a_m, b_1, \ldots, b_n\}$. Then, by assumption, there is a subgroup $\mathcal{D}$ of $\mathcal{B}$ with $B \cap C = D \cap C$ and an isomorphism $F : C \to D$ with $F(b) = b$ for all $b \in B$. It follows that $\mathcal{B} \models \theta(F(a_1), \ldots, F(a_m), b_1, \ldots, b_n)$ and therefore $\mathcal{B} \models \varphi(b_1, \ldots, b_n)$.
□

Proposition 6. *Let $\mathcal{A}$ be an Abelian p-group such that $\mathcal{A} = \mathcal{B} \oplus \mathcal{E}$ for some subgroups $\mathcal{B}$ and $\mathcal{E}$, where $\mathcal{B}$ has unbounded character. Then $\mathcal{B}$ is a Σ_1 elementary subgroup of $\mathcal{A}$.*

Proof. We prove this assertion using Proposition 5. Let C be any finite subgroup of $\mathcal{A}$. Let $\mathcal{B}_0$ be the projection of C onto $\mathcal{B}$ and let $\mathcal{E}_0$ be the projection onto $\mathcal{E}$. Since $\mathcal{B}$ has unbounded character, there is a subgroup $\mathcal{B}_1$ of $\mathcal{B}$ independent of $\mathcal{B}_0$ and isomorphism ψ from $\mathcal{E}_0$ to $\mathcal{B}_1$. Now let $\mathcal{D} = \{x + y : x \in B_0, y \in B_1\}$ and define the isomorphism from C to $\mathcal{D}$ by $\phi(b + c) = b + \psi(c)$. Then ϕ is an isomorphism from C to $\mathcal{D}$ which preserves elements of $\mathcal{B}$. We note that $\mathcal{B} \cap C = \mathcal{D} \cap C = \mathcal{B}_0$. Thus, condition (*) is satisfied, and the result follows. □

Proposition 7. *Suppose that $\mathcal{A}$ is a countable Abelian p-group which is a product of cyclic subgroups and let K be a subcharacter of $\chi(\mathcal{A})$. That is, K is a subset of $\chi(\mathcal{A})$ such that, for any n and k, $(n + 1, k) \in K$ implies $(n, k) \in K$. Then $\mathcal{A}$ has a pure subgroup $\mathcal{B}$ which is a factor of $\mathcal{A}$.*

Proof. We have $\mathcal{A} = \bigoplus_{i \in \omega}\langle a_i \rangle$, where each $\langle a_i \rangle$ is a pure cyclic subgroup of order p^{n_i}. We can select a subset I of ω so that $\mathcal{B} = \bigoplus_{i \in I}\langle a_i \rangle$ has character K and then $C = \bigoplus_{i \notin I}\langle a_i \rangle$ is a factor of $\mathcal{A}$, that is, $\mathcal{A} = \mathcal{B} \oplus C$. □

Proposition 8. *Let $\mathcal{A}$ be a countable Abelian p-group and let $\mathcal{B}$ be a Σ_1 elementary subgroup of $\mathcal{A}$. Then the following conditions hold:*

1. *$\mathcal{B}$ is a pure subgroup of $\mathcal{A}$.*
2. *$\chi(\mathcal{B}) \subseteq \chi(\mathcal{A})$.*
3. *$\mathcal{B} \models \theta_{n,k}$ for any $(n, k) \in \chi(\mathcal{A})$, that is, whenever $\mathcal{A}$ has a pure subgroup of the form $\bigoplus_{i<n} \mathbb{Z}(p^k)$, then $\mathcal{B}$ has a subgroup of the form $\bigoplus_{i<n} \mathbb{Z}(p^{k_i})$, with each $k_i \geq k$.*
4. *If $\mathcal{A}$ has a divisible component, then either $\mathcal{B}$ has a divisible component or $\chi(\mathcal{B})$ is unbounded.*

Proof. Suppose first that $\mathcal{B}$ is a Σ_1 elementary subgroup of the Abelian p-group $\mathcal{A}$.

(1) Let $b \in \mathcal{B}$ and suppose $ht^{\mathcal{A}}(b) \geq n$. Then $b = p^n a$ for some $a \in \mathcal{A}$. Thus $\mathcal{A} \models (\exists x) p^n x = b$. Since $\mathcal{B}$ is a Σ_1 elementary subgroup of $\mathcal{B}$, $\mathcal{B} \models (\exists x) p^n x = b$, so that $ht^{\mathcal{B}}(b) \geq n$ as well. It follows that $\mathcal{B}$ is a pure subgroup of $\mathcal{A}$.

(2) Suppose that $(n, k) \in \chi(\mathcal{B})$. Then $\mathcal{B}$ has a pure subgroup $\mathcal{C}$ isomorphic to $\bigoplus_{i<n} \mathbb{Z}(p^k)$. Since $\mathcal{B}$ is pure in $\mathcal{A}$, it follows that $\mathcal{C}$ is a pure subgroup of $\mathcal{A}$. Thus $(n, k) \in \chi(\mathcal{A})$.

For part (3), suppose that $(n, k) \in \chi(\mathcal{A})$. Then $\mathcal{A} \models \theta_{n,k}$. Since $\mathcal{B}$ is a Σ_1 elementary submodel of $\mathcal{A}$ and $\theta_{n,k}$ is a Σ_1 sentence, it follows that $\mathcal{B} \models \theta_{n,k}$, and therefore $\mathcal{B}$ has a subgroup of the form $\bigoplus_{i<n} \mathbb{Z}(p^{k_i})$, with each $k_i \geq k$.

For part (4), suppose that $\mathcal{A}$ has a divisible component. Then $\mathcal{A} \models \theta_{1,k}$ for each k. It follows as above that $\mathcal{B} \models \theta_{1,k}$ for all k and therefore either $\mathcal{B}$ has a divisible component or $\chi(\mathcal{B})$ is unbounded.   □

We conjecture that the converse of Proposition 8 also holds.

Proposition 9. *Let $\mathcal{A}$ be a countable Abelian p-group and let $\mathcal{B}$ be a Σ_2 elementary subgroup of $\mathcal{A}$. Then*

1. *$\mathcal{B}$ is a pure subgroup of $\mathcal{A}$.*
2. *$\chi(\mathcal{A}) = \chi(\mathcal{B})$.*
3. *If $\mathcal{A}$ has a divisible component, then either $\mathcal{B}$ has a divisible component or $\chi(\mathcal{B})$ is unbounded.*

Proof. First suppose that $\mathcal{B}$ is a Σ_2 elementary subgroup of $\mathcal{A}$.

Parts (1) and (3) follow as in the proof of Proposition 8.

(2) Suppose that $(n, k) \in \mathcal{A}$. Then by Proposition 1, $\mathcal{A}$ has a pure subgroup $\mathcal{C}$ isomorphic to $\bigoplus_{i<n} \mathbb{Z}(p^k)$. Thus $\mathcal{A} \models \psi_{n,k}$. Since $\mathcal{B}$ is a Σ_2 elementary submodel of $\mathcal{A}$ and $\psi_{n,k}$ is a Σ_2 sentence, it follows that $\mathcal{B} \models \psi_{n,k}$, and therefore $(n, k) \in \chi(\mathcal{B})$.   □

We conjecture that the converse of Proposition 9 also holds.

Theorem 7. *Let $\mathcal{A}$ be an Abelian p-group with no elements of infinite height in the reduced part. That is, $\mathcal{A}$ is a product of cyclic and quasi-cyclic components. Then $\mathcal{A}$ has a Σ_1-generically computably enumerable copy if and only if at least one of the following holds:*

(a) $\chi(\mathcal{A})$ is bounded;
(b) $\chi(\mathcal{A})$ has a Σ_2^0 subset K with a computable s_1-function.
(c) $\mathcal{A}$ has a divisible component.

Proof. First suppose that $\mathcal{A}$ has a Σ_1-generically computably enumerable copy. Then $\mathcal{A}$ has a Σ_1 elementary substructure $\mathcal{B}$ which is isomorphic to a computably enumerable structure $\mathcal{C}$. If $\mathcal{A}$ has no divisible component, then $\mathcal{C}$ has no divisible component. If $\chi(\mathcal{A})$ is unbounded, then $\chi(\mathcal{C})$ is unbounded, by Proposition 8. Thus $\mathcal{C}$ has a Σ_2^0 character K with a computable s_1-function, and it follows from Proposition 8 that $\chi(\mathcal{C}) \subseteq \chi(\mathcal{A})$.

The other direction is in three cases.

(a) If $\chi(\mathcal{A})$ is bounded, then $\mathcal{A}$ has a computable copy.

In cases (b) and (c), we will assume that $\chi(\mathcal{A})$ is unbounded and show that there is a structure $\mathcal{B} \subseteq \mathcal{A}$ which is isomorphic to a computable p-group $\mathcal{D}$. Then we will build a copy $\mathcal{C}$ of $\mathcal{A}$ with a dense computable subgroup $\mathcal{D}$ and fill out the rest of $\mathcal{C}$ to make it isomorphic to $\mathcal{A}$, as explained in (b).

(b) In this case, $\mathcal{A}$ has no divisible component, and is a product of cyclic subgroups. Thus by Proposition 7, $\mathcal{A}$ has a pure subgroup $\mathcal{B}$ with character K and $\mathcal{B}$ is a factor of $\mathcal{A}$. It follows from Proposition 6 that $\mathcal{B}$ is a Σ_1 elementary subgroup of $\mathcal{A}$.

By Lemma 1, there is a computable p-group $\mathcal{D}$ with character K isomorphic to $\mathcal{B}$. We may assume that the universe D of $\mathcal{D}$ is a computable asymptotically dense set. Let ϕ be an isomorphism from $\mathcal{D}$ to $\mathcal{B}$ and extend this to a bijection from ω to ω. Then we extend $\mathcal{D}$ to a group $\mathcal{C}$ with universe ω by letting $x +^{\mathcal{C}} y = \phi^{-1}(\phi(x) +^{\mathcal{A}} \phi(y))$. For $x, y \in D$, we have

$$x +^{\mathcal{C}} y = \phi^{-1}(\phi(x) +^{\mathcal{A}} \phi(y)) = \phi^{-1}(\phi(x +^{\mathcal{D}} y)) = x +^{\mathcal{D}} y,$$

since ϕ is an isomorphism from $\mathcal{D}$ to $\mathcal{B} \subseteq \mathcal{A}$. For arbitrary $x, y \in \omega$,

$$\phi(x +^{\mathcal{C}} y) = \phi(\phi^{-1}(\phi(x) +^{\mathcal{A}} \phi(y))) = \phi(x) +^{\mathcal{A}} \phi(y),$$

so ϕ is an isomorphism from $\mathcal{C}$ to $\mathcal{A}$. Since $\mathcal{B}$ is a Σ_1 elementary subgroup of $\mathcal{A}$, and ϕ is an isomorphism mapping $\mathcal{B}$ to $\mathcal{D}$, it follows that $\mathcal{D}$ is a Σ_1 elementary subgroup of $\mathcal{C}$. Thus $\mathcal{C}$ is Σ_1-generically computably enumerable.

(c) In this case, the divisible component $\mathcal{B}$ will be a Σ_1 elementary substructure and we proceed as in (b) to define a computable group $\mathcal{D}$ with infinitely many divisible components, and extend this to a Σ_1-generically computably enumerable structure which is isomorphic to $\mathcal{A}$.   □

We observe that the argument above also proves that $\mathcal{A}$ is Σ_1-generically computably enumerable if and only if it has a subgroup $\mathcal{B}$ which is isomorphic to a computable group.

Theorem 8. *The group $\mathcal{A}$ is Σ_2-generically computably enumerable if and only if it has a computable copy.*

Proof. Suppose that $\mathcal{A} = (\omega, +^{\mathcal{A}})$ is Σ_2-generically computably enumerable and let $\mathcal{D}$ be a dense computably enumerable set such that $\mathcal{D} = (D, +^{\mathcal{A}})$ is a computably enumerable group and also a Σ_2 elementary subgroup of $\mathcal{A}$. Then $\chi(\mathcal{D})$ is a Σ_2^0 set since D is computably enumerable and $\chi(\mathcal{D}) = \chi(\mathcal{A})$ since $\mathcal{D}$ is a Σ_2 elementary submodel of $\mathcal{A}$. If $\chi(\mathcal{A})$ is bounded, then $\mathcal{A}$ has a computable copy. So suppose that $\chi(\mathcal{A})$ is unbounded. If $\mathcal{D}$ has no divisible component, then $\chi(\mathcal{D})$ has a computable s_1-function, so that $\mathcal{A}$ has a computable copy. If $\mathcal{D}$ has a divisible component, then $\mathcal{A}$ also has a divisible component and therefore has a computable copy.   □

4   Conclusion and Future Research

We have shown that any Abelian p-group has a generically computable copy and that such a group has a Σ_2-generically computably enumerable copy if and only it has a computable copy. We also gave a partial characterization of the Σ_1-generically computably enumerable Abelian p-groups, and a non-trivial characterization of the generically computable Abelian groups. It remains to consider more general Abelian p-groups with transfinite length.

We obtained necessary conditions for a subgroup of a countable Abelian p-group to be a Σ_1 or a Σ_2 elementary substructure. The conjecture is that these conditions are also necessary. We conjecture that a subgroup of an Abelian p-group is Σ_3 elementary if and only if it is (fully) elementary. This might even hold for Σ_2 elementary substructures.

It is interesting to consider whether any appropriate class of structures (perhaps with bounded Scott rank or some similar condition) would trivialize at some level, and we propose that a general result may be possible. Perhaps a general connection can be made in terms of the level at which Σ_n elementarity implies full elementarity. To our thinking, this recalls the feature of computable categoricity by which every structure with a $\Pi_{\alpha+1}$ Scott sentence is Δ^0_α-categorical [10]. So there might be results in the general hyperarithmetic hierarchy.

Previous papers also examined coarsely computable structures, so future work should examine Σ_n-coarsely computably enumerable Abelian groups.

Generically computable and coarsely computable isomorphisms were also studied in [2]. Future plans involve the study of densely computable isomorphisms for Abelian groups. We have the following preliminary result.

Theorem 9. *Let $\mathcal{A}$ and $\mathcal{B}$ be computable Abelian p-groups each isomorphic to $\bigoplus_{i<\omega} \mathbb{Z}(p) \oplus \bigoplus_{i<\omega} \mathbb{Z}(p^2)$ such that the elements of order p^2 are asymptotically dense.*

Then $\mathcal{A}$ and $\mathcal{B}$ are generically computably isomorphic.

References

1. Calvert, W., Cenzer, D., Harizanov, V.: Densely computable structures. J. Logic Comput. **32**, 581–607 (2022)
2. Calvert, W., Cenzer, D., Harizanov, V.: Generically and coarsely computable isomorphisms. Computability **11**, 223–239 (2022). https://doi.org/10.3233/COM-210382
3. Calvert, W., Cenzer, D., Harizanov, V., Morozov, A.: Effective categoricity of Abelian p-groups. Ann. Pure Appl. Logic **159**, 187–197 (2009)
4. Fuchs, L.: Infinite Abelian groups, volume I, Academic Press (1970)
5. Jockusch, C.G., Schupp, P.E.: Generic computability, Turing degrees, and asymptotic density. J. London Math. Soc. **85**, 472–490 (2012)
6. Jockusch, C.G. Schupp, P.E.: Asymptotic density and the theory of computability: a partial survey. In: Computability and Complexity, Lecture Notes in Computer Science, vol. 10010, pp. 501–520 (2017)

7. Kaplansky, I.: Infinite Abelian groups, University of Michigan Press (1954)
8. Kapovich, I., Myasnikov, A., Schupp, P., Shpilrain, V.: Generic-case complexity, decision problems in group theory, and random walks. J. Algebra **264**, 665–694 (2003)
9. Khisamiev, N.G.: Constructive Abelian groups, Handbook of Recursive Mathematics, Vol. 2, Stud. Logic Found. Math., vol. 139, Elsevier, pp. 1177–1231 (1998)
10. Montalbán, A.: A robuster Scott rank. Proc. Am. Math. Soc. **143**, 5427–5436 (2015)
11. Rotman, J.J.: The theory of groups, Allyn and Bacon (1965)
12. Soare, R.I.: Recursively Enumerable Sets and Degrees. Springer-Verlag (1987)

Extraction Rates of Random Continuous Functionals

Douglas Cenzer[1]($\boxtimes$), Cameron Fraize[2], and Christopher Porter[3]

[1] University of Florida, Gainesville, FL 32611, USA
cenzer@ufl.edu
[2] University of Florida, Gainesville, FL 32611, USA
cameron.fraize@ufl.edu
[3] Drake University, Des Moines, IA 50311, USA
christopher.porter@drake.edu

Abstract. In this article, we study the extraction rate, or output/input rate, of algorithmically random continuous functionals on the Cantor space 2^ω. It is shown that random functionals have an average extraction rate over all inputs corresponding to the rate of producing a single bit of output, and that this average rate is attained for any (relatively) random input.

Keywords: Algorithmic randomness · random extraction · continuous functionals

1 Introduction

This paper continues the work of the authors in [CP22] on the analysis of the extraction rate, or output/input ratio, of various effective procedures. The previous paper focused on randomness extraction, starting with the classic problem, posed by von Neumann in [vN51], of extracting unbiased randomness from the tosses of a biased coin. As shown in this work, one can formalize certain randomness extraction procedures as Turing functionals and study the behavior of these functionals when applied to algorithmically random sequences. For a number of such functionals, it is known that almost every sequence attains the extraction rate. In the previous paper, we provided a sufficient level of algorithmic randomness that guaranteed this result for three classes of functionals:

1. functionals defined in terms of maps on $2^{<\omega}$ that we call block maps, which generalize von Neumann's procedure,
2. functionals derived from certain trees called discrete distribution generating trees (or DDG trees, for short), introduced by Knuth and Yao [KY76] in the study of non-uniform random number generation, and
3. a procedure independently developed by Levin [LZ70] and Kautz [Kau91] for converting biased random sequences into unbiased random sequences.

This research was partially supported by the National Science Foundation SEALS grant DMS-1362273.

In the present paper, we apply a similar methodology to the study of the extraction rates of algorithmically random continuous functionals on 2^ω, a class of functionals first introduced by Barmpalias, Brodhead, Cenzer, Remmel, and Weber in [BBC+08]. We will focus on the extraction rates of functionals that are coded by sequences that are random with respect to a Bernoulli measure. In particular, we explore the extent to which the extraction rate of a random functional depends on a certain type of representation of the functional (where a representation of a functional is given in terms of a finite map on $2^{<\omega}$ that determines the behavior of the functional on initial segments of an input sequence). Our main result shows that along sufficiently random inputs, the choice of representation of a functional does not effect the resulting extraction rate.

The remainder of the paper is as follows. In Sect. 2, we lay out the requisite background, define the extraction rate of a continuous functional, present several preliminary results, and give some basic examples. The main results on the extraction rate of random continuous functions are in Sect. 3. Conclusions and some open questions are given in the final Sect. 4.

2   Background

The set of finite binary strings will be written as $2^{<\omega}$. For a finite string $\sigma \in 2^{<\omega}$, let $|\sigma|$ denote the length of σ. For two strings σ, τ, say that τ *extends* σ and write $\sigma \preceq \tau$ if $|\sigma| \leq |\tau|$ and $\sigma(i) = \tau(i)$ for $i < |\sigma|$. For $X \in 2^\omega$, $\sigma \prec X$ means that $\sigma(i) = X(i)$ for $i < |\sigma|$. Let $\sigma^\frown \tau$ denote the concatenation of $\sigma, \tau \in 2^{<\omega}$; Let $X \upharpoonright n$ denote the string $\sigma \prec X$ with $|\sigma| = n$. The empty string will be written as ϵ.

Two sequences $X, Y \in 2^\omega$ may be coded together into $Z = X \oplus Y$, where $Z(2n) = X(n)$ and $Z(2n+1) = Y(n)$ for all n. For a finite string σ, let $[[\sigma]]$ denote $\{X \in 2^\omega : \sigma \prec X\}$. We shall refer to $[[\sigma]]$ as the *cylinder* determined by σ. The cylinder sets form a clopen basis for the standard topology on 2^ω, and the clopen sets are just finite unions of cylinders.

Next we consider the notion of a (partial) continuous function $\Phi : 2^\omega \to 2^\omega$. Such a function Φ may be defined from a function $\phi : 2^{<\omega} \to 2^{<\omega}$, which we refer to as a *representation* of Φ, satisfying the condition

(i) $\sigma \preceq \tau$, then $\phi(\sigma) \preceq \phi(\tau)$.

The function Φ will be total provided that

(ii) for all $X \in 2^\omega$, $\lim_{n \to \infty} |\phi(X \upharpoonright n)| = \infty$.

Furthermore, a representation ϕ for a total continuous function Φ must satisfy:

(iii) For all m, there exists n such that for every $\sigma \in \{0,1\}^n$, $|\phi(\sigma)| \geq m$

by compactness of 2^ω. We then have $\Phi(X) = \bigcup_n \phi(X \upharpoonright n)$. The (partial) Turing functionals $\Phi : 2^\omega \to 2^\omega$ are those which may be defined in this manner from a computable representation $\phi : 2^{<\omega} \to 2^{<\omega}$. (We will sometimes refer to total Turing functionals as *tt-functionals*.) The partial Turing functionals $\Phi :\subseteq 2^{\omega} \to 2^{\omega}$ are given by those $\phi : 2^{<\omega} \to 2^{<\omega}$ which only satisfy condition (i). In this case, we may regard $\Phi : 2^{\omega} \to 2^{\omega} \cup 2^{<\omega}$, so that $\Phi(X) = \bigcup_n \phi(X \restriction n)$ may only be a finite string.

We set $\text{dom}(\Phi) = \{X : \Phi(X) \in 2^{\omega}\}$.

Definition 1. *A continuous functional Φ is said to be* online *continuous if it has a representation ϕ with $|\phi(\sigma)| = |\sigma|$ for all strings σ; then, Φ is called* online computable *if the representation ϕ is computable.*

The *online* computable functions are an interesting class, and were studied by Cenzer and Porter [CP15] and by Cenzer and Rojas [CR18].

Next, we review some notions from algorithmic randomness. Let $\mathbb{Q}_2$ denote the dyadic rationals in $[0,1]$. Recall that a measure μ on 2^{ω} is *computable* if there is a computable function $f : 2^{<\omega} \times \omega \to \mathbb{Q}_2$ such that $|\mu([[\sigma]]) - f(\sigma, i)| \leq 2^{-i}$. For a prefix-free $V \subseteq 2^{<\omega}$ (i.e., for $\sigma \in V$, if $\sigma \prec \tau$, then $\tau \notin V$), we set $\mu([[V]]) = \sum_{\sigma \in V} \mu([[\sigma]])$. Hereafter, we will write $\mu([[\sigma]])$ as $\mu(\sigma)$ for strings σ and $\mu([[V]])$ as $\mu(V)$ for $V \subseteq 2^{<\omega}$. We also denote the *Lebesgue measure* on 2^{ω} by λ, where $\lambda(\sigma) = 2^{-|\sigma|}$ for $\sigma \in 2^{<\omega}$.

We assume that the reader is familiar with the basics of algorithmic randomness; see, for instance [Nie09, DH10, SUV17], or the more recent [FP20]. Let μ be a computable measure on 2^{ω}. Recall that a μ-*Martin-Löf test* is a sequence $(\mathcal{U}_i)_{i \in \omega}$ of uniformly effectively open subsets of 2^{ω} such that for each i,

$$\mu(\mathcal{U}_i) \leq 2^{-i}.$$

Moreover, $X \in 2^{\omega}$ *passes* the μ-Martin-Löf test $(\mathcal{U}_i)_{i \in \omega}$ if $X \notin \bigcap_{i \in \omega} \mathcal{U}_i$. Lastly, $X \in 2^{\omega}$ is μ-*Martin-Löf random*, denoted $X \in \mathsf{MLR}_{\mu}$, if X passes every μ-Martin-Löf test. When μ is the uniform (or Lebesgue) measure λ, we often abbreviate MLR_{μ} by MLR.

We are particularly interested in the interaction between Turing functionals and computable measures on 2^{ω}. For computable measure μ on 2^{ω}, a Turing functional $\Phi : 2^{\omega} \to 2^{\omega}$ is μ-*almost total* if $\mu(\text{dom}(\Phi)) = 1$. The following Lemma was proved in [CP22].

Lemma 1. *A Turing functional Φ is μ-almost total if and only if $\mathsf{MLR}_{\mu} \subseteq \text{dom}(\Phi)$.*

Next we give some definitions and results on the extraction rate of (partial) continuous functionals. This is closely related to the *use* function, an important notion in computability theory. We are interested in a version of the use function of a Turing functional Φ which arises from a given representation ϕ. Let $u_{\phi}(X, n)$ be the least m such that $|\phi(X \restriction m)| \geq n$. Then the *extraction rate* of the computation of $Y = \Phi(X)$ from X is given by the ratio

$$\frac{n}{u_{\phi}(X, n)},$$

that is, the relative amount of input from X needed to compute the first n values of Y.

There is an alternative definition which is more straightforward. The ϕ-*output/input ratio* of σ, $\mathrm{OI}_\phi(\sigma)$, is defined to be

$$\mathrm{OI}_\phi(\sigma) = \frac{|\phi(\sigma)|}{|\sigma|}.$$

The next lemma was also proved in [CP22].

Lemma 2. ([CP22]). *For any Turing functional Φ with representation ϕ and any $X \in 2^\omega$ such that $\Phi(X) \in 2^\omega$,*

$$\lim_{n\to\infty} \frac{|\phi(X \restriction n)|}{n} = \lim_{m\to\infty} \frac{m}{u_\phi(X,m)},$$

provided that both limits exist.

Let us write $\mathrm{OI}_\phi(X)$ for $\limsup_{n\to\infty} \mathrm{OI}_\phi(X \restriction n)$; we refer to this as the ϕ-*extraction rate along X*. This extraction rate certainly depends on the particular representation ϕ for a (partial) continuous function Φ. We would like to say that the extraction rate for a constant function should be very low and should approach 0 in the limit. However, consider the following example:

Example 1. Let $\Phi(X) = 0^\omega$ for all $X \in 2^\omega$ and let $\phi(\sigma) = 0^{|\sigma|}$ for all $\sigma \in 2^{<\omega}$. Then $u_\phi(X,n) = n$ for all n and thus $\lim_{n\to\infty} \frac{n}{u_\phi(X,n)} = 1$ for all X.

To avoid this problem, we can work with a maximally efficient representation ϕ which may be defined as follows:

Definition 2. *For any partial continuous function Φ, the* canonical *representation ϕ for Φ is defined by letting $\phi(\sigma)$ be the longest common initial segment of all members of $\{\Phi(X) : \sigma \prec X\}$. Let $u_\Phi = u_\phi$ denote the use function associated with the canonical representation ϕ.*

For example, the identity function on strings is the canonical representation of the identity function on 2^ω and thus the use $u_\Phi(X,n) = n$ for all n, so that $\lim_{n\to\infty} \frac{n}{u_\phi(X,n)} = 1$. As a second example, if $\Phi(X) = X \oplus X$, then $\lim_{n\to\infty} \frac{n}{u_\phi(X,n)} = \frac{1}{2}$.

Note that if ϕ is the canonical representation for a constant function $\Phi(X) = C$, then we have $\phi(\sigma) = C$, an infinite sequence, for every σ. To avoid this unpleasantness, we can restrict our functions to the non-constant functions.

Definition 3. *A partial continuous function Φ is* nowhere constant *if for any string σ, either $\Phi(X)$ is undefined (that is, it is a finite string) for some $X \in [[\sigma]]$, or there exist $X_1 \neq X_2$ both in $[[\sigma]]$ such that $\Phi(X_1) \neq \Phi(X_2)$.*

It is easy to see that if Φ is nowhere constant, then the canonical function is a well-defined map taking strings to strings and satisfies condition (i) in the definition of a representative of a functional.

Definition 4. *Let Φ be a partial Turing functional with canonical generator ϕ. The Φ-output/input ratio given by σ, $OI_\Phi(\sigma)$, is defined to be*

$$OI_\Phi(\sigma) = \frac{|\phi(\sigma)|}{|\sigma|}.$$

Similarly, for $X \in 2^\omega$ we define $OI_\Phi(X)$ to be

$$\limsup_{n\to\infty} \frac{|\phi(X \upharpoonright n)|}{n}.$$

We refer to $OI_\Phi(X)$ as the Φ-extraction rate along X.

The canonical representation of a functional has the following nice property, which is immediate from the definition.

Lemma 3. *Let Φ be a partial continuous functional on 2^ω with canonical representation $\phi : 2^{<\omega} \to 2^{<\omega}$. Then*

(∗) for all σ such that $\sigma^\frown 0, \sigma^\frown 1 \in \mathrm{dom}(\phi)$, if $\phi(\sigma 0) \succeq \tau$ and $\phi(\sigma 1) \succeq \tau$, then $\phi(\sigma) \succeq \tau$.

It was shown in [CP22] that, if Φ is a total, nowhere constant Turing functional, then the canonical representation ϕ of Φ is computable. On the other hand, if Φ is only a partial computable, nowhere constant function, then the canonical representation of Φ is not necessarily computable, but it will be computable in the complete Σ_1^0 set $\emptyset'$. See [DH10] for more background on computability theory and randomness.

We will consider the extraction rate of a continuous functional both in terms of an arbitrary representation and in terms of the canonical representation.

We would also like to define the *average Φ-output/input ratio* for a given Turing functional. However, such an average depends on an underlying probability measure on 2^ω. Since we are interested, at least in part, in Turing functionals that extract unbiased randomness from biased random inputs, we need to consider average Φ-output/input ratios parameterized by an underlying measure.

Definition 5. *The* average Φ-output/input ratio *for strings of length n with respect to μ, denoted $Avg(\Phi, \mu, n)$, is defined to be*

$$Avg(\Phi, \mu, n) = \sum_{\sigma \in 2^n} \mu(\sigma) OI_\Phi(\sigma).$$

Equivalently, we have

$$Avg(\Phi, \mu, n) = \frac{1}{n} \sum_{\sigma \in 2^n} \mu(\sigma)|\phi(\sigma)|,$$

where ϕ is the canonical representation of Φ. Note that this is the μ-average value of $OI_\Phi(X \upharpoonright n)$ over the space 2^ω, since this function is constant on each interval $[[\sigma]]$. That is, if we fix n and let $F_n(X) = OI_\Phi(X \upharpoonright n)$, then F_n is a computable map from 2^ω to $\mathbb{R}$ and the average value of F_n on 2^ω is given by

$$\int_{2^\omega} F_n(X) \, d\mu(X).$$

We consider the behavior of this average in the limit, which leads to the following definition (which is adapted from one provided by Peres in [Per92]).

Definition 6. *The μ-extraction rate of Φ, denoted $Rate(\Phi, \mu)$, is defined to be*

$$Rate(\Phi, \mu) = \limsup_{n \to \infty} Avg(\Phi, \mu, n).$$

For example, it is easy to see that the extraction rate of the functional $\Phi(X) = X \oplus X$ is exactly 2.

An interesting problem is to determine for which Turing functionals the lim sup in the definition of extraction rate actually equal to a lim. An example of a functional Φ is given in [CP22] where $\limsup_{n \to \infty} Avg(\Phi, \mu, n) = 2$ whereas $\liminf_{n \to \infty} Avg(\Phi, \mu, n) = 1.5$, so that the limit does not exist.

For the $\lim_{n \to \infty} Avg(\Phi, \mu, n)$ to exist, the functional Φ must be regular in the relative amount of input needed for a given amount of output. The authors have studied some families of functions for which this seems to be the case. First, there are the online continuous (or computable) functions. On the other hand, there are the *random* continuous functions which produce regularity in a probabilistic sense. For example, the random continuous functions as originally defined by Barmpalias et al. [BBC+08] produce outputs which are roughly $\frac{2}{3}$ as long, on average, as the inputs. We will consider such functions in greater generality below in Sect. 3.

3   The Extraction Rate of Random Functions

In this section, we study the extraction rate of *random continuous functions* on 2^ω. This collection of random continuous functions was introduced by Barmpalias, Brodhead, Cenzer, Remmel, and Weber [BBC+08] and further studied by the authors in [CP15].

An arbitrary partial continuous function $F :\subseteq 2^\omega \to 2^\omega$ may be given by a *labeled* binary tree, that is, by a function $\ell : 2^{<\omega} \setminus \{\epsilon\} \to \{0, 1, B\}$, where we use $B = 2$ to denote a blank. The function ℓ produces a map $f_\ell : 2^{<\omega} \to 2^{<\omega}$ where $f_\ell(\epsilon) = \epsilon$ and, for non-empty σ, $f_\ell(\sigma) = \tau$ is the result of deleting the B's from the sequence $(\ell(\sigma \upharpoonright i))_{i \le |\sigma|}$. Then f_ℓ is a monotone function on non-empty strings and induces a partial function F just as Turing functionals were defined above. That is, $F(X)(m) = n$ if there exists k, τ such that $f_\ell(X \upharpoonright k) = \tau$ and $\tau(m) = n$. It is not hard to see that every continuous function has such a representation, and in fact, infinitely many such representations.

We shall denote the space of such representations by $\mathcal{L} = \{0, 1, B\}^{2^{<\omega}} (= 3^{2^{<\omega}})$, and consider it to have its usual product topology and Borel σ-algebra.

We will first calculate the extraction rate with respect to the representation f_ℓ defined above and later show that, on average, this does not change for the canonical representation of F_ℓ.

We code these labelings as follows: enumerate $2^{<\omega} \setminus \{\epsilon\}$ length-lexicographically by $\sigma_0, \sigma_1, \ldots$ and, for $x \in 3^\omega$, we let $\ell_x(\sigma_n) = x(n)$. Similarly, for strings $\rho \in 3^{<\omega}$, we define a partial labeling $\ell_\rho(\sigma_n) = \rho(n)$ for $n < |\rho|$; the resulting partial function on strings f_ρ is defined, as before, by deleting all of the B's from the sequence $(\ell(\sigma \upharpoonright i))_{i \leq |\sigma|}$. It is clear that for any $x \in 3^\omega$, $\ell_x = \lim_n \ell_{x \upharpoonright n}$ and $f_{\ell_x} = \lim_n f_{\ell_{x \upharpoonright n}}$. For notational simplicity, we let $f_x = f_{\ell_x}$ and $F_x = F_{\ell_x}$. In particular, this map is a homeomorphism between 3^ω and $\mathcal{L}$, and hence is also a bimeasurable map between these two spaces, equipped with their respective Borel σ-algebras.

Definition 7. *Given $q, r, s \in [0,1]$ such that $q+r+s = 1$, consider the Bernoulli measure μ on 3^ω with Bernoulli parameters $p_0 = q$, $p_1 = r$, and $p_2 = s$. This is defined so that, for each $n \in \omega$, $\mu(\{x : x(n) = 0\}) = q$, $\mu(\{x : x(n) = 1\}) = q$, and $\mu(\{x : x(n) = 2\}) = s$. With respect to our coding, q is the probability that $\ell_x(\sigma) = 0$, r is the probability that $\ell_x(\sigma) = 1$, and $s = 1 - q - r$ is the probability that $\ell_x(\sigma) = B$. A partial continuous function F is said to be μ-Martin-Löf random if it has a μ-Martin-Löf random coding x.*

It was shown in [CP15] that as long as $s \leq 1/2$, the probability that the induced function on 2^ω is total will be one, and otherwise it will be zero. Thus in the case of $s \leq 1/2$, we may consider μ to be a measure on the space of (codes for) labels of total continuous functions. A continuous function is said to be μ-*random* if it is coded by a μ-Martin-Löf random sequence in 3^ω.

Where we may reason about labels without respect to their codes, we consider the pushforward measure μ^* on $\mathcal{L}$ induced by the bijective map $x \mapsto \ell_x$. Note that the pushforwards of these measures μ are precisely the Bernoulli measures ν on $\mathcal{L}$, for which we have, $\nu(\{\ell \in \mathcal{L} : \ell(\sigma) = i\}) = p_i$ for $i = 0, 1, 2$.

Now, for our purposes, fix $q, r, s \in [0,1]$ and let $p = q+r$, i.e., the probability that $\ell_x(\sigma) \in \{0,1\}$. (In the standard example from [BBC+08], we have $q = r = s = \frac{1}{3}$, so that $p = \frac{2}{3}$.) We will show that if F is μ-random, then the extraction rate of F with respect to the Lebesgue measure on 2^ω is exactly p. We do this whether the function F is partial or total. Given a label $\ell \in \mathcal{L}$ and $i \geq 1$, define

$$S_i(\ell) = |\{\sigma \in \{0,1\}^i : \ell(\sigma) \in \{0,1\}\}|.$$

Then the expected value of S_i is $2^i p$. Using Chernoff's Lemma [Che52], we get the following, which will prove to be useful shortly.

Lemma 4. *For any $\epsilon > 0$, we have $\mu^*\{|S_i(\ell) - p2^i| > \epsilon p2^i\} \leq 2^{-\epsilon^2 p 2^i/3}$.*

Towards calculating the rate of a random function, we first calculate the average output-input ratio for an arbitrary continuous function on 2^ω using the following lemma.

Lemma 5. *Let* $F :\subseteq 2^\omega \to 2^\omega$ *be a continuous functional and let* $\ell : 2^{<\omega} \to \{0, 1, B\}$ *label* F. *Then for any* $n \in \omega$,

$$Avg(F, \lambda, n) = \frac{1}{n} \sum_{i=1}^{n} 2^{-i} S_i(\ell).$$

Proof. For each $\sigma \in \{0,1\}^n$, $|f_\ell(\sigma)| = |\{i : \ell(\sigma \upharpoonright i) \in \{0,1\}\}|$. Thus whenever $\ell(\tau) \in \{0, 1\}$ for τ of length i, there are 2^{n-i} extensions σ of τ of length n for which we count an additional bit towards the value $f_\ell(\sigma)$. In particular, this implies that $\sum_{\sigma \in 2^n} |f_\ell(\sigma)| = \sum_{i=1}^{n} 2^{n-i} S_i(\ell)$. Thus, it follows that

$$Avg(F, \lambda, n) = \frac{1}{n} \sum_{\sigma \in 2^n} 2^{-n} |f_\ell(\sigma)| = \frac{1}{n} \sum_{i=1}^{n} 2^{-i} S_i(\ell).$$

$\square$

Note that if for each $i \geq 1$ we have $S_i(\ell) = p2^i$, the expected value of S_i, then it follows from Lemma 5 that $Avg(F, \lambda, n) = p$. Similarly, for a fixed $\epsilon > 0$, if $|S_i(\ell) - p2^i| \leq \epsilon p2^i$ for each i, then $|Avg(F, \lambda, n) - p| \leq p\epsilon$. To ensure that this average approaches p for a sufficiently random function, we consider a precise sequence of the values to plug in for ϵ, which will allow us to establish the next result.

Theorem 1. *Let* μ *be a Bernoulli measure on* 3^ω *with each* $p_i > 0$ *and let* $p = p_0 + p_1$, *that is,* p *is the probability that* $\ell_x(\sigma) \in \{0, 1\}$ *for* $x \in 3^\omega$. *Let* $F :\subseteq 2^\omega \to 2^\omega$ *be a* μ-*random continuous function. Then*

$$Rate(F, \lambda) = p.$$

Proof. For $i \geq 1$, let $\epsilon_i = \epsilon n/2i^2$. Then $\epsilon_i p2^i = \epsilon n p2^i/2i^2$, and by Lemma 4 we have

$$\mu^\star(\{|S_i(\ell) - p2^i| > \epsilon n p2^i/2i^2\}) \leq 2^{-\epsilon^2 n^2 p2^i/12i^4}.$$

It follows that the probability that $|S_i(\ell) - p2^i| > \epsilon_i p2^i$ holds for any $i \leq n$ is at most $\sum_{i=1}^{n} 2^{-\epsilon^2 n^2 p2^i/12i^4}$.

On the other hand, if $|S_i(\ell) - p2^i| \leq \epsilon_i p2^i$ holds for each $i \leq n$, then by Lemma 5, $Avg(F, \lambda, n)$ differs from p by at most

$$\frac{1}{n} \sum_{i=1}^{n} 2^{-i} \epsilon_i p2^i = \frac{1}{n} \sum_{i=1}^{n} \epsilon n p/2i^2 = p\epsilon \sum_{i=1}^{n} 1/2i^2.$$

Since $\sum_{i=1}^{\infty} 1/2i^2 < 1$, it follows in this case that $|Avg(F, \lambda, n) - p| \leq p\epsilon$.

Now we are ready to define our μ-Martin-Löf test for any function F for which $Avg(F, \lambda, n)$ stays too far from p. For $n \geq 1$, let $\epsilon = \delta_n = n^{-1/2}$. Let $\mathcal{U}_n$ be the set of codes $x \in 3^\omega$ such that $|S_i(\ell_x) - p2^i| > n^{1/2} p2^i/2i^2$ for some $i \leq n$. Then if $x \notin \mathcal{U}_n$, we have $|Avg(F_\ell, \lambda, n) - p| \leq p n^{-1/2}$. Thus, for $\epsilon = n^{-1/2}$, the calculations above show that

$$\mu(\mathcal{U}_n) = \mu^\star \left(\bigcup_{1 \le i \le n} \{\ell \in 3^{2^{<\omega}} : |S_i(\ell) - p2^i| > (\delta_n)_i p2^i\} \right) \le \sum_{i=1}^n 2^{-np2^i/12i^4}.$$

Next we observe that the function $g(i) = 2^i/12i^4$ for $i \ge 1$ has an absolute minimum at $i = 6$; denote the rational number $g(6) = 2^6/12 \cdot 6^4$ by q. Then we have $2^{-npg(i)} \le 2^{-npq}$ for all $n, i \ge 1$.

Let $t < pq$ also be a positive rational, so that $pq - t > 0$, and so that $2^{-n(pq-t)} < 1$. As $\lim_{n\to\infty} n/2^{n(pq-t)} = 0$, let $N \ge 1$ be such that for all $n \ge N$, $n \le 2^{n(pq-t)}$. Given $n \ge N$, slight rearrangement of this inequality gives us that $n2^{-npq} \le 2^{-nt} < 1$.

Now, observe that for $n \ge N$, we have

$$\sum_{i=1}^n 2^{-np2^i/12i^4} = \sum_{i=1}^n 2^{-npg(i)} \le \sum_{i=1}^n 2^{-npq} = n2^{-npq} \le 2^{-nt}.$$

Thus $\mu(\mathcal{U}_n) \le 2^{-nt}$ for every $n \ge N$.

Now, given $n \ge N$, let k_n be the index of the lexicographically-greatest $\sigma \in 2^{<\omega}$ of length n, so that if $m \in \omega$ and σ_m has length $\le n$, then $m \le k_n$. Since S_i only counts labels attached to strings of length i, $x \mapsto S_i(\ell_x)$ only requires the first k_i bits of x. Thus $x \mapsto \langle S_1(\ell_x), \ldots, S_n(\ell_x) \rangle \in \omega$ requires the first k_n bits of x, and so

$$\mathcal{U}_n = \bigcup_{1 \le i \le n} \{S_i(\ell_{x \restriction k_n}) - p2^i| > (\delta_n)_i p2^i\}$$

is clopen. In particular, the sequence $(\mathcal{U}_n)_{n \ge N} = (\mathcal{U}_{N+n})_{n \in \omega}$ is uniformly clopen. Now, if we let $\mathcal{V}_m = \bigcup_{n > m+N} \mathcal{U}_n$, then $(\mathcal{V}_m)_{m \in \omega}$ is uniformly c.e., and for $m \in \omega$ we also have $\mu(\mathcal{V}_m) \le \sum_{n > m+N} 2^{-nt} \le 2^{-(m+N)t}$. The sequence $(\mathcal{V}_m)_{m \in \omega}$ is our desired test.

If F is a Martin-Löf random function, then F must pass this test, and therefore there is some $x \in 3^\omega$ such that $F = F_x$ and $x \notin \mathcal{V}_m$ for some m. It follows that $x \notin \mathcal{U}_n$ for all $n > m + N$, and thus for all such n,

$$|Avg(F, \lambda, n) - p| \le pn^{-1/2}.$$

We then have

$$Rate(F, \lambda) = \limsup_{n \to \infty} Avg(F, \lambda, n) = p.$$

$\square$

Corollary 1. *For any online random continuous function F, $Rate(F, \lambda) = 1$.*

We can also show that for any random function F, this rate is attained by each sufficiently random input.

Theorem 2. *Let $F :\subseteq 2^\omega \to 2^\omega$ be a μ-random continuous functional for a Bernoulli measure μ on 3^ω, where μ gives probability $p = p_0 + p_1$ that $\ell_x(\sigma) \in \{0,1\}$ for a code $x \in 3^\omega$. If x is any μ-Martin-Löf random code for F and $A \in 2^\omega$ is Martin-Löf random relative to x, then*

$$\lim_{n \to \infty} \mathrm{OI}_{f_x}(A \restriction n) = Rate(F, \lambda) = p.$$

Proof. Let $x \in 3^\omega$ be a μ-Martin-Löf random code such that $F = F_x$. Given a sequence $A \in 2^\omega$ that is Martin-Löf random relative to x, it follows from the computability of the measure μ and van Lambalgen's theorem that x is μ-Martin-Löf random relative to A (see [VL90] or [DH10, Corollary 6.9.3]). Since the sequence $(A \restriction n)_{n \in \omega}$ is A-computable, we can view the values $\ell_x(A \restriction n)_{n \in \omega}$ as being randomly chosen from $\{0, 1, B\}$ with the probability that $\ell_x(A \restriction n) \in \{0, 1\}$ equal to p.

Now, we have $|f_x(A \restriction n)| = |\{i < n : \ell_x(A \restriction i) \in \{0,1\}|$. By Chernoff's Lemma (Lemma 4), we see that for any $n \in \omega$, the probability that $||f_x(A \restriction n)| - pn| < pn\epsilon$, or equivalently that

$$\left| \frac{|f_x(A \restriction n)|}{n} - p \right| < p\epsilon,$$

is at most $2^{-\epsilon^2 pn/3}$. Thus we may take $\mathcal{U}_n$ to be the set of A such that

$$\left| \frac{|f_x(A \restriction n)|}{n} - p \right| < pn^{-\frac{1}{3}},$$

and observe that $\mu(\mathcal{U}_n) \leq 2^{-pn^{1/3}/3}$.

Now we observe that for any $c > 0$, $cn^{\frac{1}{3}} > 2 \log n$ for sufficiently large n and that $2^{-2 \log n} = n^{-2}$. Let $\mathcal{V}_m = \bigcup_{n>m} \mathcal{U}_n$. Then $\mu(\mathcal{V}_m) \leq \sum_{n>m} n^{-2} < m^{-1}$, for sufficiently large m. Fix $M \in \omega$ be such that $\mu(\mathcal{V}_m) < m^{-1}$ for all $m \geq M$, and consider the sequence $(V_M + m)_{m \in \omega}$. Again we see that the $\mathcal{U}_n$ are uniformly clopen and so the $\mathcal{V}_m$ are uniformly c.e., and hence $(\mathcal{V}_{M+m})_{m \in \omega}$ is a Martin-Löf test relative to x. If A passes the test $(\mathcal{V}_{M+m})_{m \in \omega}$, then for some m, we have $A \notin \mathcal{V}_{M+m}$ and hence $A \notin \mathcal{U}_n$ for all $n > M + m$. It follows that

$$\left| \frac{|f_x(A \restriction n)|}{n} - p \right| < pn^{-\frac{1}{3}},$$

for sufficiently large n and therefore $\lim_{n \to \infty} \mathrm{OI}_F(A \restriction n) = p = Rate(F, \lambda)$. $\square$

Observe that in this result, we have not proven that $\lim_{n \to \infty} \mathrm{OI}_F(A \restriction n) = Rate(F, \lambda) = p$. Indeed, we have only proven that the output-input rate of a μ-random *representation* along a relatively random sequence agrees with the average rate of the induced random functional. As it is not necessarily the case that a random representation will be the canonical one, we will need to relate the behavior of the canonical representation and a random representation in the limit. These are the main results of the paper.

We first consider the case of *online* functionals. Recalling that our Bernoulli parameters are $p_0 = q$, $p_1 = r$ and $p_2 = s$, we first consider the case when $s = 0$. These corresponding μ-random functionals are the so-called *online* random functionals from [CP15, CR18]. We will assume without loss of generality that $q \leq r < 1$.

Recall that an *online* functional F is one that yields one bit of output for every bit of input, that is, F has a representation f with $|f(\sigma)| = |\sigma|$, for all σ. Thus each such functional F has a unique labeling $\ell : 2^{<\omega} \setminus \epsilon \to \{0,1\}$, and hence a unique code $x \in 2^\omega$. Further, when $s = 0$, 2^ω is a Π_1^0 class of μ-measure one in 3^ω; that is, the set of (codes for) online functionals form a Π_1^0 class of measure one. Thus no μ-Martin-Löf randoms have a 2, and thus all are codes for online functionals.

We now prove for every μ-random online continuous functional F and every Martin-Löf random sequence A relative to a μ-random code for F, A has F-output-input ratio that attains $Rate(F, \lambda) = 1$.

Theorem 3. *Let μ be a computable Bernoulli measure on 2^ω with $p_0, p_1 > 0$ and let F be a μ-random continuous online functional with μ-Martin-Löf random code x. Let $\phi = \phi_F$ be the canonical representation of F. Then for any $A \in 2^\omega$ Martin-Löf random relative to x,*

$$\mathrm{OI}_F(A) = \lim_{n\to\infty} \frac{|\phi_F(A \upharpoonright n)|}{n} = 1.$$

Proof. Let $p_0 = q$ and $p_1 = r$. We first note that $|f(\sigma)| = |\sigma| \leq |\phi(\sigma)|$ for all σ by the definition of an online function and of the canonical representation. The following lemma is needed.

Lemma 6. *For all sufficiently large k and all strings σ,*

$$\mu(\{y \in 2^\omega : |\phi_{F_y}(\sigma)| \geq |\sigma| + k\}) \leq 2^{-k}.$$

Proof. Given $k \in \omega$ and a string σ, let $p_{k,\sigma} = \mu(\{y \in 2^\omega : |\phi_{F_y}(\sigma)| \geq |\sigma| + k\})$. For any y, $|\phi_{F_y}(\sigma)| \geq k$ if and only if there is a string ρ of length k such that, for all τ of length k, $f(\sigma^\frown\tau) = f(\sigma)^\frown\rho$. This means that for any $i < k$, and all τ of length i, the outputs $f(\sigma^\frown\tau)$ are all the same. Now there are 2^i strings τ of length i and either the ouputs are all 0, which happens with probability q^{2^i}, or they are all 1, which happens with probability r^{2^i}. Therefore

$$p_{k,\sigma} \leq (q^2 + r^2)(q^4 + r^4) \cdot \cdots \cdot (q^{2^k} + r^{2^k}).$$

It follows that $p_k \leq 2r^2(2r^4) \cdot \cdots \cdot (2r^{2^k}) \leq 2^k r^{2^k}$. Since $r < 1$, $r = 2^{-t}$ for some $t > 0$. If k is large enough so that $t \cdot 2^k > 2k$, then $2^k r^{2^k} = 2^k 2^{-t2^k} = 2^{k-t2^k} < 2^{-k}$.

This concludes the proof of the lemma. $\qquad\square$

Now, by the lemma, we can take $K \geq 0$ be such that for all $k \geq K$ and all $m \in \omega$,

$$\mu(\{y \in 2^\omega : |\phi_{F_y}(A \restriction m)| \geq m + k\}) \leq 2^{-k}.$$

In addition to K, we require one more modulus to define the A-Martin-Löf test we wish to use. Fix $\delta \in \mathbb{Q}^+$. Since $\delta \in \mathbb{Q}$, $2^{-\delta}$ is a computable real, as is $1 - 2^{-\delta}$. In particular, $\eta = 1 - 2^{-\delta}$ is lower semicomputable; let $(x_n)_{n \in \omega}$ be an increasing computable sequence of rationals such that $\lim_n x_n = \eta$. Find the least N such that $0 < x_N < \eta$, and find the least k such that $2^{-k} \leq \eta$; denote this least k by $K_\delta \in \omega$. By construction, the function $\delta \mapsto K_\delta$ is a computable map $\mathbb{Q}^+ \to \omega$.

Now, given $\delta \in \mathbb{Q}^+$, we have that for all $k \geq K_\delta$,

$$2^{-k} < 1 - 2^{-\delta}$$

so that for all such k,

$$\frac{2^{-k}}{1 - 2^{-\delta}} < 1.$$

With this in mind, let $K'_\delta = \max\{K, K_\delta\}$. Note that $\delta \mapsto K'_\delta$ is a computable map.

For every $\delta \in \mathbb{Q}^+$ and $n, m \in \omega$, define the set

$$U_{\delta,n,m} = \{y \in 3^\omega : |\phi_{F_y}(A \restriction m)| \geq m + m\delta + K'_\delta + n\}.$$

Finally, for every $\delta \in \mathbb{Q}^+$ and n, define

$$V_{\delta,n} = \bigcup_{m > n} U_{\delta,n,m}.$$

It can be shown that, for every $\delta \in \mathbb{Q}^+$, the sequence $(V_{\delta,n})_{n \in \omega}$ is an A-Martin-Löf test, by our choice of K'_δ.

We now return to our fixed online functional F with A-Martin-Löf random code x. Given $\delta \in \mathbb{Q}^+$, x passes the A-Martin-Löf test $(V_{\delta,n})_{n \in \omega}$, so there is an index, say n, such that $x \notin V_{\delta,n}$. Thus, given $m > n$, we have

$$|\phi(A \restriction m)| < m + m\delta + K'_\delta + n.$$

Recall that because ϕ_F represents an online functional, we have $|\sigma| = |f_x(\sigma)| \leq |\phi_F(\sigma)|$ for every string σ. It follows that $m \leq |\phi(A \restriction m)|$. Dividing by m (nonzero since $m > n \geq 0$), we find that

$$1 \leq \frac{|\phi(A \restriction m)|}{m} < 1 + \delta + \frac{K'_\delta + n}{m}.$$

Since $m > n$ was arbitrary, it follows that

$$1 \leq \limsup_{m \to \infty} \frac{|\phi(A \restriction m)|}{m} \leq \limsup_{m \to \infty} \left(1 + \delta + \frac{K'_\delta + n}{m}\right)$$
$$= \lim_{m \to \infty} \left(1 + \delta + \frac{K'_\delta + n}{m}\right) = 1 + \delta.$$

Because $\delta \in \mathbb{Q}^+$ was arbitrary, it follows that

$$\limsup_{m \to \infty} \frac{|\phi(A \restriction m)|}{m} \leq 1 + \delta$$

for every such δ. But then we get that $\limsup_{m \to \infty} |\phi(A \restriction m)|/m = 1$. Finally,

$$\limsup_{m \to \infty} \frac{|\phi(A \restriction m)|}{m} \leq 1 \leq \liminf_{m \to \infty} \frac{|\phi(A \restriction m)|}{m},$$

and so $\lim_{m \to \infty} |\phi(A \restriction m)|/m = 1$, as desired.

Part (b) follows from Theorem 1 and the fact that the set of inputs A which are Martin-Löf random with respect to F has Lebesgue measure one.   □

Note that this result is a special case of the following theorem; we will reduce a more general case to this special case in the next proof.

We now generalize Theorem 3 to the case of a general Bernoulli measure.

Theorem 4. *Let μ be a Bernoulli measure on 3^ω with $p_2 < 1$ and $p_0, p_1 > 0$, and let F be a μ-random continuous functional with μ-Martin-Löf random code x and corresponding representation f_x, and let ϕ be the canonical representation of F. Then for any $A \in 2^\omega$ Martin-Löf random relative to x,*

$$\lim_{n \to \infty} \frac{|\phi_F(A \restriction n)|}{|f_x(n)|} = 1.$$

Moreover, $\lim_{n \to \infty} \mathrm{OI}_F(A \restriction n) = Rate(F, \lambda) = p$.

Proof. As before, let $q = p_0$, $r = p_1$, and $s = p_2$. We have two cases.

Case I: We first consider the case where $1/2 \leq s < 1$, so that the set of codes for total functionals does not have μ-measure 1; in this case, some μ-random functionals will be partial.

For any string τ, let $p(\tau)$ be the probability that for any $X \in 2^\omega$, $\tau \prec F(X)$. Certainly $p(\epsilon) = 1$. We calculate $p(\tau)$ by induction on string-length. This recursive calculation of p requires us to find $p(0 ^\frown \tau)$ and $p(1 ^\frown \tau)$; we will give the details for $p(0 ^\frown \tau)$, and the formula for $p(1 ^\frown \tau)$ will be similar, *mutatis mutandis*. Recall that q is the probability, for any given σ, that $\ell_x(\sigma) = 0$. Let $p = p(0 ^\frown \tau)$ and let $u = p(\tau)$.

First, observe that, for $x \in 3^\omega$ and $X \in 2^\omega$, if $i \prec F_x(X)$, then $\ell_x(0), \ell_x(1) \neq (1 - i)$. Thus $p(0) \leq (1 - r)^2$ and $p \leq (1 - q)^2$. Per our convention, we have assumed that $q \leq r < s$, so $1 - r \leq 1 - q$, and so $p(0), p(1) \leq (1 - q)^2$.

Now, assume that $p(\tau) = u$ is given. We compute $p(0^{\frown}\tau) = p$. We have three subcases:

Subcase 1: $f(0) = 0 = f(1)$ – this occurs with probability $q^2 \cdot u^2$.

Subcase 2: $f(0) = B$ and $f(1) = 0$ or $f(0) = 0$ and $f(1) = B$ – this has probability $2qsp \cdot u$.

Subcase 3: $f(0) = f(1) = B$ – this occurs with probability $s^2 \cdot p$.

Thus we obtain the quadratic equation

$$p = s^2 p^2 + 2rsup + r^2 u^2 q^2,$$

which has solution

$$p = \frac{1 - 2rsu \pm \sqrt{(1-2rsu)^2 - 4s^2 r^2 u^2}}{2s^2} = \frac{1 - 2rsu \pm \sqrt{1 - 4rsu}}{2s^2}.$$

Using the fact that $u \leq 1$ and $r < 1 - s$, it is not hard to show that $p^+ = (1 - 2rsu + \sqrt{1 - 4rsu})/2s^2 > 1$, which would contradict that μ is a probability measure, so that

$$p = \frac{1 - 2rsu - \sqrt{1 - 4rsu}}{2s^2}. \tag{1}$$

Here are the details. Since $u \leq 1$ and $r < 1-s$, we have $1 - 2rsu + \sqrt{1 - 4rsu} > 1 - 2(1-s)s + \sqrt{1 - 4(1-s)s}$. Simplifying, we get that

$$
\begin{aligned}
1 - 2(1-s)s + \sqrt{1 - 4(1-s)s} &= 1 - 2s + 2s^2 + \sqrt{1 - 4s + 4s^2} \\
&= 1 - 2s + 2s^2 + \sqrt{(2s-1)^2} \\
&= 1 - 2s + 2s^2 + 2s - 1 \quad \text{since } s \geq 1/2 \\
&= 2s^2,
\end{aligned}
$$

and so

$$\frac{1 - 2(1-s)s + \sqrt{1 - 4(1-s)s}}{2s^2} = 1.$$

We now see that $p^+ > 1$, as claimed, so that

$$p = (1 - 2rsu - \sqrt{1 - 4rsu})/2s^2$$

To obtain an upper bound for p, we first show that $1 - 2rsu + \sqrt{1 - 4rsu} \geq 1/2$. Indeed, since p is defined, we have $1 - 4rsu \geq 0$. But then $rsu \leq 1/4$, and so $-2rsu \geq -1/2$, and so $1 - 2rsu \geq 1/2$. Thus $1 - 2rsu + \sqrt{1 - 4rsu} \geq 1/2$.

Multiplying top and bottom of the RHS of (1) by the rational conjugate of the numerator and then simplifying, we find that

$$p = \frac{2r^2u^2}{1 - 2rsu + \sqrt{1 - 4rsu}}.$$

Because $1 - 2rsu + \sqrt{1 - 4rsu} \leq 1/2$, we get that $p \leq 4r^2u^2$. Because $r < 1/2$, we find that $p < u^2$. That is,

$$p(1^\frown\tau) < p(\tau)^2. \tag{2}$$

Notice that we only used that $u \leq 1$ and $r < 1/2$ to derive (2). Because $q < 1/2$, a similar argument gives that $p(0^\frown\tau) \leq p(\tau)^2$.

Thus we have that for all τ, $p(0^\frown\tau), p(1^\frown\tau) < p(\tau)^2$. Since $p(0), p(1) < (1-q)^2$, it follows by a straightforward induction that for any τ of length k,

$$p(\tau) < (1-q)^{2^k},$$

Because $1 - q < 1$, there is a positive rational $t < 1$ such that $1 - q < 2^{-t}$. Thus, a straightforward induction shows that $p(\tau) < 2^{-t2^k}$ for any string τ of length k. As there are 2^k strings of length k, the probability $p_k = \mu\{x \in 3^\omega : |\phi_{F_x}(\sigma)| \geq |f_x(\sigma)| + k\}$ is less than $2^k \cdot 2^{-t2^k} = 2^{-(t2^k-k)}$. Given k such that $2^{1-k}k \leq t$, we have $2^{-(t2^k-k)} \leq 2^{-k}$, so that $p_k < 2^{-k}$ for all such k. Let K be the least such k such that $2^{1-k}k \leq t$.

The remainder of the proof, including the construction of the μ-Martin-Löf tests, is similar to the end of the proof of Theorem 3. That is, we fix $A \in 2^\omega$ and may show that if F has a μ-Martin-Löf random code x which is random relative to A, then $\lim_{m\to\infty} |\phi_F(A \restriction m)|/|f(A \restriction m| = 1$. For $q \in \mathbb{Q}^+$, we let K_δ and K'_δ be defined similarly as in the proof of Theorem 3. We also define the classes $U_{\delta,n,m}$ and $V_{\delta,n}$ similarly as in that proof, with

$$U_{\delta,n,m} = \{y \in 3^\omega : |\phi_{F_y}(A\restriction m)| \geq |f(A\restriction m)| + m\delta + K'_\delta + n\},$$

and $V_{\delta,n} = \bigcup_{m>n} U_{\delta,n,m}$. Letting the family of $(V_{\delta,n})_{n\in\omega}$ for $\delta \in \mathbb{Q}^+$ be our desired μ-Martin-Löf tests, we will have that $\lim_{n\to\infty} |\phi_F(A\restriction n)|/|f_x(A\restriction n)| = 1$.

Case II: Next, we suppose that $s < \frac{1}{2}$, so that the set of codes for total functionals is a Σ_1^0 class of μ-measure one, and so that all μ-random functions are total. Given a code $x \in 3^\omega$ inducing a total functional $F = F_x$ with label $\ell = \ell_x$, we will first use totality of F to define an online labeling function ℓ^* with corresponding representation function $g = g_x$ and online functional $G = G_x$. We will then show that, for any string σ and any $k \in \omega$,

$$\{y \in 3^\omega : |\phi_{F_y}(\sigma)| \geq |f_y(\sigma)| + k\} \subseteq \{y \in 3^\omega : |\phi_{G_y}(\sigma)| \geq |\sigma| + k\}, \tag{3}$$

so that the measure of the left-hand set is at most the measure of the right-hand set. Lemma 6 then gives us that there is a natural, say K, such that for any string σ and for all $k \geq K$,

$$\mu(\{F_y \text{ is online and } \phi_{F_y}(\sigma) \geq |\sigma| + k\}) \leq 2^{-k},$$

and so $\mu(\{|\phi_{F_y}(\sigma)| \geq |f_y(\sigma)| + k\}) \leq 2^{-k}$ for all σ and all $k \geq K$. Given $A \in 2^\omega$ that is Martin-Löf random relative to our code x and a $\delta \in \mathbb{Q}^+$, we may yet again define the μ-Martin-Löf test $(V_{\delta,n})_{n \in \omega}$, as in the proof of Theorem 3. That $\lim_{n\to\infty} |\phi_F(A{\restriction}n)|/|f(n)| = 1$ will follow as it did in that proof, *mutatis mutandis*.

The online functional G is defined via a function $\theta : 2^{<\omega} \to 2^{<\omega}$. Let $\theta(\epsilon) = \epsilon$. For any σ, let $\theta(\sigma{}^\frown 0) = \theta(\sigma){}^\frown 0^{m+1}$, where m is the least such that $\ell(\sigma{}^\frown 0^{m+1}) \neq B$. Similarly, let $\theta(\sigma{}^\frown 1) = \theta(\sigma){}^\frown 1^{n+1}$, where n is the least such that $\ell(\sigma{}^\frown 1^{n+1}) \neq B$. Define the *online* labeling ℓ^* by setting $\ell^*(\sigma) = \ell(\theta(\sigma))$, for any string σ. Then, for $X \in 2^\omega$, let $\Theta(X) = \bigcup_n \theta(X \restriction n)$; it is easy to see that the online labeling ℓ^* induces $F \circ \Theta$, and so this composition is an online functional. Note that the map $x \mapsto G_x$ is well-defined on the set of total functionals, since if $x \in 3^\omega$ and F_x is total, then for any σ and $i \in \{0,1\}$, there is an $m \in \omega$ such that $\ell_x(\sigma{}^\frown i^{m+1}) \neq B$–otherwise, there would be some σ such that $F_x(\sigma{}^\frown i^\omega)$ is undefined. Thus $\theta_x(\sigma)$ is defined for every σ, and so the composition $G_x = F_x \circ \Theta_x$ is defined. (In particular, $x \mapsto G_x$ is almost total with respect to μ.)

To establish the inclusion (3), let $x \in 3^\omega$. Observe that for all σ, we have $\phi_{F_x}(\theta_x(\sigma)) \preceq \phi_{F_x \circ \Theta_x}(\sigma)$, and so $|\phi_F(\theta(\sigma))| \leq |\phi_{F_x \circ \Theta_x}(\sigma)|$ for all σ. Given a string σ and $k \in \omega$, suppose that $|\phi_{F_x}(\theta_x(\sigma))| \geq |\theta_x(\sigma)| + k$. Then, as $|\theta_x(\sigma)| > |\sigma|$, we have $|\phi_{F_x}(\theta_x(\sigma))| \geq |\sigma| + k$. Because $|\phi_F(\theta_x(\sigma))| \leq |\phi_{F_x \circ \Theta_x}(\sigma)|$, we have $|\phi_{F_x \circ \Theta_x}(\sigma)| \geq |\sigma| + k$. The inclusion in (3) now follows, as claimed, finishing the case.

To conclude the argument for Case II, recall from Theorem 2 that

$$\lim_{n\to\infty} \frac{|f_x(A{\restriction}n)|}{n} = \lim_{n\to\infty} \mathrm{OI}_{f_x}(A{\restriction}n) = \mathrm{OI}_{f_x}(A) = \mathrm{Rate}(F, \lambda) = p.$$

It follows that

$$\lim_{n\to\infty} \frac{|\phi_F(A{\restriction}n)|}{n} = \lim_{n\to\infty} \frac{|\phi_F(A{\restriction}n)|}{f_x(A{\restriction}n)} \cdot \frac{|f_x(A{\restriction}n)|}{n}$$

$$= \lim_{n\to\infty} \frac{|\phi_F(A{\restriction}n)|}{f_x(A{\restriction}n)} \cdot \lim_{n\to\infty} \mathrm{OI}_{f_x}(A{\restriction}n)$$

$$= 1 \cdot \mathrm{OI}_{f_x}(A) = \mathrm{Rate}(F, \lambda)$$

concluding the proof. $\qquad\square$

We also have the following corollary.

Corollary 2. *Every μ-random continuous functional F is almost total.*

Proof. Let F be a μ-random continuous functional, let x be a μ-Martin-Löf random code for F, and let $A \in 2^\omega$ be Martin-Löf random relative to x. It follows from Theorem 4 that $\lim_{n\to\infty} |\phi_F(A \upharpoonright n)|/n = \infty$ and therefore $\lim_{n\to\infty} |\phi_F(A \upharpoonright n)| = \infty$. Thus $F(A) \in 2^\omega$ and $A \in \mathrm{dom}(F)$. It is well-known that for any Z, the set of reals which are Martin-Löf random relative to Z has Lebesgue measure 1. Thus F is almost total. □

4   Conclusions and Open Questions

We showed that a random continuous functional F with representation ϕ has an average output/input rate of p, where p is the probability that $|\phi(\sigma^\frown i)| > |\phi(\sigma)|$ for a string σ. Furthermore, if A is Martin-Löf random with respect to F, then the output/input rate of F on input A is p. This result was shown to be robust in that it holds with respect to the canonical representation of F.

We conclude with some open questions. The most interesting problem would be to prove (partial) converses to the main results. For example, can we show that A is Martin-Löf random if and only if, for all online functions F such that A is Martin-Löf random relative to F and - for which $Rate(F, \lambda)$ exists, $\mathrm{OI}_F(A \upharpoonright n) = Rate(F, \lambda)$.

It is easy to see that there are computable functions for which $Rate(F, \lambda)$ exists, but is not realized by *any* input. That is, F can have an output/input rate of 0 on inputs starting with 0 and a rate of 1 on inputs starting with 1, so that $Rate(F, \lambda) = \frac{1}{2}$. Can we show that a continuous online functional F, for which $Rate(F, \lambda)$ exists, is random continuous if and only if, for all inputs A which are Martin-Löf relatively random to a code for F, $\mathrm{OI}_F(A \upharpoonright n) = Rate(F, \lambda)$?

Here is another topic to consider: one might define a variation of online computability where, say, exactly two bits of input are used to compute one bit of output. Presumably, the output/input rate would be $\frac{1}{2}$.

References

[BBC+08] Barmpalias, G., Brodhead, P., Cenzer, D., Remmel, J.B., Weber, R.: Algorithmic randomness of continuous functions. Arch. Math. Logic **46**(7–8), 533–546 (2008)

[Che52] Chernoff, H.: A measure of asymptotic efficiency for tests of a hypothesis based on the sum of observations. Annals Math. Stat. **23**(4), 493–507 (1952)

[CP15] Cenzer, D., Porter, C.P.: Algorithmically Random Functions and Effective Capacities. In: Jain, R., Jain, S., Stephan, F. (eds.) TAMC 2015. LNCS, vol. 9076, pp. 23–37. Springer, Cham (2015). https://doi.org/10.1007/978-3-319-17142-5_4

[CP22] Cenzer, D., Porter, C.P.: Randomness extraction in computability theory. Computability (2022). https://doi.org/10.3233/COM-210343

[CR18] Cenzer, D., Rojas, D.A.: Online Computability and Differentiation in the Cantor Space. In: Manea, F., Miller, R.G., Nowotka, D. (eds.) CiE 2018. LNCS, vol. 10936, pp. 136–145. Springer, Cham (2018). https://doi.org/10.1007/978-3-319-94418-0_14

[DH10] Downey, R.G., Hirschfeldt, D.R.: Algorithmic randomness and complexity. Springer (2010). https://doi.org/10.1007/978-0-387-68441-3

[FP20] Franklin, J.N.Y., Porter, C.P.: Key developments in algorithmic randomness. In Johanna N.Y. Franklin and Christopher P. Porter, editors, Algorithmic Randomness: Progress and Prospects, volume 50 of Lecture Notes in Logic. Cambridge University Press (2020)

[Kau91] Steven M. Kautz. Degrees of random sets. ProQuest LLC, Ann Arbor, MI, 1991. Thesis (Ph.D.)-Cornell University

[KY76] Knuth, D.E., Yao, A.C.: The complexity of nonuniform random number generation. In: Algorithms and complexity (Proc. Sympos., Carnegie-Mellon Univ., Pittsburgh, Pa., 1976), pp. 357–428 (1976)

[LZ70] Levin, L., Zvonkin, A.K.: The complexity of finite objects and the development of the concepts of information and randomness of means of the theory of algorithms. Uspekhi Mat. Nauk **25**, 85–127 (1970)

[Nie09] Nies, A.: Computability and randomness, volume 51 of Oxford Logic Guides. Oxford University Press (200

[Per92] Peres, Y.: Iterating von Neumann's procedure for extracting random bits. Ann. Statist. **20**, 590–597 (1992)

[SUV17] Shen, A., Uspensky, V.A., Vereshchagin., N.: Kolmogorov complexity and algorithmic randomness, vol. 220. American Mathematical Soc (2017)

[VL90] Van Lambalgen, M.: The axiomatization of randomness. J. Symbolic Logic **55**(3), 1143–1167 (1990)

[vN51] Neumann, J.v.: Various techniques used in connection with random digits. Appl. Math Series **12**, 36–38 (1951)

Reservoir Computing with Nanowire Exchange-Coupled Spin Torque Oscillator Arrays

Matt Dale[1,3], Richard F. L. Evans[2], Angelika Sebald[3],
and Susan Stepney[1,3]([✉]) (iD)

[1] Department of Computer Science, University of York, York, UK
{richard.evans,angelika.sebald,susan.stepney}@york.ac.uk
[2] School of Physics, Engineering and Technology, University of York, York, UK
[3] York Cross-disciplinary Centre for Systems Analysis, University of York, York, UK

Abstract. Spin torque oscillators (STOs) feature transient non-linear behaviour that can be exploited for computation. When combined in arrays, they can be networked to produce more complex collective behaviours than single devices alone. We simulate a physical reservoir computer comprising an array of STOs, using a macro spin approximation. We demonstrate that STOs can be networked together in arrays using nanowires, and that by altering the properties of these nanowires we can optimise the magnetic exchange coupling between the oscillators for computational purposes. We train a simulated array of coupled oscillators to compute various time-independent and time-dependent benchmark tasks. We explore the effects of array size, heterogeneous coupling, and connection topologies. We demonstrate the computational potential of programming the exchange coupling in arrays of oscillators through nanowires.

1 Introduction

Spintronics uses the spin degree of freedom of the electron to reduce power consumption and increase the data processing in electronics [38]. A spin torque oscillator (STO), a specific type of magnetic tunnel junction, is a magnetic multi-layer device, whose magnetisation oscillates when a spin polarised current is injected. STOs are CMOS (complementary metal-oxide-semiconductor) compatible [39] and have a low power draw, so they can be connected to existing devices with relative ease. Their state of dynamic equilibrium makes STOs an interesting candidate for unconventional computing models as their coupled oscillations exhibit highly nonlinear behaviour when excited by an input field.

The computational capabilities of STOs have been explored both in simulation and experimentally for various applications including neuromorphic computing [4, 12,15,18]. Various properties and modes of individual STOs have been exploited, such as frequency, phase, and amplitude to perform computation [24]. Other work has explored multiple oscillator architectures including a network of four coupled spin-torque nano-oscillators to perform vowel recognition [29], and arrays (some with different geometries) of STOs connected via dipolar fields [4,18].

© The Author(s), under exclusive license to Springer Nature Switzerland AG 2023
D. Genova and J. Kari (Eds.): UCNC 2023, LNCS 14003, pp. 64–78, 2023.
https://doi.org/10.1007/978-3-031-34034-5_5

Here we explore arrays of oscillators directly exchange coupled via connecting nanowires. Exchange coupling using nanowires enables additional degrees of freedom in array design, such as network topology, as well as the potential to reconfigure or tune coupling strengths for device training. To explore the computational power provided by direct coupling, we simulate a macro spin approximation [5] of an insulating nanowire exchange-coupled STO array. We apply the reservoir computing framework, providing the theoretical model of computation used to exploit the device. We explore different configurations of STO arrays including material properties, types of connectivity, and possible STO network topologies. The results in this work show competitive performance across four different computational tasks, highlighting the potential of these new magnetic network devices for multiple applications.

2   Spin Torque Oscillators for Reservoir Computing

2.1   Individual Oscillators

STOs are multi-layered magnetic nanostructures. These are typically three layer systems of two nanomagnets sandwiching a non-magnetic layer. The first ferromagnetic layer has a fixed magnetisation whilst the second layer's magnetisation is allowed to move freely.

When a current is injected through the device, it is spin polarised to align with the direction of the magnetisation of the fixed layer. When the polarised current passes into the non-fixed magnetic layer, there is a transfer of spin angular momentum between the conduction electrons and the magnetic layer due to the conservation of spin angular momentum [23]. This transfer of spin angular momentum, or spin torque, is called the spin transfer torque (STT) effect. It causes the magnetisation of the free layer to tilt towards or away from the fixed magnetisation depending on the direction of the current [21]. The non-magnetic layer prevents direct exchange between the two magnetic layers.

This spin torque has two normally conservative components, the in-plane and out-of-plane torque. The in-plane torque, or damping-like torque, lies anti-parallel to the Gilbert damping [25]; as such it acts to reduce the process of the free magnetisation tending towards the effective magnetic field $\mathbf{H}_{\text{eff}}$ (see Fig. 1a). Beyond a certain critical current density through the layers there is a spontaneous precession of the magnetisation due to the in-plane torque [3]. Similarly, the out-of-plane torque, or field-like torque, is anti-parallel to the field precession. These two material dependent terms provide handles on the spin precession that allows for the design of spin torque devices [21].

The spin transfer effect can be used for many novel applications, including the next generation of random access memory [20], random number generation [11], new logic components [27], and high-data-transfer readers [30].

2.2   Coupled Oscillators

It is possible to build a delay-line reservoir computer [1] using a single STO. This method creates a network of *virtual nodes* through time multiplexing [28].

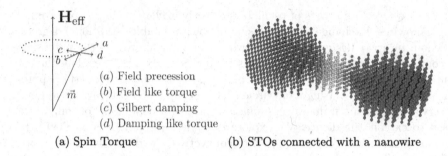

(a) Spin Torque

(a) Field precession
(b) Field like torque
(c) Gilbert damping
(d) Damping like torque

(b) STOs connected with a nanowire

Fig. 1. (a) A vector diagram showing the competing spin torque and field terms. (b) Two spin torque oscillators (blue, red) with a connecting nanowire (white). (Color figure online)

High performance has been reported on several tasks, including speech recognition [36]. Building a more standard multi-node reservoir computer, as presented here, requires coupling a network of STOs, to allow information to propagate and interact.

The coupling of STOs is typically governed by spin-wave or dipolar coupling. To exploit these effects, STOs must be placed in close proximity, within micrometer distances. They can also be connected electrically through synchronisation using self-emitted radio frequency (rf) currents [31]. Forced synchronisation can be used to suppress the thermal fluctuation of the oscillation trajectory of the STO [37].

Here we consider STOs coupled by an insulating nanowire of parameterisable width and length, giving a 'dog bone' shape (Fig. 1b). Preliminary simulation experiments (not reported here) show that the exchange coupling scales linearly with the number of atoms in the system. A wide range of exchange values are possible by changing the nanowire's width and length, demonstrating that nanowire geometry allows for controllable coupling of oscillators.

A 2D array of electrically isolated STOs can be interconnected by these non-conducting magnetic nanowires mediating the exchange coupling. Using modern deposition techniques, it is entirely plausible to fabricate such devices and nanowires in a single layer, by successive patterning and backfill. (See Fig. 2 for a schematic illustration of two connection topologies.)

Typical sizes for the applications here are nanoscale, roughly 20–50 nm in diameter so that the STOs remain a single magnetic domain. Nanowire diameters of 10 nm are possible with current deposition technology. Nanowire lengths of 5–1000 nm would give very different levels of coupling.

We assume that patterned leads can be used to allow individual excitation and measurement of each node. Although this would be challenging to fabricate, is not impossible. The focus of this work is on the computational capacity of such a device.

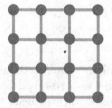 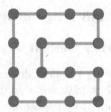

Fig. 2. Schematic STO array connectivity and topology. STOs are connected via nanowires, which control exchange coupling strength. Exchange coupling strength may be uniform across the array or varied individually by varying nanowire parameters. (left) A grid topology, with a maximum of four connection wires per STO. (right) A ring topology, with two connection wires per STO. Input signals are injected into individual STOs; here in simulation these are chosen via an evolutionary optimisation process.

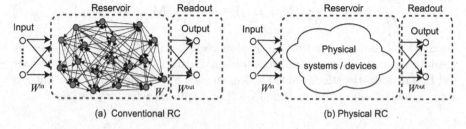

Fig. 3. (a) The Echo State Network computational model of a recurrent neural network (RNN) with random input and internal weights, and trained output weights. (b) A physical realisation of the computational model, replacing the internal RNN with a physical dynamical system. Only the outputs are trained. Figure from [33].

2.3 Physical Reservoir Computing

Reservoir Computing in general, and the Echo State Network model in particular [17], is a form of computational model that combines a random recurrent neural network (RNN) with a training algorithm that trains only the output weights (Fig. 3a). It is well-suited to tasks requiring classification of time-dependent inputs.

The internals of the RNN can be treated as a black box; this allows the RNN model to be replaced with another suitable non-linear dynamical system, and in particular, a suitable physical material (Fig. 3b); see, for example, [8].

The use of a physical material exploits the natural dynamics of the material, proving a potentially low power intrinsic computational device. This natural dynamics will have its own natural timescales, and so the input will need to be matched to these timescales.

3   Simulation Approach

3.1   Simulation Method

Before fabricating physical devices, it is helpful to simulate them, in order to determine if they have suitable dynamics for use as a reservoir computer. The VAMPIRE simulator [10] has previously been used to investigate the computational properties of magnetic films [7]. Here we apply it to STO arrays.

The simulation of magnetic systems is complex and a variety of methods can be employed. Here, we use VAMPIRE to apply both atomistic and micromagnetic simulations. In the micromagnetic simulation the Heun integration of the Landau Lifshitz Gilbert equation is used [14], which performs the time evolution of the macrospin for a magnetic material.

$$\frac{\partial \mathbf{M}}{\partial t} = -\frac{\gamma}{(1 + \alpha^2)} (\mathbf{M} \times \mathbf{H}_{\text{eff}}) - \frac{\gamma \alpha}{(1 + \alpha^2)} [\mathbf{M} \times (\mathbf{M} \times \mathbf{H}_{\text{eff}})] \tag{1}$$

where $\mathbf{M}$ is the normalised magnetisation vector, $\gamma = 1.76 \times 10^{11}$ J/T/s is the absolute value of gyromagnetic ratio, α is the intrinsic Gilbert damping constant and $\mathbf{H}_{\text{eff}}$ denotes the effective field acting on each STNO including contributions from exchange, anisotropy, external fields and spin-transfer torques [25].

3.2   Macro Spin Approximation

To explore reservoir computing, multiple oscillators and connections are needed. We approximate the nanowire structure using a macro-spin model to reduce computational time. A single oscillator is treated as a single macro spin; this is a reasonable approximation since these STOs are below the Stoner radius for a single domain particle [34,35]. The presented spin torque devices are not vortex type so there is minimal variance in the spin across a single node. The macro spin model reduces simulation run time by approximating hundreds or thousands of electrons per oscillator with a single spin represented by a unit cell. The underlying physics is identical. The devices act as two macro spins with an effective exchange.

In the preliminary nanowire model (§2.2), the exchange energy between STOs is defined by the nanowire width. Here, in the macro spin model, we generalise the effects of nanowire exchange coupling, and allow other means of exchange coupling as well. In a physical system, it is plausible to alter exchange coupling by exploiting the temperature dependence of exchange coupling [10] rather than nanowire widths. This would allow reconfiguration of the exchange coupling post-fabrication.

Using VAMPIRE's custom unit cell files describing atomic positions and interaction lists, we also investigate custom array topologies, types of STO connectivity, and individual exchange coupling strengths.

The STO reservoir array features a range of material and simulation parameters. We select appropriate parameters by using a basic optimisation algorithm

(§4.1). These parameters include the Gilbert damping of the material with a range of $[0.01, 1]$ (dimensionless), the spin transfer relaxation torque $[-1, 1]$ Tesla, precession torque $[0, 1]$ Tesla, torque asymmetry $[0, 1]$ (dimensionless), global applied field strength $[0.15, 0.25]$ Tesla, input signal scaling to each STO $[-1, 1]$, and the exchange field $0.01 - 1$ Tesla. Some parameters are fixed during simulation including the uniaxial anisotropy $(-9 \times 10^4$ J m$^{-3})$, material magnetic moment $(1.44 \times 10^6$ J T^{-1} m$^{-3})$, and temperature at zero Kelvin. This range of parameters allows us to explore a wide variety of STOs.

The arrays are initially connected in a basic Cartesian grid of STOs. Each STO is connected via bidirectional nanowires to their nearest neighbours, with each node having four connections, unless at the grid edge. Other connection topologies are explored later.

3.3   Inputs and Outputs

Input to the simulated reservoir is encoded in the magnitude of the applied field. Outputs are decoded from the z components of the spin states.

3.4   Transients and Timescales

The internal timescale of a physical system determines factors such as processing speed, transient behaviour, and memory. Matching the timescale of the task input and physical system is crucial to using such devices to solve computational problems.

Physical systems typically have a fixed internal timescale. By varying the system input and output sample frequency it is possible to exploit their rate response in different ways. For example, sampling the output faster can simulate longer transient behaviour, relative to the slower input data rate.

Here, we demonstrate how a fixed timescale system and sample-and-hold input rates can be used to tackle time-dependent and time-independent tasks. In the case of the time-dependent task, we exploit the inherent transient dynamics of continuous physical system where the influence of the previous inputs / system state affects the next state, i.e., some memory persists. With our system, we find a simulated input and readout frequency of 133 GHz (7.5 ps) produces and records desirable transient behaviour. In the time-independent case, we continuously drive the system with the same input sample, forcing the system to washout previous transient behaviour and settle to a consistent state. After an optimised number of samples, the state is then collected and used for further processing.

4 Simulation Experiments

4.1 Experimental Procedure

Here, optimisation is carried out on simulation parameters related to material properties of the oscillators, their array connectivity, and input signals.

A simple steady-state genetic algorithm (GA) [16] is used to search for optimal configurations of the STO array. Parameters under optimisation include the globally applied field strength; exchange coupling; input signal strength to individual STOs; the spin transfer relaxation, precession, and asymmetry torque; Gilbert damping; and, input sample-and-hold duration.

The GA has a population of 10 individuals and evolves for 1000 generations, where each generation consists of: *selection* – a tournament of two random individuals from the population; *cross-over* – winning individual inherits a percentage of genes from the genotype; *point-mutation* on a percentage of genes from the genotype; and, *evaluation* of new phenotype representing STO arrays – this consists of configuring the array, applying reservoir training, and evaluation of separate test data.

Results are presented for the best individual of the evolved population, for each of 10 different evolutionary runs.

We evaluate performance using two classification tasks (spiral and diabetes), system modelling (NARMA-10), and speech recognition (Japanese vowels). The classification tasks are time-independent and the others are time-dependent. A description and list of parameters relating to each task is given in the Appendix.

4.2 Effect of Array Size

We investigate the effect of array size on task performance. Two array sizes are investigated: 36 STOs in a 6×6 grid, and 64 STOs in an 8×8 grid. All nanowires are constrained to be the same size.

The results are given in Fig. 4. Typically, task performance improves significantly for the larger array size. Only the vowel recognition task shows no significant improvement, maintaining a statistically similar performance and averaging an accuracy of roughly 96.5%. The larger array (64) manages to correctly classify all classes on the spiral task, resulting in a 100% accuracy. On average, both do well miss-classifying only a few instances. Performance on the diabetes database is competitive to a range of methods in the literature [26, table 3]; the larger 64 node array can reach approximately 94% accuracy. On the NARMA-10 task, the larger array has a significantly smaller (better) normalised root mean square error (NRMSE) [22, p.661] value; performance is comparable with 50 node RNN reservoirs [32, fig 9].

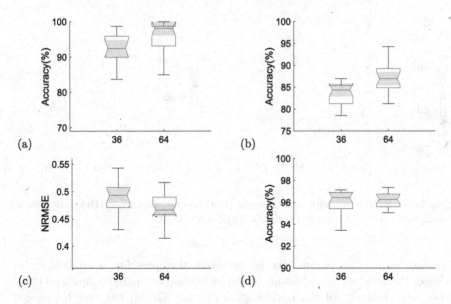

Fig. 4. Task performance against array size, for tasks (a) Spiral, (b) Diabetes, (c) NARMA-10, (d) Vowels. All four tasks are evaluated across two array sizes: 36 and 64 STOs. A large array tends to result in better performance across all tasks, although no significant improvement for vowels task is seen.

4.3   Effect of Nanowire Size

In the array size experiments above (§4.2), each nanowire is set to the same width (which is found through optimisation) resulting in a homogeneous network, i.e., all connections having the same strength. Here, we explore arrays with individual connection strengths which are now optimised.

Having more connections and free parameters in a network results in greater control, and typically improves the fit of the model to the task data. Exploring individual connection strengths provides a larger parameter space to optimise the array. However, it is unclear whether this can improve the performance of the proposed system.

Figure 5 compares homogeneous and heterogeneous networks on the spiral and NARMA-10 task. For both tasks, we see a significant difference in their performances when optimised. For the spiral task, on average, heterogeneous networks result in a lower accuracy. For the NARMA-10 task, heterogeneous networks lead to a smaller (better) normalised mean squared error. The former case is counter to what we might expect, of improved performance with more free parameters. However, the latter agrees with our expectations.

On the other tasks, we see on average an improved performance, however, these are not statistically significant. Examples of the best performing arrays are given in Fig. 6.

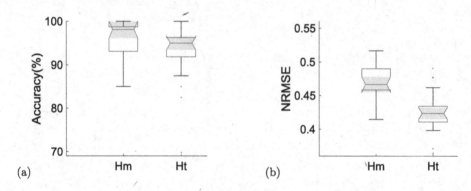

Fig. 5. Task performance with homogeneous (Hm) and heterogeneous (Ht) connections (64 node STO array), for tasks (a) Spiral, (b) NARMA-10.

Having more free parameters to optimise also presents a challenge, in this case, the random initialisation of the individual exchange couplings could increase the difficulty of the optimisation process. Giving the search process more time to explore the increased search space would likely lead to improved performances.

4.4 Effect of Connectivity Topology

Network topology has been shown to have a significant affect on the information processing of a reservoir [6,13,19]. The topologies of physical reservoirs are in many circumstances constrained by the complexity of physical wiring. Simple topologies such as rings and grids are easy to implement compared to other networks featuring nodes with many-to-many connections or long distance connections.

Here, we demonstrate the effects of topology on task performance for an STO array. The basic grid topology comprises nodes with a maximum of four connections; the ring topology has two connections for each node (Fig. 2). We consider homogeneous networks with 64 STO nodes formed into rings and grids. We assume the distance between the STOs is large enough that we can neglect any interference from dipolar interactions between unconnected nodes.

The optimised performance of each topology on the diabetes classification and vowels recognition tasks are given in Fig. 7. There is no statistically significant difference between the ring and the grid. Despite having fewer connections, the ring topology does not typically result in poorer performance. The optimisation process still manages to find comparable performances, suggesting good solutions are as abundant as grid networks.

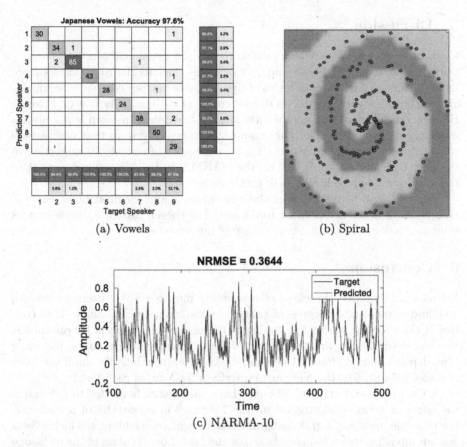

(a) Vowels

(b) Spiral

(c) NARMA-10

Fig. 6. Example of best performing STO arrays on different tasks: (a) Confusion matrix and accuracy on vowels task. (b) Trained output on the nonlinear two-class spiral dataset. Class is determined by location within the spiral pattern. Decision boundary of classes is highlighted in purple. (c) Target sequence (black) and trained output (red) of the reservoir array. (Color figure online)

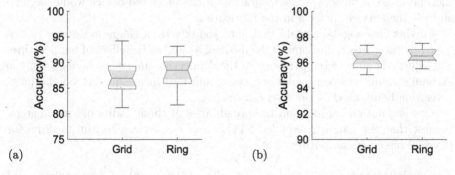

(a)

(b)

Fig. 7. Task performance versus topology, for tasks (a) Diabetes, (b) Vowels. Results are for 64 node homogeneous arrays. Two topologies are compared: grid and ring. The ring topology typically has similar performance to the grid.

5 Discussion

Connectivity and topology play critical role in the dynamical properties of networks. In [6], it is found that simpler topologies, such as the ring, possess more limited degrees of freedom in terms of dynamical behaviour compared to topologies with nodes with greater in-degree connections, e.g., a lattice or a torus. However, in terms of task complexity, greater dynamical freedom is not always necessary or even desirable. For example, a reservoir system that can possess some degree of non-linearity and a memory capacity of roughly 10 time-steps in the past typically performs well on the NARMA-10 task. Anything more than this can even begin to hinder task performance.

What we find here is that, at these array sizes, and for most tasks, there is no significant difference between topologies. The chosen tasks are simple enough to fit neatly within the dynamical range of our system.

6 Conclusions

We have investigated the effect of connecting multiple STOs using nanowires, and find a reasonable degree of control of the exchange coupling. This control of the coupling allows fine tuning of the reservoir dynamics. By optimising the array parameters we can perform different computational tasks, including time-dependent and time-independent tasks. Despite relatively small numbers of nodes (36 and 64), the STO arrays perform well across each task.

A Cartesian grid and ring are used here; more work is needed to determine the effect of array configuration on the information processing of a reservoir. For example, hexagonal grid configurations have more neighbours, which affects how an input perturbation travels across the grid. Local scaling of the exchange coupling between nodes might provide a similar effect.

The simulations performed here do not include thermal noise, which has a significant effect on the magnetisation. The effect of noise might be overcome by using multiple oscillators and averaging the output of the nodes. Along with thermal noise, a physical implementation of the proposed device would need to address the effect of defects in the fabrication.

Further investigation could look into the effects of shape anisotropy introduced by the wire on the spins of the devices, as well as the effect of temperature. The effect of non-zero temperature on the connecting nanowire should lower the exchange value between oscillators; this could also have an effect on the magnetisation being used as the reservoir output.

Our simulation results, and the possibilities of these additional parameters, suggest that the nanowire-coupled STO arrays can form a fruitful medium for physical reservoir computing.

Acknowledgements. MD, SS, and AS acknowledge funding from the SpInspired project, EPSRC grant EP/R032823/1. We thank Jed Bye for performing the preliminary coupling simulations of Sect. 2.2. All experiments were carried out using the University of York's Super Advanced Research Computing Cluster (Viking).

A Benchmark Tasks

A.1 Spiral Classification

This task involves the nonlinear classification of two spirals in Cartesian space. The dataset consists of 400 data points describing samples taken from two spirals with random noise added. The task is to classify which spiral each sample belongs to using only the (x, y) Cartesian coordinates. The spiral classes are encoded as two outputs and the predicted class is chosen as the output with highest value via a softmax function.

A.2 PIMA Indians Diabetes Classification

This dataset[1] contains real-world data related to medical diagnosis. The objective of the dataset is to diagnostically predict whether or not a patient has diabetes, based on certain diagnostic measurements. The dataset consists of several independent medical predictors including the BMI, blood pressure, and age of females at least 21 years old of Pima Indian heritage.

The database consists of 768 records. There are 268 positive and 500 negative classes. Each class is one-hot encoded into separate reservoir outputs. All input features (e.g., age) are normalised within $[0, 1]$ before use. The training set consists of 75% of samples, and test set 25%. Each sample is randomly chosen from the database and each set maintains the same percentage of each class, respectively.

A.3 NARMA-10

The NARMA (nonlinear autoregressive moving average) task [2] evaluates a reservoir's ability to model a 10-th order non-linear dynamical system. The task contains both non-linearity and a long-term dependency created by the 10-th order time-lag. The task is to predict the output $y(n + 1)$ given by eq.(2) when supplied with $u(n)$ from a uniform distribution of interval $[0, 0.5]$. For the 10-th order systems $\alpha = 0.3$, $\beta = 0.05$, $\delta = 10$ and $\gamma = 0.1$.

$$y(n + 1) = \alpha y(n) + \beta y(n) \left(\sum_{i=0}^{\delta} y(n - i) \right) + 1.5u(n - \delta)u(n) + \gamma \qquad (2)$$

A total of 5,000 values are generated and split into: 3,000 training, 1,000 validation, and 1,000 test. The first 50 values of each sub-set are discarded as an initial washout period.

---

[1] available from https://data.world/data-society/pima-indians-diabetes-database.

A.4   Japanese Vowels

The Japanese vowels dataset [9] consists of time-series data for multi-speaker classification. The data contains utterances of two Japanese vowels 'ae' by nine different male speakers. The dataset consists of 270 training utterances (30 utterances by 9 speakers) and 370 different utterances for testing (24–88 utterances by the same 9 speakers). Each utterance is pre-processed using linear prediction analysis into a discrete-time series of between 7–29 frames in length with twelve LPC cepstral coefficients.

Both the training and test data are randomly shuffled, because the original dataset groups each speaker into consecutive blocks. After every utterance is ran through the reservoir, the states of all nodes are concatenated for training. To decide on the final predicted speaker, a softmax function is used. This assigns a probability to each speaker, with the highest probability used to assign the predicted speaker.

References

1. Appeltant, L., et al.: Information processing using a single dynamical node as complex system. Nature Commun. **2**, 468 (2011). https://doi.org/10.1038/ncomms1476
2. Atiya, A.F., Parlos, A.G.: New results on recurrent network training: unifying the algorithms and accelerating convergence. IEEE Trans. Neural Netw. **11**(3), 697–709 (2000). https://doi.org/10.1109/72.846741
3. Berger, L.: Emission of spin waves by a magnetic multilayer traversed by a current. Phys. Rev. B **54**, 9353–9358 (1996)
4. Checinski, J.: Synchronization properties and reservoir computing capability of hexagonal spintronic oscillator arrays. J. Magn. Magn. Mater. **513**, 167251 (2020)
5. Chen, T., et al.: Comprehensive and macrospin-based magnetic tunnel junction spin torque oscillator model- part I: analytical model of the MTJ STO. IEEE Trans. Electron Devices **62**(3), 1037–1044 (2015). https://doi.org/10.1109/ted.2015.2390411
6. Dale, M., O'Keefe, S., Sebald, A., Stepney, S., Trefzer, M.A.: Reservoir computing quality: connectivity and topology. Natural Comput. **20**(2), 205–216 (2020). https://doi.org/10.1007/s11047-020-09823-1
7. Dale, M., et al.: Reservoir computing with thin-film ferromagnetic devices (2021), arXiv:2101.12700 [cs.ET]
8. Dale, M., Miller, J.F., Stepney, S., Trefzer, M.A.: Reservoir computing in material substrates. In: Nakajima, K., Fischer, I. (eds.) Reservoir Computing. NCS, pp. 141–166. Springer, Singapore (2021). https://doi.org/10.1007/978-981-13-1687-6_7
9. Dua, D., Graff, C.: UCI machine learning repository (2019), http://archive.ics.uci.edu/ml
10. Evans, R., Coopman, Q., Devos, S., Fan, W., Hovorka, O., Chantrell, R.: Atomistic calculation of the thickness and temperature dependence of exchange coupling through a dilute magnetic oxide. J. Phys. D Appl. Phys. **47**(50), 502001 (2014)
11. Fukushima, A., Seki, T., Yakushiji, K., Kubota, H., Yuasa, S., Ando, K.: Spin dice: random number generator using current-induced magnetization switching in mgo-mtjs. SSDM2010 Extend. Abstract pp. 1128–1129 (2010)
12. Furuta, T., et al.: Macromagnetic simulation for reservoir computing utilizing spin dynamics in magnetic tunnel junctions. Phys. Rev. Appl. **10**(3), 034063 (2018)

13. Tetko, I.V., Kůrková, V., Karpov, P., Theis, F. (eds.): ICANN 2019. LNCS, vol. 11731. Springer, Cham (2019). https://doi.org/10.1007/978-3-030-30493-5
14. Gilbert, T.: Classics in magnetics a phenomenological theory of damping in ferromagnetic materials. IEEE Trans. Magn. **40**(6), 3443–3449 (2004). https://doi.org/10.1109/tmag.2004.836740
15. Grollier, J., Querlioz, D., Camsari, K., Everschor-Sitte, K., Fukami, S., Stiles, M.D.: Neuromorphic spintronics. nature. Electronics **3**(7), 360–370 (2020)
16. Harvey, I.: The microbial genetic algorithm. In: Kampis, G., Karsai, I., Szathmáry, E. (eds.) ECAL 2009. LNCS (LNAI), vol. 5778, pp. 126–133. Springer, Heidelberg (2011). https://doi.org/10.1007/978-3-642-21314-4_16
17. Jaeger, H.: The echo state approach to analysing and training recurrent neural networks – with an erratum note. Bonn, Germany: German National Research Center for Information Technology GMD Technical Report **148**(34), 13 (2001)
18. Kanao, T., Suto, H., Mizushima, K., Goto, H., Tanamoto, T., Nagasawa, T.: Reservoir computing on spin-torque oscillator array. Phys. Rev. Appl. **12**(2), 024052 (2019)
19. Kawai, Y., Park, J., Asada, M.: A small-world topology enhances the echo state property and signal propagation in reservoir computing. Neural Netw. **112**, 15–23 (2019)
20. Khvalkovskiy, A., et al.: Basic principles of STT-MRAM cell operation in memory arrays. J. Phys. D Appl. Phys. **46**, 074001 (2013)
21. Locatelli, N., Cros, V., Grollier, J.: Spin-torque building blocks. Nature Mater **13**(1), 11–20 (2014)
22. Lukoševičius, M.: A practical guide to applying echo state networks. In: Montavon, G., Orr, G.B., Müller, K.-R. (eds.) Neural Networks: Tricks of the Trade. LNCS, vol. 7700, pp. 659–686. Springer, Heidelberg (2012). https://doi.org/10.1007/978-3-642-35289-8_36
23. Maekawa, S., Valenzuela, S.O., Kimura, T., Saitoh, E.: Spin Current. Oxford University Press (2017)
24. Marković, D.: Reservoir computing with the frequency, phase, and amplitude of spin-torque nano-oscillators. Appl. Phys. Lett. **114**(1), 012409 (2019)
25. Meo, A., Cronshaw, C.E., Jenkins, S., Winterburn, A., Evans, R.F.L.: Spin-transfer and spin-orbit torques in the Landau-Lifshitz-Gilbert equation (2022). 10.48550/arXiv.2207.12071
26. Naz, H., Ahuja, S.: Deep learning approach for diabetes prediction using PIMA Indian dataset. J. Diabete Metab. Disord. **19**(1), 391–403 (2020). https://doi.org/10.1007/s40200-020-00520-5
27. Prenat, G., Dieny, B., Guo, W., El Baraji, M., Javerliac, V., Nozieres, J.: Beyond MRAM, CMOS/MTJ integration for logic components. IEEE Trans. Magn. **45**(10), 3400–3405 (2009)
28. Riou, M., et al.: Neuromorphic computing through time-multiplexing with a spin-torque nano-oscillator. In: 2017 IEEE International Electron Devices Meeting (IEDM). pp. 36.3.1–36.3.4 (2017)
29. Romera, M., et al.: Vowel recognition with four coupled spin-torque nano-oscillators. Nature **563**(7730), 230–234 (2018)
30. Sato, R., Kudo, K., Nagasawa, T., Suto, H., Mizushima, K.: Simulations and experiments toward high-data-transfer-rate readers composed of a spin-torque oscillator. IEEE Trans. Magn. **48**(5), 1758–1764 (2012)
31. Sharma, R., et al.: Electrically connected spin-torque oscillators array for 2.4 GHz wifi band transmission and energy harvesting. Nature Commun. **12**(1), 1–10 (2021)

32. Stepney, S.: Non-instantaneous information transfer in physical reservoir computing. In: Kostitsyna, I., Orponen, P. (eds.) UCNC 2021. LNCS, vol. 12984, pp. 164–176. Springer, Cham (2021). https://doi.org/10.1007/978-3-030-87993-8_11

33. Tanaka, G., et al.: Recent advances in physical reservoir computing: a review. Neural Netw. **115**, 100–123 (2019)

34. Tannous, C., Gieraltowski, J.: The Stoner-Wohlfarth model of ferromagnetism: Static properties. arXiv preprint physics/0607117 (2006)

35. Terris, B.: Bit patterned magnetic recording media. In: Buschow, K.H.J., et al. (eds.) Encyclopedia of Materials: Science and Technology, pp. 1–6. Elsevier (2011)

36. Torrejon, J., et al.: Neuromorphic computing with nanoscale spintronic oscillators. Nature **547**(7664), 428–431 (2017)

37. Tsunegi, S., et al.: Physical reservoir computing based on spin torque oscillator with forced synchronization. Appl. Phys. Lett. **114**(16), 164101 (2019)

38. Wolf, S.A., et al.: Spintronics: a spin-based electronics vision for the future. Science **294**(5546), 1488–1495 (2001)

39. Zahedinejad, M., et al.: CMOS compatible W/CoFeB/MgO spin Hall nano-oscillators with wide frequency tunability. Appl. Phys. Lett. **112**(13), 132404 (2018)

Tight Bounds on the Directed Tile Complexity of a Just-Barely 3D $2 \times N$ Rectangle at Temperature 1

David Furcy[(✉)], Scott M. Summers, and Hailey Vadnais

Computer Science Department, University of Wisconsin Oshkosh, Oshkosh,
WI 54901, USA
{furcyd,summerss,vadnah08}@uwosh.edu

Abstract. We study the problem of determining the size of the smallest
tile set in which a given target shape uniquely self-assembles in Winfree's
abstract Tile assembly Model (aTAM), an elegant combinatorial model
of DNA tile self-assembly. This problem is also known as the directed
tile complexity problem. We work in a variant of the aTAM, restricted
to having the minimum binding strength threshold (temperature) set to
1 but mildly generalized to allow self-assembly to take place in a just-
barely 3D setting, where unit cubes are allowed to be placed in the $z = 0$
and $z = 1$ planes. Furcy, Summers and Withers recently proved lower
and upper bounds on the directed tile complexity of a just-barely 3D
$k \times N$ rectangle at temperature-1 of $\Omega\left(N^{\frac{1}{k}}\right)$ and $O\left(N^{\frac{1}{k-1}} + \log N\right)$,
respectively. However, their upper bound does not hold for $k = 2$. We
close this gap for $k = 2$ by proving an asymptotically tight bound of
$\Theta(N)$ on the directed tile complexity of a just-barely 3D $2 \times N$ rectangle
at temperature-1. The proof of our lower bound is based on an algorithm
that uses a novel projection of a given just-barely 3D assembly onto an
equivalent, 2D assembly.

1 Introduction

Self-assembly, a ubiquitous occurrence in nature, generally involves numerous
seemingly simple, fundamental components, evolving through instances of local
interaction, eventually resulting in a final structure whose complexity is greater
than the sum of the complexities of its parts. In this paper, we study the theoretical power of self-assembly in Winfree's abstract Tile Assembly Model (aTAM)
[11], which is a discrete mathematical model of DNA tile self-assembly [9] and
simple enough to intuitively describe in one paragraph, which we do next.

Winfree's aTAM is a combinatorial model of tile-based self-assembly, where
the fundamental self-assembling components are unit square tile types, to each
side of which there corresponds a glue comprised of a string label and a positive
integer strength. The aTAM restricts the number of tile types in the tile set
to be finite but infinitely many tiles of each type are assumed to exist. If two
tiles are placed next to each other at integer coordinates and the opposing glues

match, then the tiles bind with the strength of the glue, thus creating a tile assembly, or a mapping of integer coordinates to tile types, of size 2. Before the process of self-assembly begins, a positive integer temperature value is specified, which is usually 1 or 2, and a fixed seed tile is placed at a designated location defining the initial seed-containing assembly. Self-assembly then proceeds via an assembly sequence, where the seed-containing assembly may be grown by one tile during each step if there exists a tile (of some type) that can be placed at an unoccupied integer coordinate and bind to an existing tile belonging to seed-containing assembly with strength at least the temperature and perhaps via more than one glue. The steps of an assembly sequence continue until a terminal assembly is reached to which no further tiles can bind. Note that the domain of the terminal assembly technically defines a shape, or a set of connected integer coordinates, which we say uniquely self-assembles in the given tile set if every assembly sequence over the tile set results in the same terminal assembly.

One of the most widely studied optimization problems in the aTAM concerns finding the smallest tile set in which a given target shape uniquely self-assembles at some temperature, also known as the problem of determining the directed tile complexity of a given target shape $X \subseteq \mathbb{Z}^2$, at some temperature. This problem has been studied with respect to several classes of shapes, e.g., squares [1,5,8], rectangles [2] and algorithmically-specified finite shapes [10]. In this paper, we are particularly interested in studying the directed tile complexity of rectangles and in Winfree's aTAM model restricted to temperature 1 and mildly generalized to a just-barely 3D setting (see also [3], where 3D unit cubes are allowed to be placed in both the $z = 0$ and $z = 1$ planes).

In fact, this is the setting in which Furcy, Summers and Withers recently proved lower and upper bounds on the directed tile complexity of a just-barely 3D $k \times N$ rectangle at temperature 1, of $\Omega\left(N^{\frac{1}{k}}\right)$ and $O\left(N^{\frac{1}{k-1}} + \log N\right)$, respectively [4]. Note that their upper bound does not hold for $k = 2$ but it is easy to see that the directed tile complexity of a just-barely 3D $2 \times N$ rectangle at temperature 1 is $O(N)$ at temperature 1.

To that end, note that that a straightforward construction testifying to the fact that the directed tile complexity of a just-barely 3D $2 \times N$ rectangle is based on the simple idea of having N unique tile types self-assemble along the x-axis in a linear fashion, starting from the seed tile, where the east and west glues of each tile type effectively encodes the position of each tile type along the path. Assuming each tile type along the path has a glue pointing to the north and above (to the $z = 1$ plane), then two additional tile types can be used to place a tile at every other location in a just-barely 3D $2 \times N$ rectangle.

During the self-assembly of the previously described tile set, every tile that binds initially does so via a glue that points either west, south or down (to the $z=0$ plane). It is natural to ask whether it is possible to asymptotically reduce the directed tile complexity of a just-barely 3D $2 \times N$ rectangle via a tile set, the self-assembly of which follows a more convoluted pattern. One example is a zig-zag pattern, where some tiles initially bind via a glue that points either east, or up (to the $z = 1$ plane) while other tiles initially bind via a glue that points either west, or down. In our main result, we answer this question negatively: the directed tile complexity of a just-barely 3D 2 × N rectangle is $\Omega(N)$, regardless of how convoluted the self-assembly pattern might be. Our main result effectively closes the previous gap from Furcy, Summers and Withers, giving an asymptotically tight bound of $\Theta(N)$ on the directed tile complexity of a just-barely 3D 2 × N rectangle at temperature 1.

While our main result of an asymptotically tight bound of $\Theta(N)$ for the directed tile complexity of a just-barely 3D 2 × N rectangle at temperature 1 is perhaps unsurprising to the expert reader and seemingly incremental, our proof technique uses a novel projection of a just-barely 3D assembly sequence onto an equivalent 2D assembly sequence. Our projection technique essentially allows us to reason about a 3D assembly sequence as though it is self-assembling in 2D.

2 Preliminaries

In this section, we define the aTAM, as well as some specific notation needed for the proof of our main result.

2.1 The Abstract Tile Assembly Model

In this subsection, we briefly define Winfree's aTAM (see also [7,8]).

A *grid graph* is an undirected graph $G = (V, E)$, where $V \subset \mathbb{Z}^3$, such that, for all $\{\vec{a}, \vec{b}\} \in E$, $\vec{a} - \vec{b}$ is a 3-dimensional unit vector. The *full grid graph* of V is the undirected graph $G_V^f = (V, E)$, such that, for all $\vec{x}, \vec{y} \in V$, $\{\vec{x}, \vec{y}\} \in E \iff \|\vec{x} - \vec{y}\| = 1$, i.e., if and only if $\vec{x}$ and $\vec{y}$ are adjacent in the 3-dimensional integer Cartesian space.

A 3-dimensional *tile type* is a tuple $t \in (\Sigma^* \times \mathbb{N})^6$, e.g., a unit cube, with six sides, listed in some standardized order, and each side having a *glue* $g \in \Sigma^* \times \mathbb{N}$ consisting of a finite string *label* and a nonnegative integer *strength*. We assume a finite set of tile types, but an infinite number of copies of each tile type, each copy referred to as a *tile*. A *tile set* is a set of tile types and is usually denoted as T.

A *configuration* is a (possibly empty) arrangement of tiles on the integer lattice $\mathbb{Z}^3$, i.e., a partial function $\alpha : \mathbb{Z}^3 \dashrightarrow T$. Two adjacent tiles in a configuration *bind*, *interact*, or are *attached*, if the glues on their abutting sides are equal (in both label and strength) and have positive strength. Each configuration α induces a *binding graph* G_α^b, a grid graph whose vertices are positions occupied by tiles, according to α, with an edge between two vertices if the tiles at those vertices bind. An *assembly* is a connected, non-empty configuration, i.e., a partial function $\alpha : \mathbb{Z}^3 \dashrightarrow T$ such that $G_{\text{dom } \alpha}^f$ is connected and dom $\alpha \neq \varnothing$. Given $\tau \in \mathbb{Z}^+$, α is τ-*stable* if every cut-set of G_α^b has weight at least τ, where the weight of an edge is the strength of the glue it represents. When τ is clear from context, we say α is *stable*. Given two assemblies α, β, we say α is a *subassembly* of β, and we write $\alpha \sqsubseteq \beta$, if dom $\alpha \subseteq$ dom β and, for all points $\vec{p} \in$ dom α, $\alpha(\vec{p}) = \beta(\vec{p})$.

82   D. Furcy et al.

A 3-dimensional *tile assembly system* (TAS) is a triple $\mathcal{T} = (T, \sigma, \tau)$, where T is a tile set, $\sigma : \mathbb{Z}^3 \dashrightarrow T$ satisfying $|\text{dom } \sigma| = 1$ is the *seed assembly* (trivially τ-stable), and $\tau \in \mathbb{Z}^+$ is the *temperature*. Given two τ-stable assemblies α, β, we write $\alpha \to_1^{\mathcal{T}} \beta$ if $\alpha \sqsubseteq \beta$ and $|\text{dom } \beta \backslash \text{dom } \alpha| = 1$. In this case we say α $\mathcal{T}$-*produces* β *in one step*. If $\alpha \to_1^{\mathcal{T}} \beta$, dom $\beta \backslash$dom $\alpha = \{\vec{p}\}$, and $t = \beta(\vec{p})$, we write $\beta = \alpha + (\vec{p} \mapsto t)$. The $\mathcal{T}$-*frontier* of α is the set $\partial^{\mathcal{T}} \alpha = \bigcup_{\alpha \to_1^{\mathcal{T}} \beta} (\text{dom } \beta \backslash \text{dom } \alpha)$, i.e., the set of empty locations at which a tile could stably attach to α. The t-*frontier* of α, denoted $\partial_t^{\mathcal{T}} \alpha$, is the subset of $\partial^{\mathcal{T}} \alpha$ defined as $\{ \vec{p} \in \partial^{\mathcal{T}} \alpha \mid \alpha \to_1^{\mathcal{T}} \beta \text{ and } \beta(\vec{p}) = t \}$.

Let $\mathcal{A}^T$ denote the set of all assemblies of tiles from T, and let $\mathcal{A}_{<\infty}^T$ denote the set of finite assemblies of tiles from T. A sequence of $k \in \mathbb{Z}^+ \cup \{\infty\}$ assemblies $\vec{\alpha} = (\alpha_0, \alpha_1, \dots)$ over $\mathcal{A}^T$ is a $\mathcal{T}$-*assembly sequence* if, for all $1 \le i < k$, $\alpha_{i-1} \to_1^{\mathcal{T}} \alpha_i$. The *result* of an assembly sequence $\vec{\alpha}$, denoted as $\text{res}(\vec{\alpha})$, is the unique limiting assembly (for a finite sequence, this is the final assembly in the sequence). We write $\alpha \to^{\mathcal{T}} \beta$, and we say α $\mathcal{T}$-*produces* β (in 0 or more steps), if there is a $\mathcal{T}$-assembly sequence $\alpha_0, \alpha_1, \dots$ of length $k = |\text{dom } \beta \backslash \text{dom } \alpha| + 1$ such that (1) $\alpha = \alpha_0$, (2) dom $\beta = \bigcup_{0 \le i < k} \text{dom } \alpha_i$, and (3) for all $0 \le i < k$, $\alpha_i \sqsubseteq \beta$. We say α is $\mathcal{T}$-*producible* if $\sigma \to^{\mathcal{T}} \alpha$, and we write $\mathcal{A}[\mathcal{T}]$ to denote the set of $\mathcal{T}$-producible assemblies. An assembly α is $\mathcal{T}$-*terminal* if α is τ-stable and $\partial^{\mathcal{T}} \alpha = \varnothing$. We write $\mathcal{A}_\square[\mathcal{T}] \subseteq \mathcal{A}[\mathcal{T}]$ to denote the set of $\mathcal{T}$-producible, $\mathcal{T}$-terminal assemblies. If $|\mathcal{A}_\square[\mathcal{T}]| = 1$ then $\mathcal{T}$ is said to be *directed*.

In general, a 3-dimensional *shape* is a set $X \subseteq \mathbb{Z}^3$, such that G_X^f is connected. For a finite shape $X \subseteq \mathbb{Z}^3$, define $x^- = \min \{ x \mid (x, y, z) \in X \}$ and $x^+ = \max \{ x \mid (x, y, z) \in X \}$. The quantities y^-, y^+, z^- and z^+ can be defined similarly. Then, we say that the *horizontal extent* of X is $x^+ - x^-$. The *vertical* and *stacked* (vertical with respect to the z-axis) extents are defined similarly. We say X is *just-barely 3D* if it has stacked extent 1. We say the *furthest extreme column of* a shape $X \subseteq \mathbb{Z}^3$ from a location $(x, y, z) \in X$ to be $(\{x^-\} \times \mathbb{Z} \times \mathbb{Z}) \cap X$, if $|x^- - x| \ge |x^+ - x|$ and $(\{x^+\} \times \mathbb{Z} \times \mathbb{Z}) \cap X$ otherwise.

We say that a TAS $\mathcal{T}$ *self-assembles* X if, for all $\alpha \in \mathcal{A}_\square[\mathcal{T}]$, dom $\alpha = X$, i.e., if every terminal assembly produced by $\mathcal{T}$ places a tile on every point in X and does not place any tiles on points in $\mathbb{Z}^3 \backslash X$. We define the *tile complexity* of a shape X at temperature τ, denoted by $K_{SA}^\tau(X)$, as the minimum number of distinct tile types of any TAS that self-assembles it, i.e., $K_{SA}^\tau(X) = \min \{ n \mid \mathcal{T} = (T, \sigma, \tau), |T| = n \text{ and } \mathcal{T} \text{ self-assembles } X \}$. We say that a TAS $\mathcal{T}$ *uniquely self-assembles* a shape $X \subseteq \mathbb{Z}^3$ if $\mathcal{A}_\square[\mathcal{T}] = \{\alpha\}$ and dom $\alpha = X$. The *directed tile complexity* of a shape X at temperature τ is the minimum number of distinct tile types of any TAS that uniquely self-assembles (USA) X, denoted by $K_{USA}^\tau(X) = \min \{ n \mid \mathcal{T} = (T, \sigma, \tau), |T| = n \text{ and } \mathcal{T} \text{ uniquely self-assembles } X \}$.

2.2 Window Movies

The next two paragraphs contain definitions and notation that were taken directly from [6]. We include them verbatim for the sake of consistency.

A *window* w is a set of edges forming a cut-set of the full grid graph of $\mathbb{Z}^3$. Given a window w and an assembly α, a window that *intersects* α is a partitioning of α into two configurations (i.e., after being split into two parts, each part may or may not be disconnected). In this case we say that the window w cuts the assembly α into two non-overlapping configurations α_L and α_R, satisfying, for all $\vec{x} \in \text{dom } \alpha_L$, $\alpha(\vec{x}) = \alpha_L(\vec{x})$, for all $\vec{x} \in \text{dom } \alpha_R$, $\alpha(\vec{x}) = \alpha_R(\vec{x})$, and $\alpha(\vec{x})$ is undefined at any point $\vec{x} \in \mathbb{Z}^3 \setminus (\text{dom } \alpha_L \cup \text{dom } \alpha_R)$. Given a window w, its translation by a vector $\vec{\Delta}$, written $w + \vec{\Delta}$ is simply the translation of each one of w's elements (edges) by $\vec{\Delta}$. All windows in this paper are assumed to be induced by some translation of the yz-plane. Each window is thus uniquely identified by its x coordinate. For a window w and an assembly sequence $\vec{\alpha}$, we define a *glue window movie* M to be the order of placement, position and glue type for each glue that appears along the window w in $\vec{\alpha}$, regardless of whether the glue (eventually) forms a bond. Given an assembly sequence $\vec{\alpha}$ and a window w, the associated glue window movie is the maximal sequence $M_{\vec{\alpha},w} = (\vec{v}_1, g_1), (\vec{v}_2, g_2), \dots$ of pairs of grid graph vertices $\vec{v}_i$ and glues g_i, given by the order of appearance of the glues along window w in the assembly sequence $\vec{\alpha}$. We write $M_{\vec{\alpha},w} + \vec{\Delta}$ to denote the translation by $\vec{\Delta}$ of $M_{\vec{\alpha},w}$, yielding $\left(\vec{v}_1 + \vec{\Delta}, g_1 \right), \left(\vec{v}_2 + \vec{\Delta}, g_2 \right), \dots$.

If $\vec{\alpha}$ follows s, then the notation $M_{\vec{\alpha},w} \upharpoonright s$ denotes the *restricted* glue window submovie (*restricted to s*), which consists of only those steps of $M_{\vec{\alpha},w}$ that place glues that form positive-strength bonds that cross w at locations belonging to the simple path s. Let $\vec{v}$ denote the location of the starting point of s (i.e., the location of σ). Let $\vec{v}_i$ and $\vec{v}_{i+1}$ denote two consecutive locations in $M_{\vec{\alpha},w} \upharpoonright s$ that are located across w from each other. We say that these two locations define a *crossing* of w, where a crossing has exactly one direction. We say that this crossing is *away from $\vec{v}$* (or *away from σ*) if the x coordinates of $\vec{v}$ and $\vec{v}_i$ are equal or the x coordinate of $\vec{v}_i$ is between the x coordinates of $\vec{v}$ and $\vec{v}_{i+1}$.

2.3 Sufficiently Similar Restricted Glue Window Submovie Definition and a Corresponding Lemma

To prove our main result, we use a technique that relies on the following submovie similarity introduced by Furcy, Summers and Withers (Definition 3 of [4]):

Definition 1. *Assume:* $\mathcal{T} = (T, \sigma, 1)$ *is a 3D TAS,* $\alpha \in \mathcal{A}[\mathcal{T}]$, *$s$ is a simple path in G_α^b starting from the location of σ, $\vec{\alpha}$ is a sequence of $\mathcal{T}$-producible assemblies that follows s, w and w' are windows, σ is not located between w and w', $\vec{\Delta} \neq \vec{0}$ is a vector satisfying $w' = w + \vec{\Delta}$, e and e' are two odd numbers, and $M = M_{\vec{\alpha},w} \upharpoonright s = (\vec{v}_1, g_1), \dots, (\vec{v}_{2e}, g_{2e})$ and $M' = M_{\vec{\alpha},w'} \upharpoonright s = (\vec{v}_1', g_1'), \dots, (\vec{v}_{2e'}', g_{2e'}')$ are both non-empty restricted glue window submovies.*

We say that M and M' are sufficiently similar if the following constraints are satisfied:

1. *same number of crossings: $e = e'$,*
2. *same set of crossing locations (up to translation):*
$$\left\{ \vec{v}_i + \vec{\Delta} \;\middle|\; 1 \leq i \leq 2e \right\} = \left\{ \vec{v}_j' \;\middle|\; 1 \leq j \leq 2e \right\},$$
3. *same crossing directions at corresponding crossing locations:*
$$\left\{ \vec{v}_{4i-2} + \vec{\Delta} \;\middle|\; 1 \leq i \leq \tfrac{e+1}{2} \right\} = \left\{ \vec{v}_{4j-2}' \;\middle|\; 1 \leq j \leq \tfrac{e+1}{2} \right\}, \text{ and}$$

4. *same glues in corresponding "away crossing" locations:*
  for all $1 \le i, j \le \frac{e+1}{2}$, if $\vec{v}'_{4j-2} = \vec{v}_{4i-2} + \vec{\Delta}$, then $g'_{4j-2} = g_{4i-3}$.

We will invoke the following Window Movie Lemma for directed, temperature-1 self-assembly, introduced by Furcy, Summers and Withers (Lemma 5 of [4]):

Lemma 1. *Assume: $\mathcal{T} = (T, \sigma, 1)$ is a directed, 3D TAS, $k \in \mathbb{Z}^+$, $X_k \subseteq \mathbb{Z}^3$ is any finite just-barely 3D shape with vertical extent k and finite horizontal extent, $s \subseteq X_k$ is a simple path in the full grid graph of X_k from the location of the seed of $\mathcal{T}$ to some location in the furthest extreme column of X_k such that there exists a $\mathcal{T}$-assembly sequence $\vec{\alpha}$ that follows s, w and w' are windows, such that, $\vec{\Delta} \neq \vec{0}$ is a vector satisfying $w' = w + \vec{\Delta}$, and e is an odd number satisfying $1 \le e < 2k$. If $M = M_{\vec{\alpha},w} \upharpoonright s = (\vec{v}_1, g_1), \ldots, (\vec{v}_{2e}, g_{2e})$ and $M' = M_{\vec{\alpha},w'} \upharpoonright s = (\vec{v}'_1, g'_1), \ldots, (\vec{v}'_{2e}, g'_{2e})$ are sufficiently similar non-empty restricted glue window submovies, then $\mathcal{T}$ does not self-assemble X_k.*

3   Main Result

In this section, we prove that the directed tile complexity of a just-barely 3D $2 \times N$ rectangle at temperature 1 is $\Theta(N)$. This proof uses a new definition of submovie similarity (with an associated, simplified counting argument) and a new pumping argument. Before we define our simplified notion of submovie similarity, we make the following observation:

Observation 1. *When $k = 2$, each window cuts the just-barely 3D $k \times N$ rectangle in at most 4 locations. Therefore, the length of any restricted glue window submovie is either 1 or 3. This observation extends to any shape with a vertical extent equal to 2.*

The following notion of "almost sufficient similarity" is a relaxed form of the more general sufficient similarity (Definition 1), where only the first glues of the two movies have to match.

Definition 2. *Assume: $\mathcal{T} = (T, \sigma, 1)$ is a 3D TAS, $\alpha \in \mathcal{A}[\mathcal{T}]$, s is a simple path in G^b_α starting from the location of σ, $\vec{\alpha}$ is a sequence of $\mathcal{T}$-producible assemblies that follows s, w and w' are windows, σ is not located between w and w', $\vec{\Delta} \neq \vec{0}$ is a vector satisfying $w' = w + \vec{\Delta}$, $e, e' \in \{1, 3\}$, and $M = M_{\vec{\alpha},w} \upharpoonright s = (\vec{v}_1, g_1), \ldots, (\vec{v}_{2e}, g_{2e})$ and $M' = M_{\vec{\alpha},w'} \upharpoonright s = (\vec{v}'_1, g'_1), \ldots, (\vec{v}'_{2e'}, g'_{2e'})$ are both non-empty restricted glue window submovies.*

We say that M and M' are almost sufficiently similar if the following constraints are satisfied:

1. *same number of crossings: $e = e'$,*
2. *same ordered crossing locations (up to translation): for each $1 \le i \le 2e$, $\vec{v}_i + \vec{\Delta} = \vec{v}'_i$, and*
3. *same glue at the first crossing: $g_1 = g'_1$*

Note that the definition of "almost sufficiently similar submovies" is both: (1) stronger than that of "sufficiently similar submovies" since the former assumes that all ordered crossing locations match pairwise after translation by $\vec{\Delta}$ and that there are exactly either one or three crossings and (2) weaker since the former assumes that only the glues at the first crossings match.

We now show that we need only examine a "very small" number of restricted glue window submovies in order to find two almost sufficiently dissimilar ones.

Lemma 2. *Assume:* $\mathcal{T} = (T, \sigma, 1)$ *is a 3D TAS, G is the set of all glues in T, X is a just-barely 3D shape with a vertical extent equal to 2, s is a simple path starting from the location of σ such that $s \subseteq X$, $\vec{\alpha}$ is a $\mathcal{T}$-assembly sequence that follows s, $m \in \mathbb{Z}^+$, for all $1 \le l \le m$, w_l is a window, for all $1 \le l < l' \le m$, $\vec{\Delta}_{l,l'} \ne \vec{0}$ satisfies $w_{l'} = w_l + \vec{\Delta}_{l,l'}$, and for all $1 \le l \le m$, there exists $e_l \in \{1, 3\}$ such that $M_{\vec{\alpha}, w_l} \upharpoonright s$ is a non-empty restricted glue window submovie of length $2e_l$. If $m > 28|G|$, then there exist $1 \le l < l' \le m$ such that $e_l = e_{l'} = e$ and $M_{\vec{\alpha}, w_l} \upharpoonright s = (\vec{v}_1, g_1), \ldots, (\vec{v}_{2e}, g_{2e})$ and $M_{\vec{\alpha}, w_{l'}} \upharpoonright s = (\vec{v}_1', g_1'), \ldots, (\vec{v}_{2e}', g_{2e}')$ are almost sufficiently similar non-empty restricted glue window submovies.*

Note that the "almost sufficiently similar" relation is an equivalence relation. The proof of Lemma 2 counts the number of distinct equivalence classes this relation defines using a simplified version of the counting argument in the proof of Lemma 1 [4]:

Proof. Let e be an element of $\{1, 3\}$ and w be any window such that $M = M_{\vec{\alpha}, w} \upharpoonright s = (\vec{v}_1, g_1), \ldots, (\vec{v}_{2e}, g_{2e})$ is a non-empty restricted glue window submovie. e represents the number of times that $\vec{\alpha}$ crosses w (going either away from or toward the seed) as it follows s. We now consider two disjoint cases:

- If $e = 1$, there are four ways to choose the crossing location and, for each one of them, there are $|G|$ ways to choose the two glues that are placed at this crossing. Hence, the number of distinct equivalence classes of almost sufficiently similar submovies with one crossing is $4|G|$.
- If $e = 3$, there are (as above) $4|G|$ ways to choose the location and glue of the first crossing and, for each one of them, there are $3 \times 2 = 6$ ways to choose the locations of the two other crossings. Hence, the number of distinct equivalence classes of almost sufficiently similar submovies with three crossings is $24|G|$.

Therefore, the almost sufficiently similar relation partitions the set of all possible restricted glue window submovies into $28|G|$ distinct equivalence classes. Thus, if $m > 28|G|$, then there are two numbers $1 \le l < l' \le m$, such that, for $e = e_l = e_{l'}$, $M = M_{\vec{\alpha}, w_l} \upharpoonright s = (\vec{v}_1, g_1), \ldots, (\vec{v}_{2e}, g_{2e})$ and $M' = M_{\vec{\alpha}, w_{l'}} \upharpoonright s = (\vec{v}_1', g_1'), \ldots, (\vec{v}_{2e}', g_{2e}')$ are two different, non-empty, almost sufficiently similar restricted glue window submovies.

We now prove that the existence of two almost sufficiently similar restricted glue window submovies is enough to prevent the unique self-assembly of any finite shape with a vertical extent equal to 2.

Lemma 3. *Assume:* $T = (T, \sigma, 1)$ *is a directed, 3D TAS,* $X \subseteq \mathbb{Z}^3$ *is any finite just-barely 3D shape with finite horizontal extent and a vertical extent equal to 2,* $s \subseteq X$ *is a simple path in the full grid graph of* X *from the location of the seed of* T *to some location in the furthest extreme column of* X *such that there exists a* T*-assembly sequence* $\vec{\alpha}$ *that follows* s, w *and* w' *are windows, such that,* $\vec{\Delta} \neq \vec{0}$ *is a vector satisfying* $w' = w + \vec{\Delta}$, *and* $e \in \{1, 3\}$. *If* $M = M_{\vec{\alpha}, w} \upharpoonright s = (\vec{v}_1, g_1), \ldots, (\vec{v}_{2e}, g_{2e})$ *and* $M' = M_{\vec{\alpha}, w'} \upharpoonright s = (\vec{v}_1', g_1'), \ldots, (\vec{v}_{2e}', g_{2e}')$ *are almost sufficiently similar non-empty restricted glue window submovies, then* T *does not self-assemble* X.

The proof of this lemma is split into two cases, namely $e = 1$ or $e = 3$. In each case, we show that the two almost sufficiently similar submovies must actually be sufficiently similar, thereby reducing each case to an application of Lemma 5 of [4].

To facilitate the proof of the non-trivial second case, we use the *projection* of an assembly whose shape is a just-barely 3D rectangle (or, more generally, any finite shape with a vertical extent equal to 2) onto the 2D xy-plane, as defined visually in Fig. 1.

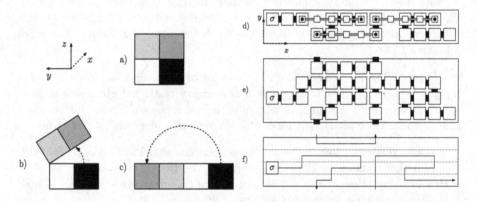

Fig. 1. a) Actual cross-section of the $2 \times N$ rectangle b) After splitting the two halves of the rectangle and performing a small rotation of its top half c) After the complete 180° rotation of the top half d) Sample assembly viewed from the top (as in the rest of the paper) e) Same sample assembly shown (again, viewed from the top) in our 2D projection. Note that, the assembly is the result of an assembly sequence placing tiles along a simple path, and when the path exits through the south (resp., north) side of the rectangle, it must re-enter the rectangle from the north (resp., south) side and at the same x coordinate, which corresponds to a move up from the $z = 0$ plane to the $z = 1$ plane (resp., down from the $z = 1$ plane to the $z = 0$ plane) in the actual rectangle f) The path of the same projected assembly, shown as a polyline with arrow(s), when individual tiles need not be differentiated.

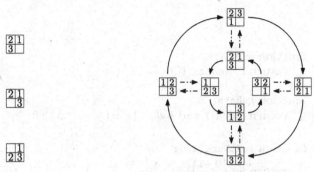

(a) The three representative crossing patterns

(b) Each solid arrow represents a counter-clockwise 90° rotation around the x axis. Each dash dotted arrow represents a 180° end-to-end rotation of the shape around the axis that crosses the section from its top-left corner to its bottom-right corner.

Fig. 2. Taxonomy of crossing patterns for 3-crossing submovies in a just-barely 3D shape with a vertical extent equal to 2. All twenty-four possible crossing patterns are equivalent (up to rotation) to one of the representative patterns shown on the left. The figure on the right depicts the 8 crossing patterns that are equivalent to the topmost representative pattern shown on the left.

Proof. If $e = 1$, then each submovie contains only one pair of attached glues. In this case, almost sufficient similarity implies sufficient similarity, since both definitions assume that the first glues match.

The rest of the proof deals with the case $e = 3$, for which we now prove that, if the glues at the first crossing are the same in both submovies, then the glues at the third crossing of both submovies must also match, thereby making the two submovies sufficiently similar.

Note that there exist $4 \times 3 \times 2 = 24$ different ways of choosing the locations and ordering of the crossings in a 3-crossing submovie. Figure 2 shows how each one of these 24 crossing patterns is identical (up to rotation) to one of three distinct "representative" crossing patterns. The rest of this proof deals explicitly with the representative pattern shown at the bottom of Fig. 2a but can easily be adapted to apply to either one of the other two representatives.

The top of Fig. 4 depicts a simple path s from the seed tile on the left side of the shape (in this case, a projected just-barely 3D $2 \times N$ rectangle) to the black tile on the right side of the rectangle. It also assumes the existence of two almost sufficiently similar submovies called M (resp., M') with six positions labeled $\vec{v}_1$ through $\vec{v}_6$ (resp., $\vec{v}'_1$ through $\vec{v}'_6$) along the window labeled w (resp., w'). Since M and M' are almost sufficiently similar, the glues on the east side of the tiles at positions $\vec{v}_1$ and $\vec{v}'_1$ are identical.

The main algorithm in Fig. 3 builds a new assembly sequence $\vec{\beta}$ that starts when the sub-assembly sequence of $\vec{\alpha}$ that ends in position $\vec{v}'_1$ has just finished

```
1  function onP'(i):
2  |   return i > index_ᾱ(v⃗'₃)
3
4  function onBoth(i):
5  |   return onP'(i) and index_ᾱ(Pos(ᾱ[i]) − Δ⃗) ≥ 0
6
7  function leftTurn(a⃗,b⃗):
8  |   return b⃗ = ( 0 −1 ) · a⃗
   |                ( 1  0 )
9
10 function main():
11 |   β⃗ ← (ᾱ[index_ᾱ(v⃗'₁)])
12 |   i ← index_ᾱ(v⃗₂)
13 |   while Pos(ᾱ[i]) ≠ v⃗₃ do
14 |   |   β⃗ ← β⃗ + (ᾱ[i] + Δ⃗)
15 |   |   i ← i + 1
16 |   i ← index_ᾱ(v⃗'₄)
17 |   while Pos(ᾱ[i]) ≠ v⃗'₅ do
18 |   |   if onBoth(i) then     // in this case, the position of ᾱ[i] is on P'
19 |   |   |   β⃗ ← β⃗ + ᾱ[i]
20 |   |   |   c⃗ ← Pos₂(ᾱ[i])
21 |   |   |   n⃗' ← Pos₂(ᾱ[i + 1])
22 |   |   |   n⃗ ← Pos₂(ᾱ[index_ᾱ(Pos(ᾱ[i]) − Δ⃗) + 1])
23 |   |   |   d⃗ ← n⃗ − c⃗
24 |   |   |   d⃗' ← n⃗' − c⃗
25 |   |   |   if leftTurn(d⃗',d⃗) then   // switch to P; get off P'
26 |   |   |   |   i ← index_ᾱ(n⃗)
27 |   |   |   else    // stay on both P' and P
28 |   |   |   |   i ← i + 1
29 |   |   else if onP'(i) then   // stay on P' and off P
30 |   |   |   β⃗ ← β⃗ + ᾱ[i]
31 |   |   |   i ← i + 1
32 |   |   else    // stay on P and off P'
33 |   |   |   β⃗ ← β⃗ + (ᾱ[i] + Δ⃗)
34 |   |   |   i ← i + 1
```

Fig. 3. The algorithm that proves that the glues between positions $\vec{v}'_5$ and $\vec{v}'_6$ in $\vec{\alpha}$ are identical to the glues between positions $\vec{v}_5$ and $\vec{v}_6$ in $\vec{\alpha}$. $Pos_2(\vec{\alpha}[i])$ is the location in the 2D xy plane of the projection of $Pos(\vec{\alpha}[i])$ according to the projection defined in Fig. 1. The reader must be aware that the algorithm is embedded in the proof of Lemma 3 and thus has direct access to terms defined therein. This is why we do not explicitly pass $\vec{\alpha}$, and $\vec{v}_1, \ldots, \vec{v}_6$ in as input to the algorithm.

assembling. This is represented, on Line 11 of the algorithm, by the initialization of $\vec{\beta}$ to the tile placement step at position $\vec{v}_1'$ in $\vec{\alpha}$ and of the index of the next tile placement step (on Line 12) to the (to-be-translated) tile placement step at position $\vec{v}_2$ in $\vec{\alpha}$. We now show that the glues on the east side of the tiles at positions $\vec{v}_5$ and $\vec{v}_5'$ must also be identical by tracing this algorithm, which will end up placing at position $\vec{v}_5'$ the same tile that was placed at position $\vec{v}_5$ in $\vec{\alpha}$.

First, since $\vec{v}_1'$ is part of the first crossing of w', no tiles have been placed on the east side of w' yet. Since the glue that sticks out on its east side is identical to the east-side glue of the tile at position $\vec{v}_1$, Loop 1 of the algorithm (Lines 13 through 15) makes a translated copy of the sub-assembly sequence from $\vec{v}_2$ to $\vec{v}_3$ and adds it to $\vec{\beta}$. Since $\mathcal{T}$ is directed, the type of tile that it places at location $\vec{v}_3'$ is unique. Therefore, the type of tile that $\vec{\alpha}$ places at position $\vec{v}_3'$ must be the same type of tile that $\vec{\beta}$ just placed at that location. As a result, the west-facing glue that sticks out at the second crossing of w' in $\vec{\beta}$ is identical to the glue between the tiles at locations $\vec{v}_3$ and $\vec{v}_4$ in $\vec{\alpha}$. $\vec{\beta}$ can now be extended using the tile type that $\vec{\alpha}$ placed at $\vec{v}_4'$, which must be the same tile type that $\vec{\alpha}$ placed at $\vec{v}_4$, since $\mathcal{T}$ is directed and could have (and therefore must have) placed that tile after crossing w for the second time.

The second loop in our algorithm (see Lines 16 through 34 in Fig. 3) builds a sub-assembly sequence from $\vec{v}_4'$ to $\vec{v}_5'$ that is appended to $\vec{\beta}$ and guarantees that the type of tile placed at $\vec{v}_5'$ is the same as the type of tile that was placed by $\vec{\alpha}$ at $\vec{v}_5$. To explain how this sub-assembly sequence is built, we call P (resp., P') the projected sub-path from $\vec{v}_4$ to $\vec{v}_5$ (resp., from $\vec{v}_4'$ to $\vec{v}_5'$) in $\vec{\alpha}$. Since our projection maintains the adjacency of positions (modulo an invisible link between the north and south sides of the shape), and P (resp., P') is a simple path, the union of the positions in P (resp., P') and the positions on the west side of w (resp., w') between $\vec{v}_5$ and $\vec{v}_4$ (resp., $\vec{v}_5'$ and $\vec{v}_4'$) together define a closed curve in the binding graph of the shape. By the Jordan curve theorem, each one of these paths divides the projection plane between an interior region and an exterior region. Both of these interior regions are free of tiles, by construction of $\vec{\alpha}$ along the simple path s.

In the example of Fig. 4a, each interior region of P and P' appears shaded as two disconnected components labeled P_a and P_b (resp., P_a' and P_b') due to the fact that our projection splits and rotates the top half of the 3D shape.

Nevertheless, P is a continuous path whose interior region always lies to its left. The same holds for P'. As a result, any one-tile left turn made when following one of these paths is guaranteed to belong to its interior region. This is the crux of the proof of correctness of the second loop in our algorithm. Loop 2 in Fig. 3 builds and adds to $\vec{\beta}$ a sub-assembly sequence whose path defines a new closed region that remains entirely inside the intersection of the interior regions defined by P' and the translation of $P + \vec{\Delta}$, which guarantees that this path cannot be blocked.

Each iteration of Loop 2 in our algorithm adds one tile placement step to $\vec{\beta}$ (on Line 19, 30, or 33). All of the other lines in Loop 2 are used to compute the location of the next tile placement step in $\vec{\beta}$. The position of each placement step lies either on P' (marked by a • in Fig. 4), or $P + \vec{\Delta}$ (marked by a ▲ in Fig. 4), or on both (marked by a + in Fig. 4). In the latter case, the tile being placed was the same at the corresponding locations in P and P', which is how we end up getting the correct tile in position $\vec{v}_5'$, since both the first and last positions in $\vec{\beta}$ must be shared by $P + \vec{\Delta}$ and P' (since the two movies M and M' are almost sufficiently similar and thus always cross the windows in the same row of the projected rectangle).

In the first iteration of Loop 2, $\vec{\beta}$ is on both $P + \vec{\Delta}$ and P' and places at $\vec{v}_4'$ the tile shared by these two paths, indicated by a + in Fig. 4b. At this point, P' turns right to the north, whereas P keeps going straight towards the west, as shown by the two arrows anchored at the +. Lines 20 through 25 of the algorithm detect that P is making a left turn away from P'. In order for $\vec{\beta}$ to remain within the interior regions of both paths, it decides, on line 28, to follow P only, as indicated by the second + in Fig. 4c[1].

In the second iteration, β finds itself back on both $P + \vec{\Delta}$ and P', with only one direction it could move along, as indicated by the arrow in Fig. 4c. So, β makes this move, as indicated by the middle + in Fig. 4d. In fact, $\vec{\beta}$ remains on both paths for two additional iterations. When in the position marked by the westernmost + in Fig. 4d, there is a split between $P + \vec{\Delta}$ (which moves to the south) and P' (which keeps moving to the west). The correctness of the algorithm requires that β make a left turn and follow $P + \vec{\Delta}$, as shown in Fig. 4e, which also depicts the three following iterations. Note that the easternmost • corresponds to the sixth iteration where, for the first time, β is only following $P + \vec{\Delta}$ (see Line 33). This remains the case for the seventh iteration whereas, on the eighth iteration, $\vec{\beta}$ is back on both paths with only one direction to move in (see Line 28). However, in the following iteration, $\vec{\beta}$ will have to make a left turn again (Line 26).

Skipping ahead, Fig. 4f shows the changes in β after seven more iterations, the last one of which shows the first time β follows P' exclusively (see Line 30 in the algorithm and the ▲ in Fig. 4f).

Figure 4g shows the last three iterations of the algorithm, ending at position $\vec{v}_5'$.

Since each and every path segment making up $\vec{\beta}$ has to be unblocked (because each segment is either on P' or inside the (empty) interior region defined by P'), $\vec{\beta}$ can always be assembled. In addition, since each and every subsequence of $\vec{\beta}$ was (or could have been) placed on P, it follows that this is the case as well for the last tile placement in $\vec{\beta}$. In conclusion, the tile placed at $\vec{v}_5'$ must be identical to the tile placed by $\vec{\alpha}$ at $\vec{v}_5$ and M' is thus sufficiently similar.

The following result chains Lemmas 2 and 3 in this order. We will use the contrapositive of the following lemma to prove our lower bound for $K_{USA}^1 \left(R_{2,N}^3 \right)$.

Lemma 4. *Assume: $T = (T, \sigma, 1)$ is a 3D TAS, G is the set of all glues in T, X is a just-barely 3D shape with finite horizontal extent and a vertical extent equal*

---

[1] This is a + because, at this location, both paths come together again.

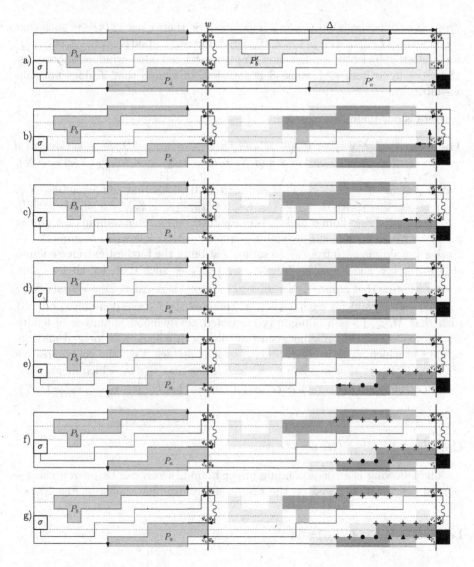

Fig. 4. Tracing the algorithm in Fig. 3 on a sample $\vec{\alpha}$ with two almost sufficiently similar glue window submovies whose crossing pattern is the bottommost representative in Fig. 2a.

to 2, $s \subseteq X$ is a simple path in the full grid graph of X from the location of σ to some location in the furthest extreme column of X in either z plane such that there exists a $\mathcal{T}$-assembly sequence $\vec{\alpha}$ that follows s, $m \in \mathbb{Z}^+$, for all $1 \le l \le m$, w_l is a window, for all $1 \le l < l' \le m$, $\vec{\Delta}_{l,l'} \ne \vec{0}$ satisfies $w_{l'} = w_l + \vec{\Delta}_{l,l'}$, and for all $1 \le l \le m$, there is $e_l \in \{1,3\}$ such that $M_{\vec{\alpha},w_l} \upharpoonright s$ is a non-empty restricted glue window submovie of length $2e_l$. If $m > 28|G|$, then $\mathcal{T}$ does not self-assemble X.

Proof. The hypothesis of Lemma 2 is satisfied. So there exist $1 \le l < l' \le m$ such that $e = e_l = e_{l'}$ and $M_{\vec{\alpha}, w_l} \upharpoonright s = (\vec{v}_1, g_1), \ldots, (\vec{v}_{2e}, g_{2e})$ and $M_{\vec{\alpha}, w_{l'}} \upharpoonright s = (\vec{v}_1', g_1'), \ldots, (\vec{v}_{2e}', g_{2e}')$ are almost sufficiently similar non-empty restricted glue window submovies. Thus, the hypothesis of Lemma 3 is satisfied. It follows that $\mathcal{T}$ does not self-assemble X.

Here is our main lower bound:

Theorem 1. *Let* $N \in \mathbb{Z}^+$. *If* X_N *is any finite just-barely 3D shape with vertical and horizontal extents equal to 2 and* N, *respectively, then* $K^1_{USA}(X_N) = \Omega(N)$.

Proof. Assume $\mathcal{T} = (T, \sigma, \tau = 1)$ is a directed, 3D TAS that self-assembles X_N. Assume $\alpha \in \mathcal{A}_\square[\mathcal{T}]$ with dom $\alpha = X_N$. Let $s = (\vec{x}_0, \vec{x}_1, \ldots, \vec{x}_n)$ be a simple path in G^b_α, such that, $\{\vec{x}_0\} = $ dom σ and $\vec{x}_n$ is in the furthest extreme column of X_N from $\vec{x}_0$. Since $\tau = 1$, there is a $\mathcal{T}$-assembly sequence $\vec{\alpha}$ that follows s. Assume $N \ge 3$. Since s is a simple path from $\vec{x}_0$ to some location in the furthest extreme column of X_N, there is some positive integer $m \ge \lfloor \frac{N}{2} \rfloor \ge \frac{N}{3}$ such that, for all $1 \le l \le m$, w_l is a window that cuts X_N, for all $1 \le l < l' \le m$, there exists $\vec{\Delta}_{l,l'} \ne \vec{0}$ satisfying $w_{l'} = w_l + \vec{\Delta}_{l,l'}$, and for each $1 \le l \le m$, there exists a corresponding $e_l \in \{1, 3\}$ such that $M_{\vec{\alpha}, w_l} \upharpoonright s$ is a non-empty restricted glue window submovie of length $2e_l$. Moreover, w_l cuts X_N between the column in which $\vec{x}_0$ is located and the column in which $\vec{x}_n$ is located. Since $\mathcal{T}$ self-assembles X_N, (the contrapositive of) Lemma 4 says that $m \le 28|G|$. We also know that $\frac{N}{3} \le m$, which means that $\frac{N}{3} \le 28|G|$. Thus, we have $N \le 3 \cdot 28|G|$ and it follows that $|T| \ge \frac{|G|}{6} \ge \frac{1}{6}\frac{N}{3 \cdot 28} = \frac{N}{504} = \Omega(N)$.

We get the following new, lower bound for $K^1_{USA}(R^3_{2,N})$.

Corollary 1. $K^1_{USA}(R^3_{2,N}) = \Omega(N)$.

The following is a corresponding upper bound, which can be proven using a general construction based on the tile assembly example shown in Fig. 2(b) of [8].

Lemma 5. $K^1_{USA}(R^3_{2,N}) = O(N)$.

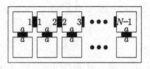

Fig. 5. An $N + 1$-tile construction for $R^3_{2,N}$ with the 1-tile as the seed tile

Proof. A $2 \times N$ rectangle can easily be constructed using $N + 1$ tiles (see Fig. 5), thereby establishing a linear upper-bound on the temperature-1 tile complexity of a just-barely 3D $2 \times N$ rectangle.

Combining this lemma and the preceding corollary yields the following new tight bound on the directed tile complexity of a just-barely 3D $2 \times N$ rectangle at temperature 1.

Corollary 2. $K^1_{USA}\left(R^3_{2,N}\right) = \Theta(N)$.

4   Conclusion

In this paper, we proved a tight bound of $\Theta(N)$ on the directed tile complexity of a just-barely 3D $2 \times N$ rectangle at temperature 1. The proof of our lower bound is based on an algorithm that uses a novel projection of a given just-barely 3D assembly onto an equivalent, 2D cylindrical assembly. While the projection technique that we use in this paper is limited to a just-barely 3D $2 \times N$ setting, future research endeavors could uncover more general projections and study the extent to which they could be applied to tile self-assembly.

References

1. Adleman, L.M., Cheng, Q., Goel, A., Huang, M.D.A.: Running time and program size for self-assembled squares. In: Proceedings of the Thirty-Third Annual ACM Symposium on Theory of Computing (STOC), pp. 740–748 (2001)
2. Aggarwal, G., Cheng, Q., Goldwasser, M.H., Kao, M.Y., de Espanés, P.M., Schweller, R.T.: Complexities for generalized models of self-assembly. SIAM J. Comput. (SICOMP) **34**, 1493–1515 (2005)
3. Cook, M., Fu, Y., Schweller, R.T.: Temperature 1 self-assembly: deterministic assembly in 3D and probabilistic assembly in 2D. In: Proceedings of the Twenty-Second Annual ACM-SIAM Symposium on Discrete Algorithms (SODA), pp. 570–589 (2011)
4. Furcy, D., Summers, S.M., Withers, L.: Improved lower and upper bounds on the tile complexity of uniquely self-assembling a thin rectangle non-cooperatively in 3d. In: 27th International Conference on DNA Computing and Molecular Programming, DNA 27, 13–16 September 2021, Oxford, UK (Virtual Conference). LIPIcs, vol. 205, pp. 1–18. Schloss Dagstuhl - Leibniz-Zentrum für Informatik (2021)
5. Manuch, J., Stacho, L., Stoll, C.: Two lower bounds for self-assemblies at temperature 1. J. Comput. Biol. **17**(6), 841–852 (2010)
6. Meunier, P.E., Patitz, M.J., Summers, S.M., Theyssier, G., Winslow, A., Woods, D.: Intrinsic universality in tile self-assembly requires cooperation. In: Proceedings of the Twenty-Fifth Annual ACM-SIAM Symposium on Discrete Algorithms (SODA), pp. 752–771 (2014)
7. Rothemund, P.W.K.: Theory and experiments in algorithmic self-assembly, Ph. D. thesis, University of Southern California (2001)
8. Rothemund, P.W.K., Winfree, E.: The program-size complexity of self-assembled squares (extended abstract). In: The Thirty-Second Annual ACM Symposium on Theory of Computing (STOC), pp. 459–468 (2000)
9. Seeman, N.C.: Nucleic-acid junctions and lattices. J. Theor. Biol. **99**, 237–247 (1982)
10. Soloveichik, D., Winfree, E.: Complexity of self-assembled shapes. SIAM J. Comput. (SICOMP) **36**(6), 1544–1569 (2007)
11. Winfree, E.: Algorithmic self-assembly of DNA, Ph. D. thesis, California Institute of Technology (1998)

Exploring the Robustness of Magnetic Ring Arrays Reservoir Computing with Linear Field Calibration

David Griffin[1]([✉])[ID], Susan Stepney[1][ID], and Ian Vidamour[2][ID]

[1] University of York, York, UK
{david.griffin,susan.stepney}@york.ac.uk
[2] University of Sheffield, Sheffield, UK
i.vidamour@sheffield.ac.uk

Abstract. One of the challenges for reservoir computing is the robustness of the implementation in the face of fabrication error. If a system is too sensitive to fabrication error, then each manufactured reservoir becomes a unique artefact with unique computational properties. Under most circumstances, this is undesirable as it makes reproduction of results, or useful systems, complicated. This paper uses simulation to examine the properties of nano-scale magnetic ring arrays as reservoir computers under parameters corresponding to a wide variety of physically derived parameters, and investigates the effectiveness of linear field calibration to minimise the difference in unexpected behaviour of the systems.

1 Introduction

Reservoir computing seeks to exploit the complex dynamic behaviour of systems to accomplish useful computation. By providing a dynamical system with an appropriate time series input, the system will progress and can be measured to extract useful information, such as categorising the input or predicting the next value of a time series. *In materio* Reservoir Computing places an additional constraint in that the dynamical system is expected to be a physical system grounded in the real world. However, a physical dynamical system is subject to error. Error can take many forms:

- Error inherent in the limitations of the equipment used to measure the system or provide input
- Error dependent on the operating environment of the system, such as temperature
- Error due to unpredictable behaviour of the system
- Error due to limitations when fabricating the system

This paper focuses on the last of these types of error. A physical system must be fabricated in some fashion, and there will always be limitations on how accurately the system can be fabricated. Examples of such limitations include purity of substances used in fabrication, and the precision of equipment used in fabrication. As fabrication error is incorporated into the system when it is made, it must be accounted for in the analysis of the system. If fabrication error is not accounted for, then the behaviour of the system may depend on the specific error introduced through fabrication, which would make results difficult to reproduce. Further, if intending to deploy multiple instances of a system to perform the same task, it is necessary for multiple physical instances of the system to be capable of the same behaviour; unmitigated fabrication error may make this difficult or impossible.

While one approach to fabrication error might be to improve the fabrication process until it is negligible, this is not necessarily practical. For example, the physical device on which the work in this paper is based [17] uses systems fabricated via electron beam lithography. This process involves multiple analogue steps that are challenging to reproduce perfectly and thus can lead to fabrication errors. The first of these error prone steps is applying the layers of magnetic material and polymer to the substrate; slight variations in thickness are unavoidable, and result in variations in thickness on the finished product. The focus of the electron beam can introduce further variation; incorrect focusing results in the electron beam having a slightly warped shape depending on position, which in turn impacts how accurately it can cut shapes. The next step is removing the material that is no longer protected by the polymer, which involves wet chemicals and is therefore difficult to reproduce exactly. Finally, even removing the remaining polymer can cause errors as small particles of magnetic material can be lifted from the substrate with the polymer, producing further irregularities.

Where it is not practical to reduce the effects of fabrication error to the point where they are negligible, effects of fabrication error can be mitigated by calibration. If calibration is sufficient, each device can be individually calibrated to have uniform logical behaviour. This paper examines nano-scale magnetic ring arrays, which can be calibrated by adjusting the strength of the magnetic field they are subjected to. By applying a simple linear search it is possible to find the optimal strength of magnetic field for a given ring array that maximises its performance. This technique has been demonstrated on a physical system [17], but it has not been explored in depth to see how calibration can compensate for a wide variety of fabrication errors.

This paper investigates the effectiveness of calibration to compensate for fabrication error by simulating a wide variety of physically derived parameters. These parameters are simulated through the phenomenological level simulator of RingSim [17]. The search is carried out by PyCHARC/SpatialGA [9], a novelty search method that seeks novel behaviours of the system. By characterising the space of possible behaviours under a wide variety of parameters, it is possible to infer the size of this space and therefore how many different uncontrolled behaviours the Ring Array can exhibit within reasonable fabrication error[1].

---

[1] This differs from controlled behaviours, which under normal circumstances it is desirable to have as many different types of behaviour as possible.

The main purpose of the search of behaviours under calibration is to show under which circumstances the same behaviours can be achieved. The sensitivity of the ring array to fabrication errors is not directly explored by this search. This is in part due to the current method of utilising the ring array requiring calibration [17], which makes it difficult to extract the effects of fabrication errors in isolation as the correct input values for a given use are dependent on the effects of fabrication error. However, the search also yields some information on the sensitivity of the ring array by identifying areas where calibration is insufficient to provide useful behaviours.

1.1 Organisation

Section 2 gives an overview of relevant concepts as well as the current state of the art of the magnetic ring array system evaluated in this paper. Section 3 outlines the details of the design of the experiment, with a particular focus on the measures used. The experiment itself is presented in Sect. 4, and the results follow in Sect. 5. An evaluation of the results in presented in Sect. 6, with a detailed discussion of how the results can be interpreted. Finally, conclusions are given in Sect. 7.

2 Background

Error in a system can be attributable to a number of factors that increase the uncertainty in using a system. Uncertainty [13] can be characterised as one of two types: aleatory uncertainty, which represents the inherent randomness of processes, and epistemic uncertainty, which represents the effect of incomplete knowledge of a system. While aleatory uncertainty is normally unavoidable, epistemic uncertainty can be reduced by a better understanding of the system under consideration [13].

Fabrication error of a physical system falls under the category of epistemic uncertainty. While it may not be practical, a system can be modelled at a higher fidelity that encompasses the effect of fabrication error; for example, using a microscope to detect physical defects and compensate for them. However, identifying and compensating for defects in this manner is a time consuming and difficult process and relies upon understanding physical phenomena that may be difficult to model [17]. An alternative to this approach is to calibrate the system [8], by applying some modification to the input or output such that a known or optimal result can be reached. This allows the epistemic uncertainty of the system to be reduced without having to identify the precise nature of defects in the system.

Reservoir computing [15] takes the behaviour of a dynamical system and attempts to extract useful computation from it. The Echo State Network (ESN) [12] is one of the archetypal artificial reservoirs, consisting of a neural network where the hidden layer consists of sparse, random connections.

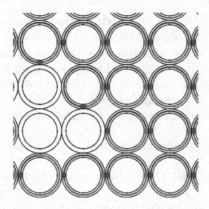

Fig. 1. Simulated segment of Nano-scale Magnetic Ring Array Reservoir under consideration

In materio Reservoir Computing takes the basic idea of reservoir computing and applies it to physical dynamical systems. These can be any physical system that exhibits dynamical behaviours, with examples as diverse as origami-based robotic feedback systems [1] or magnetic thin film arrays [5].

This paper investigates the Nano-scale Magnetic Ring Array reservoir, as defined by Dawidek et al. [7]. The mano-scale magnetic ring array utilises the phenomena of constrained domain walls to obtain reservoir properties. In the presence of a sufficiently strong magnetic field, domain walls nucleate in pairs on the rings. These domain walls can then be driven around the rings by a rotating magnetic field, exhibiting stochastic pinning behaviour at the junctions between rings. If a domain wall is pinned and comes into contact with its counterpart, it annihilates. By modulating the strength of the rotating magnetic field it is possible to provide an input to the system, and by measuring the electrical resistance of the ring array it is possible to measure some of the properties of the Domain Wall population using techniques such as anisotropic magnetoresistance [2].

While it is possible to model magnetic rings using general purpose micromagnetic simulators [16], such an approach is computationally too expensive for systems with a large number of rings. To address this, RingSim [17] was developed, which is a phenomological model of the behaviour of Domain Walls in the magnetic ring array. RingSim uses a number of physically derived parameters to characterise the behaviour of the Domain Walls, and by varying these parameters it is possible to model the behaviour of a wide variety of physical systems. As such, RingSim is a useful model for exploring fabrication error.

Both the hardware implementation of the magnetic ring array and RingSim are designed with calibration in mind [17], and in both cases a search is conducted on the magnetic field strength to maximise the response of the physical or simulated ring array. The only constraints on this search are the strength of magnetic field that can be produced by the equipment.

CHARC [6] is a novelty search algorithm that seeks to explore a behaviour space. Novelty search [14] algorithms seek to find new or novel behaviours, in contrast to optimising search algorithms that seek to optimise for a given problem. The goal of exploration as opposed to optimisation is useful for characterising a behaviour space, i.e. the set of behaviours that can be expressed by the various configurations of a system considered by CHARC. CHARC, by default, characterises the behaviour of reservoirs by three measures:

- Kernel rank (KR): the degree to which different inputs produce different outputs [4].
- Generalisation rank (GR): the degree to which similar inputs produce similar outputs [4].
- Linear Memory Capacity (LMC): the ability of a system to reproduce inputs [11].

3   Design

3.1   Search Method

To explore the behaviour of the Ring Array as characterised by RingSim, PyCHARC was used. PyCHARC is an evolution of the CHARC novelty search with an emphasis on extensibility. PyCHARC was used to conduct a novelty search over the characterisation of RingSim as given by KR, GR and LMC. As the Ring Array provides only a single output in its native configuration, the Ring Array was set up with time multiplexed outputs where multiple measurements of the ring array over the rotation of the magnetic field were used as input to the readout layer of the reservoir.

One of the differences between PyCHARC and CHARC is the ability to use different types of search algorithms to explore the behaviour space. The original search algorithm used by CHARC is based on the Microbial Genetic Algorithm [10], which, although elegantly simple, suffers from poor parallelisability. This lack of parallelisability limits how many input parameters CHARC can explore.

To counter this, these experiments used a new approach called SpatialGA. SpatialGA explores by first partitioning the behaviour space and identifying partitions that have high levels of diversity from the initial population, as characterised by the density of individuals in the partition. Once the most diverse partition is identified, multiple individuals are generated by applying crossover and mutation operators to the individuals in that partition, with the hope of finding more individuals within the partition. Once the number of individuals within the partition exceeds a threshold, it is divided into sub-partitions and the process starts over[2].

---

[2] For brevity some details, such as penalty terms on selecting the partition to explore that ensure that all areas of the behaviour space are explored rather than focusing on a infinitesimally small but interesting area, are omitted.

Algorithm 1. Pseudocode for Kernel Rank (KR)

1: $input\_length := system.washout + kr\_input\_size$
2: $input\_signal := [uniform(0.0, 1.0)$ **for** each **input** to system, **for** $input\_length]$
3: $output := system.run(input\_signal)$
4: remove first $system.washout$ elements from $output$
5: $KR := matrix\_rank(output)$
6: **return** KR

Algorithm 2. Pseudocode for Generalisation Rank (GR)

1: $input\_length := system.washout + gr\_input\_size$
2: $input\_signal := [uniform(0.4, 0.6)$ **for** each **input** to system, **for** $input\_length]$
3: $output := system.run(input\_signal)$
4: remove first $system.washout$ elements from $output$
5: $GR := matrix\_rank(output)$
6: **return** GR

3.2 Measures

While KR, GR, and LMC are "standard" measures of the behaviour of reservoirs, we are aware that there are multiple divergent implementations of these measures. The specific versions of the measures used in this work are defined here.

Kernel Rank (KR) is a measure of the ability of a reservoir to produce different outputs for different inputs. It is calculated by supplying the system under consideration with a uniform random input stream between 0 and 1, and calculating the rank of the matrix of outputs (with a threshold on SVD values of 0.01). A pseudocode implementation is given in Algorithm 1.

Generalisation Rank (GR) is a measure of the ability of a reservoir to generalise similar inputs to similar outputs. It is calculated in a similar manner to Kernel Rank, only the random input stream is over the much smaller range of 0.4 to 0.6. A pseudocode implementation is given in Algorithm 2.

Linear Memory Capacity (LMC) is a measure of how much linear memory can be stored within the reservoir. This is calculated by attempting to construct a readout layer for the reservoir that can reproduce the last n inputs. The LMC is defined as a measure of how well the outputs of the reservoir correspond to the inputs that it is supposed to represent. A pseudocode implementation is given in Algorithm 3.

3.3 Ring Array Calibration

As in prior work [17], the Ring Array requires calibration to maximise its ability to conduct useful work. In physical systems, this is in part due to the fabrication error causing intra-device variation.

The Ring Array takes a single input in the form of a global rotating magnetic field. The magnetic field drives the domain walls in the system, causing them to rotate with it unless they become pinned at a junction.

Algorithm 3. Pseudocode for Linear Memory Capacity (LMC)

1: **def** $output\_signal(input\_signal, system)$:
2: **return** [[$input\_signal$ shifted back by $x + 1$] **for** x **in** $range(system.outputs)$]

3: $input\_length := system.washout + lmc\_input\_length + system.outputs$
4: $train\_input\_signal = [uniform(0.0, 1.0)$ **for** $input\_length]$
5: $system.train($ $train\_input\_signal$ broadcast to all inputs of $system$, $output\_signal(train\_input\_signal)$)
6: $test\_input := [uniform(0.0, 1.0)$ **for** $input\_length]$
7: $test\_output := output\_signal(test\_input)$
8: $predictions := system.run($ $test\_input\_signal$ broadcast to all inputs of $system$)
9: remove first $system.washout$ values from $test\_input, predictions, test\_output$
10: $LMC := 0$
11: $inpvar = variance(test\_input)$
12: **for** each output of system **do**
13:     $covar := covariance(predictions, test\_output)$
14:     $pvar := variance(predictions)$
15:     $mc := (covar ** 2) / (inpvar * pvar)$
16:     **if** $mc \ge min\_memory\_capacity$ **then**
17:         $LMC += mc$
18:     **end if**
19: **end for**
20: **return** LMC

Calibration is accomplished by using a simple linear search over the available ranges of magnetic field strengths, retraining the output layer for each new field strength, and picking the magnetic field with the best response. If necessary, the process can be adapted into a depth-first search to refine the calibration further. The physical implementation used in the work of Vidamour et al. [18] was constrained to a maximum magnetic field strength of approximately 60 Oe.

Simulation differs from physical systems in that any magnetic field can be simulated, even if it is not something that is practical to realise in a physical system. This allows us to explore across a wider range of magnetic fields and conduct analysis on both realistic magnetic fields and unrealistic magnetic fields.

An additional effect of simulation is that parameters can also be consolidated: in a physical system, multiple physical parameters affect the probability of events. For example, the probability of pinning at a junction is influenced by edge roughness, any imperfections, temperature, material, and potentially other parameters. RingSim simplifies these parameters to a description of the required energy barriers [17], which are still represented by a large number of "physically derived" parameters. This paper explores a further simplification that directly exposes the probabilities of pinning to PyCHARC for exploration.

Table 1. Parameters used in RingSim for Experiment 1

Parameter	Range	Explanation
E0	$[1.0 \times 10^{-19}, 3.0 \times 10^{-19}]$	Characterises properties of the geometry of
E0D	$[0.5 \times 10^{-21}, 1.5 \times 10^{-21}]$	the rings
H0	$[80, 90]$	
H0D	$[10, 20]$	
ER	$[20, 30]$	Characterisation of the minimum
ERD	$[0.5, 3.0]$	propagation field of the system
PCE	$[0.5, 1.0]$	Characterisation of behaviour of two
PCH	$[0.5, 1.0]$	domain walls occupy one junction
alpha	$[1.0, 2.0]$	Value characterising how energy barrier varies with magnetic field

4 Experiments

Two primary experiments were conducted for this work. Both experiments used PyCHARC/SpatialGA to search over input parameters for RingSim. These configurations of RingSim were then calibrated using a linear search, and the calibrated system was measured to determine its KR, GR and LMC. These measurements were then fed back into PyCHARC/SpatialGA to inform the algorithm on where to explore next.

The two experiments differed in the parameters that were used as follows:

- Experiment 1: The default set of 9 parameters that characterises the energy barriers required, which control the probabilities of pinning at junctions. Parameters for this experiment are given in Table 1. The ranges of these parameters were initially selected to cover the full range of parameters that have been observed in fitting RingSim parameters to various physical devices, such as the device used in [17]. These ranges were then expanded to those shown in Table 1 to cover a range of values that are plausible given the currently fabricated devices, to allow PyCHARC/SpatialGA to search over a wider area.
- Experiment 2: An alternate set of 3 parameters that exposes the probabilities derived from the energy barriers. Parameters for this experiment are given in Table 2. Parameters for this experiment were selected to roughly correspond to the parameters of Experiment 1.

For each experiment, PyCHARC/SpatialGA was run for 250 generations with a target population of 25 individuals per region, to find configurations spanning as much of the behaviour space as possible. For each of the measures KR, GR and LMC, an optimisation pass was run to optimise the transformation function between the logical inputs of the system, which are specified between 0 and 1

Table 2. Parameters used in the simplified form of RingSim for Experiment 2

Parameter	Range	Explanation
BP	$[0, 1]$	Distribution of the probability of pinning at
PD	$[0, 0.5]$	junction.
DE	$[1, 3]$	Modifier for when two domain walls occupy a junction.

and the simulated magnetic field, $f(x) = ax + b$. This optimisation was restricted so that the image of the function was between 15 Oe and 65 Oe.[3]

The purpose of the second experiment is to determine if reducing the number of dimensions is possible. This is desirable for a number of reasons; Firstly, reducing the parameter set results in a more robust search as there are fewer dimensions of the input space of PyCHARC.

The second reason for why a reduction in dimensionality is desirable is more subtle: if the number of input dimensions can be reduced, then this implies that there is a many-to-one relationship between the default set of parameters and the reduced set. Given that the differences in behaviour are the result of fabrication error, in the absence of correlation between parameters one would assume that their relative independence. This in turn implies that the principles of the Central Limit Theorem [3] can be applied to some extent, and therefore that extreme behaviour due to fabrication error is less likely.

5   Results

5.1   Presentation of Results

The results of the experiment are presented as a graph matrix. Each graph in the matrix is a plot of one parameter against one measure. For each parameter, the individuals found by PyCHARC were placed in bins by the value of the parameter. The plots show a line representing the median measure score for individuals in each of these parameter bins against the value of the measure after calibration, and a region showing the 90% range of the individuals found. This allows the reader to judge the spread of values for the given parameter, which shows how other parameters can affect the plotted parameter.

5.2   Results of Experiment 1

Figure 2 shows the results of the exploration, broken down by the effects of each input dimension. There are two broad categories of effect seen.

In the case of H0, E0, PCE, PCH and alpha, calibration results in the following outcomes:

---

[3] These limits are somewhat arbitrary, but approximately reflect the limitations of the current physical implementation with regard to sustained magnetic fields.

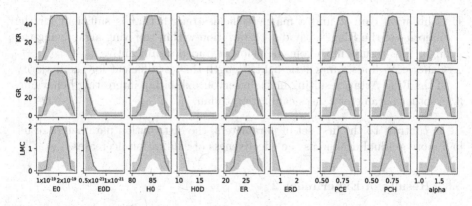

Fig. 2. Results Matrix for Experiment 1. Each graph plots one of the RingSim model parameters against one of the three metrics used by PyCHARC, showing the median and 90% range of individuals found by PyCHARC.

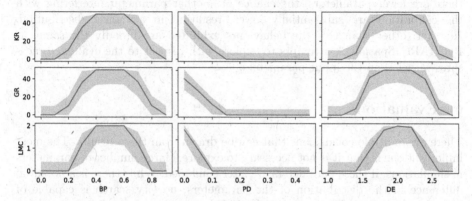

Fig. 3. Results Matrix for Experiment 2. Each graph plots one of the simplified RingSim model parameters against one of the three metrics used by PyCHARC, showing the median and 90% range of individuals found by PyCHARC.

1. Calibration cannot find a sufficiently weak magnetic field, resulting in domain walls not ever pinning at junctions, and therefore no interesting response.
2. Calibration cannot find a sufficiently strong magnetic field, resulting in domain walls always pinning at junctions, and therefore no interesting response.
3. Calibration succeeds, resulting in the reservoir exhibiting interesting behaviour.
4. Another parameter causes calibration to fail.

For these parameters, the transitions between the three outcomes are relatively abrupt.

In the case of the distribution parameters, H0D, E0D, and ERD calibration results in the following outcomes:

1. Calibration cannot find a magnetic field strength that is sufficient for the majority of the Ring Array due to variation within the Ring array being too high. This results in the output being degraded significantly.
2. Calibration finds a magnetic field strength that is sufficient for the majority of the Ring Array, resulting in the reservoir exhibiting interesting behaviour.
3. Another parameter causes calibration to fail.

In contrast to the first set of parameters, the distribution parameters result in a more gradual decline as the effectiveness of calibration decreases.

5.3   Results of Experiment 2

Figure 3 shows the results of the second experiment, using the further simplified model. The results are broadly the same as the first experiment, albeit with a lower number of dimensions. The most notable difference is that as there are fewer parameters, the chance of another parameter interfering with the calibration are substantially lower, resulting in a tighter distribution. However, other than this the behaviours exhibited are broadly the same, as PyCHARC/SpatialGA attempts to explore with respect to the evaluated measures rather than the input parameters.

6   Evaluation

There are multiple conclusions that can be drawn from these results. The most important one is that it is not necessary to explore a large number of parameters in simulations, if these parameters are later combined. While there is a potential difference in the distribution of the parameters, novelty search is capable of identifying unique behaviours regardless of the number of parameters.

One downside to simplifying the model in this way is that as the abstraction of the parameters increases, it may become difficult to determine what is physically realisable. However, provided there is some understanding of the relation between the abstract parameters and the physical system it should be possible to derive bounds for the abstract parameters that keep the exploration within realistic bounds.

Calibration on the magnetic ring array reservoir was in general very effective at finding a consistent optimal magnetic field strength, assuming such a magnetic field was possible within the bounds of the exploration. However, it was less effective when the distribution of parameters increased. This is likely due to the properties of individual junctions within the ring array becoming so divergent that a single global magnetic field was unable to compensate for their differences, resulting in some junctions always pinning or never pinning domain walls.

Given the results of calibration, it can be stated that the magnetic ring array reservoir is somewhat robust to fabrication error. This is especially true in the case that the fabrication error is uniform across the ring array; for example, a small amount of contamination of the material or an imperfection in the design.

Calibration is less effective when individual junctions with the ring array have substantially different properties. However, given that for previous experiments with real devices, the distribution parameters are between 1 and 4 orders of magnitude smaller that the base values [17], the results here suggest that for any realistic manufacturing process calibration should perform well.

The consistency of results with calibration may seem surprising; however, Experiment 2 does shed some light on why it was so successful. Assuming that the distribution of probability values within the system is relatively tight, and therefore that there exists a magnetic field that has similar effects over the entire ring array, there are only two remaining parameters. Therefore, the system only has two degrees of freedom with respect to its characterisation. As the system is a reservoir, it contains a trained linear output layer, and the calibration process effectively provides a trained linear input layer. These two linear layers allow calibration plus training to counteract the two degrees of freedom the parameters expose, leading to consistent results providing the optimal magnetic field is within the range of fields searched.

Experiment 2 also lends some credence to the idea that as in the real system multiple parameters are combined to single probability values, there is a lower chance of experiencing extreme behaviours. This can be seen to an extent with the spread of values shown in the Fig. 2 graphs; if multiple values contribute to a behaviour, then it is possible for one anomalous value to be compensated for by another. The nature of this experiment did not allow us to verify the degree to which the physical parameters are independent within the actual fabrication process, and so it is not possible to make a definitive claim that this is the case. However, if the parameters have a degree of independence then this allows a further degree of robustness for physical systems by virtue of multiple things having to go wrong for extreme behaviour to manifest.

These results also show that multiple sets of parameters can yield useful results, which suggests that it will be possible in future to use heterogeneous ring arrays, where different rings in the array have different properties. By allowing substantially different ring properties within an array, these results show that not all rings will be driven with their optimum magnetic field. There are a number of implications of this:

- Rings with relatively high energy barriers could be used as memory when the magnetic field drops too low, causing the domain walls in the rings to enter a pinned state.
- Rings with relatively low energy barriers could be used to restore portions of the ring array to a known state using a stronger than required magnetic field to cause domain walls to move with high probability, causing nucleation of domain walls in adjacent empty rings.

Hence, even though these behaviours are not useful for a global uniform ring array, it may be possible to exploit them in a heterogeneous ring array. This also highlights the usefulness of novelty search based approaches, as they can identify behaviours that would not be found with optimisation based techniques.

7 Conclusion

This paper explored the robustness of magnetic ring array reservoir computing with a calibration step by applying a novelty search approach to ring array parameters. The paper found that the behaviour of the ring array was relatively robust after calibration provided that the ring parameters resulted in a desired magnetic field that lay within the range of values obtainable. In the case that this was not possible, then the ring array would either abruptly fail or gradually degrade, depending on whether the failing was due to a global effect across the ring array or due to too much variance within the ring array. However, for the latter to cause a substantial problem would require an order of magnitude increase in variance over currently used manufacturing techniques.

The paper also demonstrated that simplifying a model to the minimum required still produces useful results with novelty search. While this may not be true with other types of search, due to the simplification having the potential to change the distribution of parameters, as novelty search seeks different behaviours it is able to largely overcome this difference.

Finally, this paper also exhibited one of the features of novelty search, in being able to capture non-optimal behaviours. In particular, the non-optimal behaviours found, while not useful for the homogeneous ring arrays considered in this paper, may have use in future work exploring the properties of heterogeneous ring arrays.

Acknowledgments. The authors wish to thank Chalres Vidamour for sharing insight into challenges of the fabrication process of the magnetic ring arrays used in prior work [17]. DG and SS acknowledge funding from the MARCH project, EPSRC grant numbers EP/V006029/1 and EP/V006339/1. IV acknowledges a DTA-funded PhD studentship from EPSRC.

References

1. Bhovad, P., Li, S.: Physical reservoir computing with origami and its application to robotic crawling. Sci. Rep. **11**(1), 1–18 (2021)
2. Bordignon, G., et al.: Analysis of magnetoresistance in arrays of connected Nano-rings. IEEE Trans. Magn. **43**(6), 2881–2883 (2007)
3. Brosamler, G.A.: An almost everywhere central limit theorem. Math. Proc. Cambridge Philos. Soc. **104**, 561–574 (1988)
4. Büsing, L., Schrauwen, B., Legenstein, R.: Connectivity, dynamics, and memory in reservoir computing with binary and analog neurons. Neural Comput. **22**(5), 1272–1311 (2010)
5. Dale, M., et al.: Reservoir computing with thin-film ferromagnetic devices. arXiv preprint arXiv:2101.12700 (2021)
6. Dale, M., Miller, J.F., Stepney, S., Trefzer, M.: A substrate-independent framework to characterise reservoir computers. Proceed. Royal Soc. A **475**, 2226 (2019). https://doi.org/10.1098/rspa.2018.0723
7. Dawidek, R.W., et al.: Dynamically driven emergence in a nanomagnetic system. Adv. Func. Mater. **31**(15), 2008389 (2021)

8. Franklin, A.: Calibration. Perspect. Sci. **5**(1), 31–80 (1997)
9. Griffin, D.: PyCHARC. https://github.com/dgdguk/pycharc/
10. Harvey, I.: The microbial genetic algorithm. In: Kampis, G., Karsai, I., Szathmáry, E. (eds.) ECAL 2009. LNCS (LNAI), vol. 5778, pp. 126–133. Springer, Heidelberg (2011). https://doi.org/10.1007/978-3-642-21314-4_16
11. Jaeger, H.: Short term memory in echo state networks. GMD-report 152. In: GMD-German National Research Institute for Computer Science (2002). http://www.faculty.jacobs-university.de/hjaeger/pubs/STMEchoStatesTechRep pdf (2002)
12. Jaeger, H., Haas, H.: Harnessing nonlinearity: predicting chaotic systems and saving energy in wireless communication. Science **304**(5667), 78–80 (2004)
13. Kendall, A., Badrinarayanan, V., Cipolla, R.: Bayesian segNet: model uncertainty in deep convolutional encoder-decoder architectures for scene understanding. In: Kim, T.-K., Stefanos Zafeiriou, G.B., Mikolajczyk, K. (eds.) Proceedings of the British Machine Vision Conference (BMVC), pp. 1-512. BMVA Press (2017). https://doi.org/10.5244/C.31.57
14. Lehman, J., Stanley, K.O.: Exploiting open-endedness to solve problems through the search for novelty. In: ALife XI, Boston, MA, USA, pp. 329–336. MIT Press (2008)
15. Schrauwen, B., Verstraeten, D., Van Campenhout, J.: An overview of reservoir computing: theory, applications and implementations. In: Proceedings of the 15th European Symposium on Artificial Neural Networks, pp. 471–482 (2007)
16. Vansteenkiste, A., Leliaert, J., Dvornik, M., Garcia-Sanchez, F., Van Waeyenberge, B.: The design and verification of mumax3. AIP Adv. **4**, 107133 (2014)
17. Vidamour, I.T., et al.: Quantifying the computational capability of a nanomagnetic reservoir computing platform with emergent magnetisation dynamics. Nanotechnology **33**(48), 485203 (2022). https://doi.org/10.1088/1361-6528/ac87b5
18. Vidamour, I., et al.: Reservoir computing with emergent dynamics in a magnetic metamaterial (2022). https://doi.org/10.48550/ARXIV.2206.04446

Undecidability of the Topological Entropy of Reversible Cellular Automata and Related Problems

Toni Hotanen$^{(\boxtimes)}$

University of Turku, Turku, Finland
`tonhot@utu.fi`

Abstract. Topological entropy is an important invariant of topological dynamical systems. It is often regarded as the measure of complexity of the system and can be used to tell non-conjugate systems apart from each other. We will show that the decision problem that asks whether the topological entropy is zero or not is undedicable in the class of reversible one-dimensional cellular automata. We will also show that some related decision problems are also undecidable in the setting of reversible cellular automata and reversible and complete Turing machines.

Keywords: cellular automata · Turing machines · decision problem · undecidable · computable · entropy · Lyapunov exponents

1 Introduction

Topological entropy is an important invariant of topological dynamical systems. Invariant meaning it is preserved under taking conjugacies of the system. Therefore if two systems have different entropy, one can immediately say that they are non-conjugate. It would therefore be interesting and useful to have an algorithm that calculates the entropy for a given system. Interestingly it was recently proven that the conjugacy problem is undecidable among reversible cellular automata in [10].

In this paper we will prove some open decision problems concerning reversible Turing machines and cellular automata.

It was shown in [2], that it is undecidable whether the topological entropy is zero or not for a given reversible and complete Turing machine. We will show that it is also undecidable whether the speed of a given machine is non-zero and whether a given machine has a strictly weakly periodic configuration or not. Fascinatingly in [6] the author constructs algorithms that estimate the values of topological entropy and speed for a given Turing machine and a precision.

The situation is entirely different when considering cellular automata. In [5] it was shown that there does not exist an algorithm that estimates the topological entropy of a given cellular automata and a precision. In [1] the analogous problem was suspected to be open in the case of reversible cellular automata and

D. Genova and J. Kari (Eds.): UCNC 2023, LNCS 14003, pp. 108–123, 2023.
https://doi.org/10.1007/978-3-031-34034-5_8

a more general. In Question 1 of [10] it also asked if the topological entropy of reversible cellular automata is computable. We will answer both of these questions in Theorem 11. In [8] it was further shown that one can not estimate the values of global Lyapunov exponents of a given reversible cellular automaton and a precision.

In [5] it was shown that the decision problem, that asks whether the topological entropy is zero for a given cellular automaton, is undecidable. We show the problem undecidable in Theorem 10. In Theorem 8 we answer negatively to Problem 2 of [8], which asks whether the decision problem, that asks whether the value of both left and right Lyapunov exponents of a given cellular automaton is zero, is decidable or not. As a somewhat related matter we will also show that it is undecidable if a given cellular automaton has a configuration that is a glider.

2   Preliminaries

A *relation* is a subset $R \subseteq X \times X$, where X is a set. We will use the standard notation aRb if $(a,b) \in R$. We will denote the complement of R as R^c, i.e. $R^c = (X \times X) \setminus R$.

An *alphabet* Σ is a finite set of *symbols*. A *word* of length n over an alphabet Σ is any element $w = (w_0, w_1, \ldots, w_{n-1}) = w_0 w_1 \cdots w_{n-1}$ from the set $\Sigma^{[0,n)} = \Sigma^n$ and $|w| = n$ is the *length* of a word w. The *empty word* is denoted as ϵ and it is the unique word of length zero. A set of all finite words i.e. $\bigcup_{n \in \mathbb{N}} \Sigma^n$ is denoted as Σ^* and a set of all finite non-empty words $\Sigma^* \setminus \{\epsilon\}$ is denoted as Σ^+. A *concatenation* $\cdot : (\Sigma^*)^2 \to \Sigma^*$ is a mapping such that $u \cdot v = u_0 u_1 \ldots u_n v_0 v_1 \ldots v_m$, where $u = u_0 u_1 \ldots u_n$ and $v = v_0 v_1 \ldots v_m$. We will adapt the shorthand notation uv for the concatenation of any two words. Elements from the sets $\Sigma^{\mathbb{N}}$, $\Sigma^{\mathbb{Z}-}$ and $\Sigma^{\mathbb{Z}}$ are called *right-infinite, left-infinite* and *bi-infinite* words, respectively. Furthermore we define a set $\Sigma^{\Omega} = \Sigma^+ \cup \Sigma^{\mathbb{N}} \cup \Sigma^{\mathbb{Z}-} \cup \Sigma^{\mathbb{Z}}$. A concatenation of elements $u \in \Sigma^{\Omega}$ and $v \in \Sigma^{\Omega}$ is defined when u is finite or left-infinite and v is finite or right-infinite. Let $u \in \Sigma^{\Omega}$ and $w \in \Sigma^{\Omega}$, we will denote $u \sqsubset w$ if there exists such $j \in \mathbb{Z}$, that $u_{i+j} = w_i$ for each i in the domain of u, and say that u is a *subword* of w. If Σ and Γ are two alphabets, we will denote the set $\{uv \mid u \in \Sigma^{\alpha}, v \in \Gamma^{\beta}\}$ as $\Sigma^{\alpha} \Gamma^{\beta}$. where $\alpha \in \{\mathbb{Z}_-, *, +\}$ and $\beta \in \{\mathbb{N}, *, +\}$. In this notation, if $\Sigma = \{a\}$, we will omit the brackets. If $w \in \Sigma^*$, we will use the notation w^{∞} for the right-infinite word $ww \cdots$ and $^{\infty}w$ for the left-infinite word $\cdots ww$. If $A \subseteq \Sigma$ and $w \in \Sigma^{\Omega}$, then $w_A = |\{i \mid w_i \in A\}|$. If $A = \{a\}$ then we denote this as w_a.

A *topological dynamical system* is a pair (X, f), where X is a compact metric space and f is a continuous function $f \colon X \to X$. A *cover* is a collection $\mathcal{C}$ of open subsets of X, such that $X \subseteq \bigcup_{U \in \mathcal{C}} U$. For a given cover $\mathcal{C}$, let $|\mathcal{C}|$ denote its cardinality. A cover is a *finite cover* if its cardinality is finite. A *subcover* of a cover is any subset that is also a cover. A *join* of n finite covers $\mathcal{C}_0, \mathcal{C}_1, \ldots, \mathcal{C}_{n-1}$ is defined as $\bigvee_{i=0}^{n-1} \mathcal{C}_i = \{\bigcap_{i=0}^{n-1} U_i \mid U_i \in \mathcal{C}_i \, \forall i \in \{0, 1, \ldots, n-1\}\}$. For a given finite cover, let $H(\mathcal{C}) = \log(\min\{|\mathcal{C}'| \mid \mathcal{C}' \text{ is a subcover of } \mathcal{C}\})$. A *topological entropy* of a finite cover $\mathcal{C}$ is defined as $H_{f,\mathcal{C}} = \lim\limits_{n\to\infty} \dfrac{H(\bigvee\limits_{i=0}^{n-1} f^{-i}(\mathcal{C}))}{n}$, where $f^{-i}(\mathcal{C}) = \{f^{-i}(U) \mid U \in \mathcal{C}\}$. A *topological entropy of a dynamical system* (X, f) is defined as $h_f = \sup_{\mathcal{C}} H_{f,\mathcal{C}}$. A point $x \in X$ is called *periodic* if there exists such $n \in \mathbb{Z}_+$ that $f^n(x) = x$.

A *shift dynamical system* is a dynamical system $(\Sigma^{\mathbb{Z}}, \sigma)$, where Σ is a finite set of symbols, $\Sigma^{\mathbb{Z}}$ is the space called the *full shift* and σ, called the *shift*, is defined in a way that $\sigma(x)_i = x_{i+1}$. The *metric* d of the space $\Sigma^{\mathbb{Z}}$ is defined as $d_\sigma(x, y) = 2^{-\inf\{|i| \in \mathbb{N}\,|\,x_i \neq y_i\}}$. It is not difficult to see that the space $\Sigma^{\mathbb{Z}}$ is compact and that the function σ is continuous. An *endomorphism* is a continuous function $f \colon \Sigma^{\mathbb{Z}} \to \Sigma^{\mathbb{Z}}$, such that $f \circ \sigma = \sigma \circ f$.

A *one-dimensional cellular automaton* is a 3-tuple $\mathcal{A} = (\Sigma, N, h)$, where Σ is a finite set of symbols called *states*, N is a *neighbourhood* $(i_0, i_1, \ldots, i_{n-1}) \in \mathbb{Z}^n$ and $h \colon \Sigma^n \to \Sigma$ is a *local rule*. If $N = [-r, r]$, we call N a *radius-r neighbourhood*. In the context of cellular automata, we call the full shift $\Sigma^{\mathbb{Z}}$ a *configuration space* and refer to its elements as *configurations*. The local rule together with the neighbourhood induces a global rule $f \colon \Sigma^{\mathbb{Z}} \to \Sigma^{\mathbb{Z}}$, which is defined in such a way that $f(c)_i = h(c_{i+i_0}, c_{i+i_1}, \cdots, c_{i+i_{n-1}})$. We make no distinction between a cellular automaton and its global rule. A *quiescent state* is a state satisfying $h(q, q, \ldots q) = q$. A configuration c such that $|\{c_i \neq q\}| < \infty$ is called *q-finite* or just *finite* if q is clear from the context. We will call a configuration c *weakly periodic* if there exists such $m \in \mathbb{N}$ and $n \in \mathbb{Z}_+$, that $f^n(c) = \sigma^m(c)$. A weakly periodic configuration is called *strictly weakly periodic* if it is not periodic. A finite strictly weakly periodic configuration is called a *glider*. By the Curtis-Hedlund-Lyndon theorem, the cellular automata, abbreviated as CA, are exactly the endomorphisms of the shift dynamical systems.

A *Turing machine* is a 3-tuple $\mathcal{M} = (Q, \Gamma, \delta)$, where $Q = Q_w \cup Q_m$ is a finite set of *states*, Γ is a finite set of *symbols* and $\delta = \delta_w \cup \delta_m$ is a set of *instructions*, where $\delta_w \subseteq Q_w \times \Gamma \times \Gamma \times Q$ is a set of *write instructions* and $\delta_m \subseteq Q_m \times \Delta \times Q$ is a set of *move instructions*, where $\Delta = \{-1, 0, 1\}$. Furthermore the following two implications must hold: (1) If $(q, d, r) \in \delta$ and $(q, d', r') \in \delta$ then $d = d'$ and $r = r'$. (2) If $(q, a, b, r) \in \delta$ and $(q, a, b', r') \in \delta$ then $b = b'$ and $r = r'$. A Turing machine is *reversible* if $\mathcal{M}^{-1} = (Q, \Gamma, \delta^{-1})$ is a Turing machine, where $(r, -d, q) \in \delta^{-1}$ if $(q, d, r) \in \delta$ and $(r, b, a, q) \in \delta^{-1}$ if $(q, a, b, r) \in \delta$. We will call $\mathcal{M}^{-1}$ the inverse machine of $\mathcal{M}$. A *configuration* is a 3-tuple (w, i, q), where $w \in \Gamma^{\mathbb{Z}}$ is the *tape*, $i \in \mathbb{Z}$ is the location of the *Turing machine head* and $q \in Q$. If a write instruction is applied to the configuration we will write $(w, i, q) \vdash (w', i, r)$ if $(q, w_i, w'_i, r) \in \delta_w$, where $w' \in \Gamma^{\mathbb{Z}}$ is such that $w'_k = w_k$ for each $k \neq i$. If a move instruction is applied to the configuration we will write $(w, i, q) \vdash (w, i + d, r)$ if $(q, d, r) \in \delta_m$. Inductively we define $\vdash^n$, where $\vdash$ is applied n times. Furthermore we will write $(w, i, q) \vdash^+ (w', j, r)$ if there exists such $n \in \mathbb{Z}_+$, that $(w, i, q) \vdash^n (w', j, r)$ holds. A Turing machine is *complete* if for each configuration (w, i, q), there exists (w', j, r), such that $(w, i, q) \vdash (w', j, r)$. We will call a configuration (w, i, q) *periodic* if $(w, i, q) \vdash^+ (w, i, q)$ and *weakly periodic* if there exists such $j \in \mathbb{Z}$, that $(w, i, q) \vdash^+ (\sigma^j(w), i - j, q)$. Furthermore we will call a configuration *strictly weakly periodic* if it is weakly periodic, but not periodic. We will call a Turing machine *periodic* if all its configurations are periodic, and *aperiodic* if none of its configurations are weakly periodic.

2.1   Construction Techniques for Turing Machines

In this subsection we will recall some useful methods for constructing new Turing machines from existing ones.

Let $\mathcal{M} = (Q, \Gamma, \delta)$ be a Turing machine. We will call a TM $\mathcal{M}' = (Q', \Gamma, \delta')$ a *copy* of $\mathcal{M}$ if there exists a bijection $\varphi : Q \rightarrow Q'$, such that $(\varphi(q), d, \varphi(r)) \in \delta'_m$ if and only if $(q, d, r) \in \delta_m$ and $(\varphi(q), a, b, \varphi(r)) \in \delta'_w$ if and only if $(q, a, b, r) \in \delta_w$. We call Q' the *copied state set* and $\varphi(q)$ the *copied state* of q. It is of course a trivial process to make copies of existing Turing machines. To simplify the notation and if it is clear from context, we might denote the states sets of multiple TMs by the same set despite the state sets being disjoint.

A TM $\mathcal{M} = (Q, \Gamma, \delta)$ is an *union of n Turing machines $\mathcal{M}_i = (Q_i, \Gamma, \delta_i)$*, where $i \in \{0, 1, ..., n-1\}$, if $Q = \bigcup_{i=0}^{n-1} Q_i$ and $\delta = \bigcup_{i=0}^{n-1} \delta_i$. When constructing larger Turing machines by taking unions of them, one might want to be able to move between the sets of states of the different machines. Next we introduce special set of states and state-symbol pairs where such transitions can naturally take place.

Definition 1. *If $q \in Q_w$ and $a \in \Gamma$ are such that $(q, a, b, r) \notin \delta$ for each pair $b \in \Gamma$ and $r \in Q$, then we call (q, a) an error pair. If $q \in Q_m$ and $(q, d, r) \notin \delta$ for each $d \in \{-1, 0, 1\}$ and $r \in Q$, we call q an error state.*

Definition 2. *If $r \in Q$ and $b \in \Gamma$ are such that $(q, a, b, r) \notin \delta$ for each pair $a \in \Gamma$ and $q \in Q$, then we call (r, b) a defective pair. Furthermore we call a state $r \in Q$ a defective state if $(q, d, r) \notin \delta$ for each $q \in Q$ and $d \in \{-1, 0, 1\}$.*

Now when taking unions of Turing machines one can add transitions from error pairs of one machine to defective pairs of another one and similarly with error states and defective states. We will see an especially useful example of this construction method in Definition 3. The technique was developed in [7] to prove the undecidability of the periodicity problem for reversible and complete Turing machines. It is also applied extensively in [3], and [2] in the proofs of undecidability of the transitivity problem, the minimality problem and the zero entropy problem, for example. We will also apply it to prove undecidability of a problem considering strictly weakly periodic points in Theorem 5.

Definition 3. *Let $\mathcal{M} = (Q, \Gamma, \delta)$ be a reversible Turing machine. Let $\mathcal{M}^+ = (Q^+, \Gamma, \delta^+)$ and $\mathcal{M}^- = (Q^-, \Gamma, \delta^-)$ be the copies of $\mathcal{M}$ and its inverse machine respectively. For each $q \in Q$ we denote as $q^x \in Q^x$ the copied states of q, where $x \in \{+, -\}$. Let $\delta' = \{(q^x, a, a, q^y) \mid (q^x, a) \text{ is an error pair of } Q^x_w \text{ and } x \neq y\}$ and $\delta'' = \{(q^x, 0, q^y) \mid q^x \text{ is an error state of } Q^x_m \text{ and } x \neq y\}$. Let $\mathcal{M}^0 = (Q^0, \Gamma, \delta^0)$ be the union of $\mathcal{M}^+$ and $\mathcal{M}^-$. Define a TM $\mathcal{M}'' = (Q^0, \Gamma, \delta^1)$, where $\delta^1 = \delta^0 \cup \delta' \cup \delta''$. The TM $\mathcal{M}''$ is referred as a TM constructed from $\mathcal{M}$ by reversing the computation.*

Notice that in previous definition the error pairs (q^x, a) of $\mathcal{M}^x$ are the defective pairs (q^y, a) of $\mathcal{M}^y$, when $x \neq y$ and analogously a similar statement is true for the error and defective pairs. It is easy to see that machine constructed via reversing the computation is a reversible and complete Turing machine.

2.2   Turing Machines as Dynamical Systems

Kůrka introduced two ways of defining complete Turing machines as dynamical systems in [9]. Both of them are straightforward constructions from the standard definition. We simply adjust the configuration space slightly to achieve a compact metric space and then we define a continuous function that remains faithful to the transition rule.

The first system is called *Turing machine with moving tape* or *TMT* for short. In TMT, the location of the Turing machine head is fixed to the origin and the tape moves instead of the Turing machine head. For example if the machine reads a right move, the tape moves left, i.e. the content at each cell gets shifted left by one cell. More specifically, the space is defined as $X = \Gamma^{\mathbb{Z}} \times Q$ and the function $f : X \to X$ works as follows: If $(q, d, r) \in \delta_m$ then $f(w, q) = (\sigma^d(w), r)$ for each $(w, q) \in \Gamma^{\mathbb{Z}} \times Q_m$. The write instruction reads the tape content at origin and rewrites it according to the instructions, i.e. for each $(q, a, a', r) \in \delta_w$ we have that $f(w, q) = (w', r)$, where $w_0 = a$, $w'_0 = a'$, and $w_i = w'_i$ for each $i \neq 0$. The distance $d : X \to \mathbb{R}$ is defined as $d((w, q), (w', q')) = 2$ if $q \neq q'$ and $d_\sigma(w, w')$ if $q = q'$.

The second system is called *Turing machine with moving head* or *TMH* for short. The function of this system works more like a computation of a traditional Turing machine. The space is defined as $X = \{w \in ((Q \times \Gamma) \cup \Gamma)^{\mathbb{Z}} \mid \exists! \, i \in \mathbb{Z} : w_i \in Q \times \Gamma\} \cup \Gamma^{\mathbb{Z}}$ equipped with the distance d_σ. The function $f : X \to X$ is defined as follows: If $w \in \Gamma^{\mathbb{Z}}$, then $f(w) = w$. Otherwise if $w_j = (q, a)$ and $(q, a, a', r) \in \delta_w$, then $f(w) = w'$, where $w'_j = (r, a')$ and $w_i = w'_i$ for each $i \neq j$. Finally if $w_j = (q, a)$ and $(q, d, r) \in \delta_m$, then $f(w) = w'$, where $w'_{j+d} = (r, w_{j+d})$, $w_j = (q, w'_j)$ and $w_i = w'_i$ for each $i \notin \{j, j + d\}$.

One can check that the spaces are indeed compact metric spaces and the functions are continuous in their respective spaces.

2.3   Simulating Turing Machines Inside Cellular Automata

We can simulate the computations of Turing machines inside cellular automata by using the construction of TMH. The only issue that needs to be dealt with is the question of what should the CA do when a configuration has multiple states depicting Turing machine heads. This is typically dealt with the introduction of arrows, which subdivide each configuration into independent simulation areas. Then we just have to decide what should happen when the simulations run out of space. Furthermore we do not require the TMs to be complete to be able to use this kind of construction as we can add rules that deal with the cases when the TM transition is undefined. We will describe a way how a given Turing machine can be simulated in sets of simulation words.

Definition 4. *Let $\mathcal{M} = (Q, \Gamma, \delta)$ be a Turing machine and denote $A = \{\rightarrow, \leftarrow\}$. Let $\Sigma_{\mathcal{M}} = Q_1 \cup T_1$, where $Q_1 = \Gamma \times Q$ and $T_1 = \Gamma \times A$. We call elements in Q_1 the head symbols and elements in T_1 the tape symbols. The alphabet $\Sigma_{\mathcal{M}}$ is called the TM alphabet.*

We define a relation R_1 in a following way: Let $a \in \Sigma_{\mathcal{M}}$ and $b \in \Sigma_{\mathcal{M}}$ then

$$aR_1b \text{ if } \begin{cases} a \in \Gamma \times \{\rightarrow\} \wedge b \in (\Gamma \times \{\rightarrow\}) \cup Q_1 \\ \vee \quad a \in Q_1 \wedge b \in \Gamma \times \{\leftarrow\} \\ \vee \quad a \in \Gamma \times \{\leftarrow\} \wedge b \in \Gamma \times \{\leftarrow\}. \end{cases}$$

Define $S_{\mathcal{M}}^{\alpha} = \{w \in \Sigma_{\mathcal{M}}^{\alpha} \mid w_j R_1 w_{j+1} \forall j \text{ and } w_{Q_1} = 1\}$, where $\alpha \in \{\mathbb{Z}, \mathbb{Z}_-, \mathbb{N}, *\}$. Elements in any of these sets will be called *simulation words*. Next we will define a semi-function on these sets, which simulates the computations of a given Turing machine.

Let $w \in S_{\mathcal{M}}^{\Omega}$. If j is such an index that $w_j \in Q_1$, then we define $f_L(w) = j$. If furthermore $w_j = (a, q)$, then $f_Q(w) = q$.

Let $\# \notin \Sigma$. We define a padding function $p: S_{\mathcal{M}}^{\Omega} \rightarrow (\Sigma \cup \{\#\})^{\mathbb{Z}}$, such that $p(w)_i = w_{i,1}$, when $w \in S_{\mathcal{M}}^{\alpha}$, $i \in \alpha$, where $\alpha \in \{\mathbb{Z}, \mathbb{Z}_-, \mathbb{N}, *\}$ and $p(w)_i = \#$ otherwise.

Using these notations we can define an injective mapping from the simulation words to Turing machine configurations.

Definition 5. *Let $\mathcal{M}$ be a TM. Define $\tau: S_{\mathcal{M}}^{\Omega} \rightarrow \Gamma^{\mathbb{Z}} \times \mathbb{Z} \times Q$ in such a way that $\tau(w) = (p(w), f_L(w), f_Q(w))$.*

Finally we can define a function that simulates the computation of a Turing machine in the simulation words:

Definition 6. *Let $\mathcal{M}$ be a TM. Define $f_{S_{\mathcal{M}}}: S_{\mathcal{M}}^{\Omega} \rightarrow S_{\mathcal{M}}^{\Omega}$ in such a way that $f_{S_{\mathcal{M}}}(w) = \tau^{-1} \circ \vdash \circ \tau(w)$ if $\vdash$ is defined for $\tau(w)$ and $\vdash \circ \tau(w) = (w', j, q)$ and $w'_j \neq \#$.*

The function of the above definition behaves on the simulation words just as the Turing machine does on configurations as long as the Turing machine head stays inside the domains of the simulation words.

If the set of states of a given CA contains a TM alphabet as a subset, we can recognize simulation areas in the configurations of such CA and use this function to simulate Turing machine computations in those areas. We will describe this process next.

Let $\mathcal{M} = (Q, \Gamma, \delta)$ be a Turing machine. Let Σ_1 be such a set of symbols that $\Sigma_{\mathcal{M}} \subseteq \Sigma_1$.

For each configuration $c \in \Sigma_1^{\mathbb{Z}}$, we define a set of locations for the Turing machine heads as
$$H_c = \{j \in \mathbb{Z} \mid c_j \in Q_1\}.$$
Next we define the *simulation bounds* as functions $l_c : H_c \to \mathbb{Z} \cup \{-\infty\}$ and $r_c : H_c \to \mathbb{Z} \cup \{\infty\}$ in the following way:
$$l_c(j) = \sup\{k \in \mathbb{Z} \mid k \le j \text{ and } c_{k-1}R_1^c c_k\}$$
and
$$r_c(j) = \inf\{k \in \mathbb{Z} \mid j \le k \text{ and } c_k R_1^c c_{k+1}\}.$$
From these bounds we can define the set of cells that are not part of any simulation area as
$$U_c = \mathbb{Z} \setminus \left(\bigcup_{j \in H_c} [l_c(j), r_c(j)] \right).$$

Using the simulation bounds, we can define a function, which simulates the computations of the given Turing machine in their designated simulation areas as $f_{\mathcal{M}} : \Sigma_1^{\mathbb{Z}} \to \Sigma_1^{\mathbb{Z}}$, where
$$\begin{aligned} f_{\mathcal{M}}(c)_{[l_c(j),r_c(j)]} &= f_{S_{\mathcal{M}}}(c_{[l_c(j),r_c(j)]}) \ \forall j \in H_c \text{ and} \\ f_{\mathcal{M}}(c)_k &= c_k \ \forall k \in U_c. \end{aligned}$$
Clearly $f_{\mathcal{M}}$ is a cellular automaton since we can extract a radius-1 local rule from its definition.

2.4   Speed of Turing Machines

We first define a function that tracks the location of the Turing machine head given some initial configuration and a time step.

Definition 7. *Let $\mathcal{M} = (Q, \Gamma, \delta)$ be a Turing machine. Let X be the configuration space of the TM. Define $f_T : X \times \mathbb{N} \to \mathbb{N}$ as $f_T((w, i, q), n) = j$ if $(w, i, q) \vdash^n (w', j, r)$.*

Using the tracking function we define a set of visited locations given some initial configuration and a time step.

Definition 8. *Let $\mathcal{M} = (Q, \Gamma, \delta)$ be a Turing machine. Let X be the configuration space of the TM. Define $f_V : X \times \mathbb{N} \to \mathbb{N}$ as $f_V(x, n) = \{f_T(x, j) \mid j \le n\}$.*

Finally we can calculate the maximum amount of visited locations by any computation by a given time and define the notion of speed.

Definition 9. *Let $\mathcal{M} = (Q, \Gamma, \delta)$ be a Turing machine. Let X be the configuration space of the TM. Define the movement bound $f_M : \mathbb{N} \to \mathbb{N}$ as $f_M(n) = \max_{x \in X} |f_V(x, n)|$. The speed of the TM $\mathcal{M}$ is defined as $f_S(\mathcal{M}) = \lim_{n \to \infty} \frac{f_M(n)}{n}$.*

Theorem 1. *[6] Let $\mathcal{M}$ be a Turing machine, and f_M be its movement bound. If $\mathcal{M}$ is aperiodic, then f_M is sublinear.*

The above Theorem implies that any aperiodic Turing machine $\mathcal{M}$ have zero speed, i.e. $f_S(\mathcal{M}) = 0$.

Theorem 2. *[4] Let $\mathcal{M}$ be a Turing machine, then $f_S(\mathcal{M}) > 0$ if and only if there exists a strictly weakly periodic configuration.*

2.5 Lyapunov Exponents of Cellular Automata

Definition 10. *Let (Σ, N, h) be a one-dimensional cellular automaton, with a global rule $f : \Sigma^{\mathbb{Z}} \to \Sigma^{\mathbb{Z}}$. For every $c \in \Sigma^{\mathbb{Z}}$, we define*

$$W_m^+(c) = \{c' \in \Sigma^{\mathbb{Z}} \mid \forall i \geq m, c_i' = c_i\}$$

and

$$W_m^-(c) = \{c' \in \Sigma^{\mathbb{Z}} \mid \forall i \leq m, c_i' = c_i\}.$$

Furthermore we define

$$I_n^+(c) = \min\{m \in \mathbb{N} \mid f^i(W_{-m}^+(c)) \subseteq W_0^+(f^i(c)), \forall i \leq n\}$$

and

$$I_n^-(c) = \min\{m \in \mathbb{N} \mid f^i(W_m^-(c)) \subseteq W_0^-(f^i(c)), \forall i \leq n\}$$

Finally we define the pointwise Lyapunov exponents as

$$\lambda^+(c) = \liminf_{n \to \infty} \frac{I_n^+(c)}{n}$$

and

$$\lambda^-(c) = \liminf_{n \to \infty} \frac{I_n^-(c)}{n}$$

and the global Lyapunov exponents as

$$\lambda^+ = \lim_{n \to \infty} \max_{c \in \Sigma^{\mathbb{Z}}} \frac{I_n^+(c)}{n}$$

and

$$\lambda^- = \lim_{n \to \infty} \max_{c \in \Sigma^{\mathbb{Z}}} \frac{I_n^-(c)}{n}.$$

2.6 Topological Entropy of Cellular Automata

Definition 11. *Let $f : \Sigma^{\mathbb{Z}} \to \Sigma^{\mathbb{Z}}$ be a CA. Define $\tau_k : \Sigma^{\mathbb{Z}} \to (\Sigma^k)^{\mathbb{N}}$ such that $\tau_k(c)_i = f^i(c)_{[0,k-1]}$. The mapping τ_k is called the k-trace shift*

Definition 12. *Let $f : X \to X$ be a CA. Define $L_{\tau_k(X)}(j) = \{u \sqsubset w \mid w \in \tau_k(X) \text{ and } |u| = j\}$ and $P_k(j) = |L_{\tau_k(X)}(j)|$.*

Theorem 3. *Let $f : X \to X$ be a CA. Then $h_f = \lim_{k \to \infty} h_{\tau_k}$, where $h_{\tau_k} = \lim_{j \to \infty} \frac{\ln(P_k(j))}{j}$.*

It is easy to see that $P_k'(j) \geq P_k(j)$ for any $k' \geq k$ and hence for any k we have that $h_{\tau_k} \leq h_f$.

3   Decision Problems

3.1   Decision Problems for Turing Machines

Decision problems that we are interested in:

ARTM reachability: Given an aperiodic and reversible Turing machine and two states q_α and q_ω, decide whether q_ω is reachable from q_α.

RCTM strictly weakly periodic configuration: Given a reversible and complete Turing machine, decide if there exists a strictly weakly periodic configuration.

RCTM zero speed: Given a reversible and complete Turing machine, decide if its speed is zero.

RCTM zero entropy: Given a reversible and complete Turing machine, decide if its entropy is zero.

The first and fourth have already been proven in [7] and [2] respectively. We use the reduction from the first decision problem to the second and third and show that they are undecidable. The fourth follows easily from the third one, although this result is not new in itself.

Theorem 4. *[7] ARTM reachability is undecidable.*

Theorem 5. *RCTM strictly weakly periodic configuration is undecidable.*

Proof. Let $\mathcal{M} = (Q, \Gamma, \delta)$ be an aperiodic and reversible Turing machine. We will prove the theorem via reduction to the ARTM reachability problem, which is known to be undecidable by Theorem 4. To this end, for a given two states q_α and q_ω of Q, we will construct a Turing machine $\mathcal{M}_{wp}$, such that q_ω is reachable from q_α in $\mathcal{M}$ if and only if $\mathcal{M}_{wp}$ has a strictly weakly periodic configuration.

Without loss of generality, we can assume that q_α is a defective state and q_ω is an error state. The reason for that is that if we can reach q_ω from q_α during finitely many steps, then there exists a last time that the computation sees the state q_α and hence we can just begin the computation from that point. Furthermore we can assume that when starting from q_α, the first two instructions are move to the right $(q_\alpha, +, q'_\alpha)$ and a move to the left $(q'_\alpha, -, q''_\alpha)$. If that is not the case, we add these moves to δ and the states q'_α and q''_α to Q. After that if $q_\alpha \in \delta_m$, we replace (q_α, d, r_0) with (q''_α, d, r_0) and if $q_\alpha \in \delta_w$, we replace each $(q_\alpha, a, b, r_a) \in \delta$ with (q''_α, a, b, r_a). We will also assume that there exists a special symbol #, such that $(q, \#)$ is both an error and a defective pair for each $q \in Q$.

We will construct three copies of $\mathcal{M}$ and three copies of its inverse machine $\mathcal{M}^-$ to achieve six new TMs $\mathcal{M}_y^x = (Q_y^x, \Gamma, \delta_y^x)$, for given pairs of subscripts and superscripts that we will introduce in the following paragraphs. The superscript x is either $+$ or $-$ depending on whether the machine is a copy of the original machine or its inverse, respectively. If we need to specify from which machine the state is, we will add the name of the Turing machine as a subscript. We will describe how to modify each copy to suit our needs. We will say that we will replace an instruction $(q, d, r) \in \delta_y^x$ with a sub-routine as described by a transition graph depicted in a given figure. What we will mean by this is that we will add all such states to the new machine's state set Q_y^x, which are depicted in the same color in the transition graph as the states q and r. Additionally we will then remove (q, d, r) from δ_y^x and add to it all the instructions that are between nodes of the same color.

We will first construct three copies of the machine $\mathcal{M}$ as follows. First we will construct a TM $\mathcal{M}_R^+ = (Q_R^+, \Gamma, \delta_R^+)$ by replacing each instruction $(q, +, r) \in \delta_R^+$, where $q \neq q_\alpha$ with the sub-routine in Fig. 1. We will also replace the instruction $(q_\alpha, +, q_\alpha') \in \delta_R^+$ with the sub-routine in Fig. 2. We then construct a TM $\mathcal{M}_L^+ = (Q_L^+, \Gamma, \delta_L^+)$ by replacing each instruction $(q, -, r) \in \delta_L^+$ with the sub-routine in Fig. 3. The third TM $\mathcal{M}_F^+ = (Q_F^+, \Gamma, \delta_F^+)$ is just the exact copy of the original machine $\mathcal{M}$.

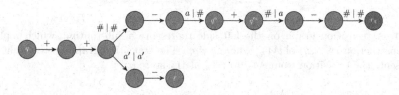

Fig. 1. A transition graph that represents a sub-routine, which replaces each instruction $(q, +, r)$ of $\mathcal{M}_R^+$, where $q \neq q_\alpha$. The states q^a and q'^a are unique for each $a \in \Gamma$. The last pair of nodes on the top-right corner represents a transition from $\mathcal{M}_R^+$ to $\mathcal{M}_R^-$.

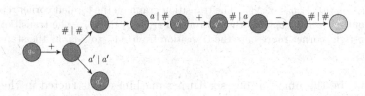

Fig. 2. A transition graph that represents a sub-routine, which replaces the instruction $(q_\alpha, +, q_\alpha')$ of $\mathcal{M}_R^+$. The states q^a and q'^a are unique for each $a \in \Gamma$. The last pair of nodes on the top-right corner represents the transition from $\mathcal{M}_R^+$ to $\mathcal{M}_L^-$.

We will then construct three copies of the inverse machine $\mathcal{M}^-$ as follows. The first TM $\mathcal{M}_R^- = (Q_R^-, \Gamma, \delta_R^-)$ is constructed by replacing each instruction $(r, -, q) \in \delta_R^-$ with the sub-routine in the left side of Fig. 4. The second TM $\mathcal{M}_L^- = (Q_L^-, \Gamma, \delta_L^-)$ is constructed by replacing each instruction $(r, +, q) \in \delta_L^-$ with the sub-routine in the top-left corner of Fig. 5 and additionally $(q_\alpha', -, q_\alpha) \in \delta_L^-$ is replaced with the sub-routine in the bottom of Fig. 5. Finally the third TM $\mathcal{M}_F^- = (Q_F^-, \Gamma, \delta_F^-)$ is constructed by replacing each instruction $(r, +, q) \in \delta_F^-$ with the sub-routine in Fig. 6.

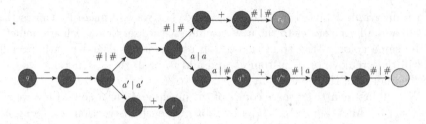

Fig. 3. A transition graph that represents the sub-routine, which replaces the instruction $(q, -, r)$ of $\mathcal{M}_L^+$. The states q^a and q'^a are unique for each $a \in \Gamma$. The last pair of nodes on the top-right corner represents a transition from $\mathcal{M}_L^+$ to $\mathcal{M}_F$ and the last pair of nodes on the middle represents a transition from $\mathcal{M}_L^+$ to $\mathcal{M}_L^-$.

Fig. 4. A transition graph on the left side represents a sub-routine, which replaces each instruction $(r, -, q)$ of $\mathcal{M}_R^-$, where $r \neq q'$. The transition graph on the right side represents the transition from $\mathcal{M}_R^-$ to $\mathcal{M}_R^+$ at the state q_α.

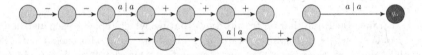

Fig. 5. The transition graph on the bottom represents the sub-routine, which replaces the instruction $(q'_\alpha, -, q_\alpha)$ of $\mathcal{M}_L^-$. The transition graph on the top-left corner represents the sub-routine, which replaces the instruction $(r, +, q)$ of $\mathcal{M}_L^-$. The transition graph on the top-right corner represents the transition from $\mathcal{M}_L^-$ to $\mathcal{M}_L^+$ at the state q_α.

Let $\mathcal{M}'$ be the union of our six Turing machines constructed in the previous two paragraphs. We will add transitions between the different state sets by adding such instructions from Figs. 1, 2, 3, 4, 5, 6 and 7, where the pairs of nodes are depicted by two different colors. Our final construction is the Turing machine $\mathcal{M}_{wp}$, which is constructed from $\mathcal{M}'$ and the inverse machine $\mathcal{M}'^-$ by the method of reversing the computation. Notice that the constructed machine $\mathcal{M}_{wp}$ is complete and reversible.

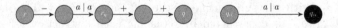

Fig. 6. The transition graph on the left side represents a sub-routine, which replaces each instruction $(r, +, q)$ of $\mathcal{M}_F^-$. The transition graph on the right side represents the transition from $\mathcal{M}_F^-$ to $\mathcal{M}_F^+$ at the state q_α.

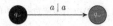

Fig. 7. A transition graph that represents the only transition from $\mathcal{M}_F^+$ to $\mathcal{M}_R^-$.

We will first assume that q_ω is reachable from q_α. Since the computation is finite, there exists such $n \in \mathbb{N}$, that exactly n indices of the tape is visited during the computation. By shifting, if necessary, we can assume that the visited indices are in the interval $[1, n]$. Let $w \in \Gamma^{\mathbb{Z}}$, $w' \in \Gamma^{\mathbb{Z}}$, $i_\alpha \in [1, n]$ and $i_\omega \in [1, n]$ be such that $(w, i_\alpha, q_\alpha) \vdash^+ (w', i_\omega, q_\omega)$ in $\mathcal{M}$.

Following the instructions of the machine it is fairly straightforward now to show $(x\#w\#y, i_\alpha, q_{\alpha, \mathcal{M}_R^+}) \vdash^+ (x\#\#wy, i_\alpha + 1, q_{\alpha, \mathcal{M}_R^+})$ and thus $^{-\infty}\#w_{[1,n]}\#^{\infty}$ is a strictly weakly periodic configuration.

Suppose then that there exists a strictly weakly periodic configuration. It is fairly easy to show that the computations needs to pass through all the machines $\mathcal{M}_X^x$ for $X \in \{L, R, F\}$ and $x \in \{-, +\}$. Therefore we have that q_ω is reachable from q_α. $\qquad\square$

Immediately we get the two following corollaries:

Theorem 6. *RCTM zero speed is undecidable.*

Proof. From Theorem 2 we know that a Turing machine has non-zero speed if and only if there exists a weakly periodic configuration. From Theorem 5 we have that RCTM strictly weakly periodic configuration is undecidable and hence RCTM zero speed is also undecidable. $\qquad\square$

Theorem 7. *RCTM zero entropy is undecidable.*

Proof. By the methods in [6], for a given TM $\mathcal{M}$, we can build another TM $\mathcal{M}^A$, such that $\frac{h_{\mathcal{M}^A}}{\log|A|} \geq s(\mathcal{M}) = s(\mathcal{M}^A) \geq \frac{h_{\mathcal{M}^A}}{\log|\Gamma \times A|}$, where Γ is the alphabet of $\mathcal{M}$ and A is a finite set of symbols such that $|A| > 1$. Then if we would have an algorithm, which tells if a given ARCTM has an entropy of value zero or not, we would also have an algorithm that tells whether a given TM has a speed zero or not. Therefore the claim follows by Theorem 6. $\qquad\square$

3.2 Decision Problems for Cellular Automata

RCA glider: Given a reversible cellular automaton, decide if there exists a glider.

RCA zero global Lyapunov exponents: Given a reversible cellular automaton, decide if $\lambda_+ = \lambda_- = 0$.

RCA zero entropy: Given a reversible cellular automaton, decide if the entropy is zero.

Theorem 8. *RCA zero global Lyapunov exponents is undecidable.*

Proof. Let $\mathcal{M}$ be a TM and let us consider the CA $f = f_{\mathcal{M}}$. Let $c \in \Sigma_1^{\mathbb{Z}}$. If there exists such $j \in H_c$, that $l_c(j) \in \mathbb{Z}_-$ or $r_c(j) \in \mathbb{Z}_-$, then for any $c' \in W_m^+(c)$, where $m = \max\{l_c(j), r_c(j)\}$, it holds that $f^i(c') \in W_m^+(f^i(c)) \subseteq W_0^+(f^i(c))$ for each $i \in \mathbb{N}$. Suppose then that there exists $j \in H_c$ such that $l_c(j) = -\infty$ and $r_c(j) \geq 0$. Let $n \in \mathbb{N}$ and $c' \in W_m^+(c)$, where $m = \min\{j, 0\} - f_M(n) - 1$. Then by definition of $f_{\mathcal{M}}$ we have that $f^i(c') \in W_{\min\{j,0\}}^+(f^i(c)) \subseteq W_0^+(f^i(c))$ for each $i \leq n$. This is clear because any change can not propagate faster than the movement bound of the Turing machine inside a single simulation area. Similar argument can be used if the origin of c is not part of a simulation area. Therefore for each configuration c and time step n, $I_n^+(c)$ is bounded above by $f_M(n) + a$ for some constant a. Analogous statement holds for $I_n^-(c)$.

On the other hand it is easy to show that $\max\{I_n^+(c), I_n^-(c)\}$ is bounded below by $\frac{f_M(n)}{2}$. This is because there exists a configuration, such that the Turing machine head will visit origin within n steps starting from either index $-\frac{f_M(n)}{2}$ or $\frac{f_M(n)}{2}$. Then we take as a simulation word c over $\mathbb{Z}$ any such configuration. Then let j be the unique index such that $j \in H_c$ and let c' be such that $c_i = c_i'$ for each $i \neq j$ and $c_j' \in T_1$. In other words we keep the configuration same otherwise except we removed the only head symbol. Now $f^i(c) \in Q_1$ and $f^i(c') \in T_1$ for some $i \leq n$.

We have that $\lambda^+ = \lambda^- = 0$ if and only if $f_S(\mathcal{M}) = 0$. Therefore by Theorem 6 we have that RCA zero global Lyapunov exponents is undecidable. □

Theorem 9. *RCA glider is undecidable.*

Proof. Let $\mathcal{M}_{wp} = (Q, \Gamma, \delta)$ be a Turing machine as constructed in Theorem 5. Let $\mathcal{A} = (\Sigma, N, h)$ be a cellular automaton, where $\Sigma = \Sigma_{\mathcal{M}}$ and $(\#, \to)$ is the quiescent state. Let $S = \{(a, q) \in Q_1 \mid (q, +, r) \in \delta_{\mathcal{M}_R^+}\}$. We define a global rule $g : \Sigma^{\mathbb{Z}} \to \Sigma^{\mathbb{Z}}$ in such a way that

$$g(c)_i = \begin{cases} (\#, \leftarrow) & \text{if } c_{[i-1,i]} \in S(\#, \to)(\#, \to), \\ (\#, \to) & \text{if } c_{[i-1,i]} \in S(\#, \leftarrow)(\#, \to) \text{ and} \\ c_i & \text{otherwise.} \end{cases}$$

It is easy to see that g is reversible. Let $f = f_{\mathcal{M}} \circ g$.

Assume first that q_ω is reachable from q_α. Let $w \in \Gamma^{\mathbb{Z}}$ be as in Theorem 5. Let $c =^{-\infty} (\#, \to)(w_1, \to)(w_2, \to) \cdots (w_{i_\alpha-1}, \to)(w_{i_\alpha}, q_\alpha)(w_{i_\alpha+1}, \leftarrow) \cdots (w_n, \leftarrow)(\#, \to)^\infty$. Now $^{-\infty}\#w_{[1,n]}\#^\infty$ is a strictly weakly periodic configuration. We saw in the proof of Theorem 5, that during the computation $(c, i_\alpha, q_\alpha) \vdash^k (\sigma^{-1}(c), i_\alpha + 1, q_\alpha)$, there is a unique time $k' \in [0, k)$, such that $(c, i_\alpha, q_\alpha) \vdash^{k'} (c, n, q)$, where $q \in Q$, such that $(q, +, r) \in \delta_{\mathcal{M}_R^+}$ for some $r \in Q$. Hence during the k iterations of f, the time-step k' is the only time, when g affects the computation by extending the simulation area from the right side by one cell. Hence the computation works as if each cell belonged into a single simulation area. Therefore c is a strictly weakly periodic configuration and since it is also finite, it is a glider.

If q_ω is not reachable from q_α, then there are no strictly weakly periodic configuration in $\mathcal{M}_{wp}$. On the other hand, it is easy to see a glider would require an existence of a strictly weakly periodic configuration of $\mathcal{M}_{wp}$. Hence by Theorem 5 we have that RCA glider is undecidable.   □

Theorem 10. *RCA zero entropy is undecidable.*

Proof. Let $\mathcal{M} = (Q, \Gamma, \delta)$, we construct $\mathcal{M}_{wp}$ almost the same way, except we add two new symbols $\#_0$ and $\#_1$ instead of $\#$, such that both behave as they would if they were just $\#$. Furthermore we add four more copies of $\mathcal{M}$ and four more copies of its inverse machine. We denote the new machines as $\mathcal{M}_y^x$, where $x \in \{+, -\}$ describing whether the copy is of the original or the inverse machine and $y \in \{F_2, F_3, S, S_2\}$. We remove the transitions of Fig. 7. Then we add transitions $(q_\omega, a, a, q_\omega)$ from $\mathcal{M}_F^+$ to $\mathcal{M}_S^-$, $\mathcal{M}_S^+$ to $\mathcal{M}_{F_2}^-$, $\mathcal{M}_{F_2}^+$ to $\mathcal{M}_{S_2}^-$, $\mathcal{M}_{S_2}^+$ to $\mathcal{M}_{F_3}^-$ and $\mathcal{M}_{F_3}^+$ to $\mathcal{M}_R^-$ for each $a \in \Gamma$. We also add transitions $(q_\alpha, a, a, q_\alpha)$ from $\mathcal{M}_{F_2}^-$ to $\mathcal{M}_{F_2}^+$ and $\mathcal{M}_{F_3}^-$ to $\mathcal{M}_{F_3}^+$. Finally we finish the construction by reversing the computation and denote the machine as $\mathcal{M}_E$.

Let Σ_1 be the TM alphabet of $\mathcal{M}_E$. And let $\Sigma = \Sigma_1 \cup \{(\#_0, \cdot), (\#_1, \cdot)\}$. Let $\# \in \{\#_1, \#_2\}$ and define g as:

$$g(c)_{[i,i+1]} = \begin{cases} (\#, \cdot)(q_{S_1^+}, a) & \text{if } c_{[i-1,i+1]} = (\#, \cdot)(\#, \rightarrow)(q_{S_1^-}, a), \\ (\#, \rightarrow)(q_{S_1^-}, a) & \text{if } c_{[i-1,i+1]} = (\#, \cdot)(\#, \cdot)(q_{S_1^+}, a), \\ (q_{S_2^+}, a)(\#, \leftarrow) & \text{if } c_{[i,i+2]} = (q_{S_2^-}, a)(\#, \cdot)(\#, \cdot), \\ (q_{S_2^-}, a)(\#, \cdot) & \text{if } c_{[i,i+2]} = (q_{S_2^+}, a)(\#, \leftarrow)(\#, \cdot) \text{ and} \\ c_{[i,i+1]} & \text{otherwise.} \end{cases}$$

It is easy to see that g is reversible. Let $f = f_\mathcal{M} \circ g$.

We will now prove the claim by a reduction to Theorem 6. Suppose q_ω is not reachable from q_α. We will show that then $\lambda^+ = \lambda^- = 0$. It then follows from Theorem x that $h_f = 0$.

Let c be a configuration such that $j \in H_c$ and $j' = \max\{k \in H_c \mid k < j\}$. We will show that any change in the simulation bounds of j does not affect the left simulation bound of j'.

Suppose $t > 0$ is such that $f^k(c)_{[l_c(j)-k_1, r_c(j)+k_2]}$ is the largest simulation word in the interval $[l_c(j) - k_1, r_c(j) + k_2]$ for each $k < t$ if and only if $k_1 = k_2 = 0$ and at time step t this no longer holds.

Suppose first that $f^t(c)_{[l_c(j)-k_1, r_c(j)+k_2]}$ is the largest simulation word in the interval $[l_c(j) - k_1, r_c(j) + k_2]$ if $k_1 = 0$ and $k_2 \in \{-1, 1\}$. By definition of g this mean that $f^{t-1}(c)_n = (q_{S_2^x}, a)$ for $x \in \{-, +\}$ some q in the set of states of $\mathcal{M}_E$ and where $a = r_c(j)$ if $k_2 = 1$ and $a = r_c(j) - 1$ if $k_2 = -1$. Now by the definition of g to have any affect in the left border the head symbol should transition into $r_{S_1^x}, b)$. By how $\mathcal{M}_E$ was constructed this is possible only if the computation goes through machines $\mathcal{M}_{F_2}^+$ or $\mathcal{M}_{F_3}^+$. But only way it can do this, is if q_ω is reachable from q_α.

Suppose then that $f^t(c)_{[l_c(j)-k_1,r_c(j)+k_2]}$ is the largest simulation word in the interval $[l_c(j)-k_1,r_c(j)+k_2]$ if $k_1 \in \{-1,1\}$ and $k_2 = 0$. By definition of g this mean that $f^{t-1}(c)_n = (q_{S_1^x}, a)$ for $x \in \{-,+\}$ some q in the set of states of $\mathcal{M}_E$ and where $a = l_c(j)$ if $k_1 = 1$ and $a = l_c(j) - 1$ if $k_1 = -1$. Now by definition of g the only way this affects the computation in the simulation bounds of j' is if there is a time step $t' > t$, such that the head symbol inside the simulation bounds of j' at time stept' is $(q'_{S_1^x}, a')$. This then reduces to the earlier case and we that the left border of the simulation area of j' does not change as q_ω is not reachable from q_α.

Similarly we can see that any change in the simulation bounds of j' does not affect the right bound of j.

Now if c is a configuration such that the origin is contained in one simulation area and there are more than one simulation areas on the left side of it, then information can not propagate to the simulation area that contains origin. Same is true for the right side, hence one only needs to analyze the cases when there is only one additional simulation area on the left or right side. This is straightforward and can be done as in Theorem 8.

Hence if q_ω is not reachable from q_α then $\lambda^+ = \lambda^- = 0$ and so $h_f = 0$.

Suppose then that q_ω is reachable from q_α.

It is easy to see that there exists $t > 0$ such that $f^t(c)_{[1,|w|]} = w'$, where $w = (\#_{k_1}, \cdot)u(\#_{k_2}, \cdot)(\#_{k_3}, \cdot)$, $w' = (\#_{k_1}, \cdot)(\#_{k_2}, \cdot)u(\#_{k_3}, \cdot)$ and u is a simulation word where q_ω is reached from q_α. This is because the machine $\mathcal{M}_E$ works as the one in the proof of Theorem 5 except the CA will modify the states $(\#, \cdot)$ as needed.

Now let $w_i = u(\#_{k_{i_1}}, \cdot)(\#_{k_{i_2}}, \cdot)(\#_{k_{i_3}}, \cdot)(\#_{k_{i_4}}, \cdot)$. Let $c = \ldots w_{-2}w_{-1}w_0w_1 w_2 \ldots$, where $c_{[0,|w_0|-1]} = w_0$. Let $t' = t * |w_0|$. Then $f^{t'*k}(c)_{[0,|w_0|-1]} = w_k$. Then $P_{|w_0|}(t' * k) \geq 2^{4*k}$. Then $h_f \geq \lim_{k\to\infty} \frac{\ln(P_{|w_0|}(t'*k))}{t'k} \geq \frac{4\ln(2)}{t'}$. □

Theorem 11. *The topological entropy h_f of a given f can not be approximated to a given precision, especially it is not computable.*

Proof. We saw in the proof of Theorem 10 that it was undecidable whether the entropy of the constructed cellular automaton was 0 or $m \geq \frac{4\ln(2)}{t'}$ for some constant t'. Hence if $0 < \epsilon < \frac{\ln(2)}{t'}$ one cannot decide if $h_f \in (\frac{3\ln(2)}{t'}, \frac{5\ln(2)}{t'})$ for example. □

Acknowledgements. The author acknowledges the emmy.network foundation under the aegis of the Fondation de Luxembourg for its financial support.

References

1. Boyle, M.: Open problems in symbolic dynamics. Contemp. Math. **469** (2008). https://doi.org/10.1090/conm/469/09161
2. Gajardo, A., Ollinger, N., Torres-Avilés, R.: Some undecidable problems about the trace-subshift associated to a Turing machine. Discrete Math. Theor. Comput. Sci. **17**(2), 267–284 (2015). https://doi.org/10.46298/dmtcs.2137, https://hal.inria.fr/hal-01349052
3. Gajardo, A., Ollinger, N., Torres-Avilés, R.: The Transitivity Problem of Turing Machines (2015)
4. Guillon, P., Salo, V.: Distortion in one-head machines and cellular automata. In: Dennunzio, A., Formenti, E., Manzoni, L., Porreca, A.E. (eds.) AUTOMATA 2017. LNCS, vol. 10248, pp. 120–138. Springer, Cham (2017). https://doi.org/10.1007/978-3-319-58631-1_10
5. Hurd, L.P., Kari, J., Culik, K.: The topological entropy of cellular automata is uncomputable. Ergodic Theory Dynam. Systems **12**(2), 255–265 (1992). https://doi.org/10.1017/S0143385700006738
6. Jeandel, E.: Computability of the entropy of one-tape Turing machines. In: Leibniz International Proceedings in Informatics, vol. 25. LIPIcs, February 2013. https://doi.org/10.4230/LIPIcs.STACS.2014.421
7. Kari, J., Ollinger, N.: Periodicity and Immortality in Reversible Computing. In: Ochmański, E., Tyszkiewicz, J. (eds.) MFCS 2008. LNCS, vol. 5162, pp. 419–430. Springer, Heidelberg (2008). https://doi.org/10.1007/978-3-540-85238-4_34
8. Kopra, J.: The Lyapunov exponents of reversible cellular automata are uncomputable. In: McQuillan, I., Seki, S. (eds.) UCNC 2019. LNCS, vol. 11493, pp. 178–190. Springer, Cham (2019). https://doi.org/10.1007/978-3-030-19311-9_15
9. Kůrka, P.: On topological dynamics of Turing machines. Theor. Comput. Sci. **174**(1), 203–216 (1997). https://doi.org/10.1016/S0304-3975(96)00025-4, http://www.sciencedirect.com/science/article/pii/S0304397596000254
10. Salo, V.: Conjugacy of reversible cellular automata and one-head machines (2020). https://doi.org/10.48550/ARXIV.2011.07827, https://arxiv.org/abs/2011.07827

Fault Pruning: Robust Training of Neural Networks with Memristive Weights

Ceca Kraišniković[1] , Spyros Stathopoulos[2] , Themis Prodromakis[2] ,
and Robert Legenstein[1(✉)]

[1] Institute of Theoretical Computer Science, Graz University of Technology,
Graz, Austria
{ceca.kraisnikovic,robert.legenstein}@igi.tugraz.at
[2] School of Engineering, University of Edinburgh, Edinburgh, UK
{s.stathopoulos,t.prodromakis}@ed.ac.uk

Abstract. Neural networks with memristive memory for weights have
been proposed as an energy-efficient solution for scaling up of neural
network implementations. However, training such memristive neural networks is still challenging due to various memristor imperfections and
faulty memristive elements. Such imperfections and faults are becoming
increasingly severe as the density of memristor arrays increases in order
to scale up weight memory. We propose fault pruning, a robust training scheme for memristive neural networks based on the idea to identify
faulty memristive behavior on the fly during training and prune corresponding connections. We test this algorithm in simulations of memristive neural networks using both feed-forward and convolutional architectures on standard object recognition data sets. We show its ability to
mitigate the detrimental effect of memristor faults on network training.

Keywords: Neural networks · Memristors · Robust training ·
Memristor faults · Network pruning

1 Introduction

Nano-scale electronic elements have recently gained increased attention for
machine learning applications and neuromorphic devices [8,9,27]. In particular,
memristive crossbar arrays have been proposed as a replacement for conventional
memory technology in hardware implementations of neural networks [1,4,26]. A
memristor is a resistor with memory in the sense that the charge that flows
through a memristor changes its resistance. Resistive Random Access Memories
(RRAM) are a common expression of devices that exhibit memristive behavior and can be realized using different architectures ranging from metal-oxides
[7] and perovskites [10] to fully organic solutions [22]. Memristors possess several advantages over conventional memory elements when their resistive state
is utilized to store weights of a neural network: First, their resistive state is
non-volatile and therefore, only memory changes but not retention consumes

D. Genova and J. Kari (Eds.): UCNC 2023, LNCS 14003, pp. 124–139, 2023.
https://doi.org/10.1007/978-3-031-34034-5_9

energy. Second, memristors can be integrated with ultra-high density, allowing to scale up neural networks. Third, several implementations of memristors have been demonstrated to present many densely packed resistive states [20] allowing them to operate in an analog fashion. This allows for greater flexibility in storing weight values with high resolution. Finally, memristors arranged in a crossbar array architecture are ideally suited to implement the fundamental mathematical operation in neural networks in $O(1)$ time: vector-matrix multiplication. This can significantly speed up computations. These advantages render them the ideal candidate for the realization of synaptic memory in neural networks. However, memristive neural networks still face substantial challenges. The programming of their resistances is noisy and their behavior is faulty. Faults exhibited by the memristor are primarily associated with issues related to the fabrication and secondarily because of operational constraints. For the former case, these include non-uniformity of the active layer, interface defects, or thermal effects during processing. As a consequence, devices might become inoperable or operate outside expected specifications. However, devices can also fail during operation as, depending on the technology, the endurance of the devices is limited. Yield and repeatability issues also affect the reliability of large crossbars when compared to established memory technologies. In order to scale up such memristive computing systems, it is necessary to increase the integration density of memristive arrays and thus scale down memristor elements. Unfortunately, the aforementioned problems become particularly pronounced in this case.

In this article, we consider the question of memristive neural network training. Such training in particular suffers from faulty memristor behaviors. Typical faulty behavior includes stuck memristors (i.e., devices that do not change their resistance), memristors with an unexpected change rate (i.e., the memristance change is stronger or weaker than expected), or even memristors with an inverted plasticity behavior (i.e., memristors that change their resistance in the wrong direction). We first analyze the impact of such faulty behavior on neural network training. We find that faulty behavior can significantly impact the resulting network performance. Based on recent findings which show that neural network connectivity can be significantly sparsified with minor loss in performance [2,6,16,19], we then propose a novel training strategy (fault pruning) where faulty memristor behavior is detected during training and corresponding devices are pruned on the fly. We evaluate fault pruning on the MNIST and CIFAR-10 data sets and show that this simple strategy is able to recover effective network optimization for both feed-forward and convolutional memristive neural networks. Further analysis reveals that the algorithm can adaptively adjust network sparsity to make use of the functional memristive resources.

2 Results

When memristive elements are used to store weight parameters of artificial neural networks, each weight w_i of the network is maintained in the resistance R_i of a corresponding memristor. More precisely, the weight is in the simplest case given by a linear mapping from the conductance $G_i = \frac{1}{R_i}$

$$w_i = \alpha\left(\frac{1}{R_i} - \frac{1}{R_C}\right), \tag{1}$$

where α represents the scaling parameter of memristive weight, and R_C represents the bias resistance value. In this simplest case, a single memristor is used to represent both positive and negative weight values in some range $[-w_{min}, w_{max}]$. More elaborated designs utilize separate memristors for positive and negative weight values, but we adopted here this scheme for simplicity. We assumed that $w_{min} = -w_{max}$, and let the weight $w_i = 0$ map to $\frac{1}{R_C}$. Hence, for a given range $[R_{min}, R_{max}]$ of resistance values, the bias resistance was given by $R_C = 2R_{min}R_{max}/(R_{min} + R_{max})$ and the scaling parameter was $\alpha = \frac{w_{max}}{1/R_{min} - 1/R_C}$. Consequently, the inverse mapping from the weight to resistance was given by

$$R_i = \frac{1}{\frac{1}{R_C} + \frac{w_i}{\alpha}}, \tag{2}$$

see Sect. 3.1 for details. We simulated training of memristive neural networks using an in-the-loop training setup [5,18,24], see Fig. 1. Here, the memristive network was simulated using non-ideal noisy memristive updates (see below). In addition, a copy of the network architecture was simulated using high-precision weights (high-precision network). Gradients were computed using backpropagation in the high-precision network and weight updates were accumulated. When significant weight changes were accumulated, memristors in the memristive network were updated [24,25]. More precisely, a resistance R_i was updated when a weight change Δw_i^{ideal} resulting in a resistance change of 2% was reached. In addition, an update of all resistances was forced every 100 training batches (see Sect. 3.2 for details). Since such updates were non-ideal due to switching noise and faulty memristors, resulting resistances were read out, mapped to weight values according to Eq. (1), and the high-precision network was updated. This procedure was iterated until the number of target epochs was reached.

Non-ideal memristor updates of the memristive network were modeled as follows. Let $\Delta w_i^{ideal,(k)}$ denote the proposed update for weight i at update step k, entailing a resistance update $\Delta R_i^{ideal,(k)}$. Due to a number of nonidealities, memristors, when programmed, often show deviations from the intended behavior. Stuck memristors do not change their resistance regardless of the magnitude of the desired resistance change, and we refer to these faults as *stuck faults*. Other memristors underestimate or overestimate the magnitude of resistance change, or even produce updates in the opposite direction of the one predicted by the underlying model of the memristor. We refer to faults where the magnitude of the resistance change is under-/over-estimated as *concordant switching faults* and to faults of memristors that produce resistance change in the opposite direction of the desired one as *discordant switching faults*. In addition, when programming the devices, i.e., switching the devices to different resistive states, the achieved resistance states are noisy due to switching noise.

High-precision network   **Memristive network**

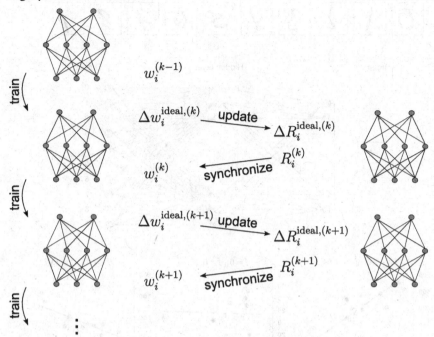

Fig. 1. In-the-loop training setup. In this setup, training is performed on two networks in parallel. In the memristive network (right), weights are implemented by unreliable and faulty memristors (simulated in our case). The high-precision network (left) has identical architecture, but weights are stored in high precision. The high-precision network is trained until significant weight changes are available. At the kth update step, such weight changes $\Delta w_i^{\text{ideal},(k)}$ are then used to update resistances in the memristive network by the desired amount $\Delta R_i^{\text{ideal},(k)}$. The resulting resistances $R_i^{(k)}$ are read out and used to synchronize the high-precision network. These steps are repeated until training ends.

We modeled faulty memristors by introducing fault factors f_i that modulated the desired (expected) resistance change $\Delta R_i^{\text{ideal},(k)}$ and added a switching noise term

$$\Delta R_i^{(k)} = f_i \cdot \Delta R_i^{\text{ideal},(k)} + \eta_i^{(k)}. \tag{3}$$

Fault factors were chosen according to the corresponding memristor fault type: a fault factor $f_i = 0$ for a stuck fault, $f_i < 0$ for a discordant switching fault, and $f_i > 0$ for a concordant switching fault. The switching noise $\eta_i^{(k)}$ was drawn independently for each memristor i and each update step k from a normal distribution with zero mean and a magnitude up to 1% of the current resistance.

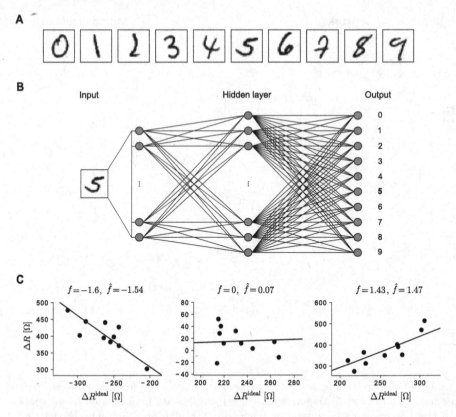

Fig. 2. Feed-forward neural network trained on the MNIST data set. (A) Example images representing 10 digits. (B) Schematic of the feed-forward architecture used to learn the task. (C) Examples of discordant switching fault (left), stuck fault (middle), and concordant switching fault (right). The noisy achieved resistance change (y-axis) is plotted against the desired change (x-axis). Line indicates linear fit for $\hat{f}$ estimate.

2.1   Training of Memristive Neural Networks with Faulty Memristors

We first investigated how faulty memristors impact the training of neural networks. We started with a simple feed-forward architecture trained on the MNIST data set [14]. The MNIST data set consists of 70 thousand $28{\times}28$ gray-scale images of handwritten digits. The goal is to classify these images into 10 classes according to the written digit, see Fig. 2A for one example image per class. The neural network architecture is shown in Fig. 2B. It consisted of one hidden layer with 128 neurons with a rectified linear (ReLU) activation function and one softmax output layer for classification. We first trained this network in the in-the-loop training setup with switching noise but without faulty memristors. In this case, the network achieved a test classification accuracy of $96.28 \pm 0.32\%$ (percentage of correctly classified test examples; mean and STD over 10 training runs with random initial conditions). We next performed training with switching noise and faulty memristors. The behavior of three example simulated faulty memristors is shown in Fig. 2C, one with a discordant switching fault (left), one with a stuck fault (middle), and one with a concordant switching fault (right). To test the effect of fault type on the network performance, we varied the proportion of fault types, see Fig. 3A (left). The figure shows test performance for a relative number of p_{stuck} stuck faults (x-axis) and a relative number of $p_{\text{discordant}}$ discordant switching faults (y-axis). The remaining simulated memristors had concordant switching faults, that is a proportion of $1 - (p_{\text{stuck}} + p_{\text{discordant}})$. We observe that even with 80% concordant switching faults (e.g., cell $(0.1, 0.1)$), the network shows good performance. This is not surprising as the parameter change is still in the correct direction although somewhat distorted. Also, stuck memristors can be tolerated up to some point. Only after 50% stuck faults in the bottom row does the performance fall below 95%. The effect of discordant memristors is more severe. At 30% discordant faults and 10% stuck faults, the performance drops below 94% and then declines rapidly.

The same trend but more strongly pronounced can be observed for the more challenging CIFAR-10 data set [13] using a convolutional network. This data set consists of color images of size (32×32) from ten different classes representing: airplanes, automobiles, birds, cats, deers, dogs, frogs, horses, ships, and trucks [13], see Fig. 4A for example images. The schematic of the architecture used to learn the task is shown in Fig. 4B. It consisted of two convolutional-pooling layers, a convolutional layer that after flattening connected to a dense layer, and finally, a softmax output layer with 10 neurons, one per class. Training without memristor faults, we achieved a test classification accuracy of $60.61 \pm 3.15\%$ (mean and STD over 10 training runs). Again, we varied the proportion of fault types as above for the MNIST data set, see Fig. 4C (left). When compared to the MNIST results, we can observe a clear performance decrease already for small proportions of stuck- and discordant switching faults (cell $(0.1, 0.1)$), and a more rapid decline of performance for increasing discordant switching faults.

2.2 Fault Pruning for Memristive Neural Networks

As the integration density of memristive arrays increases, one can expect more and more unreliable and faulty memristive elements in the array. In principle, one could characterize memristors before training and adapt the training process accordingly. However, memristors can change their characteristics after characterization and in particular memristor faults can appear during training due to limited endurance [25]. Therefore, we propose a robust training scheme (fault pruning) for memristive neural networks that detects unreliable memristors online during training using information available in the in-the-loop training setup. We will consider two alternatives to deal with faulty memristors: first, to discard them and set the connection to 0, and second, to continue using the connection but requesting from them no change in resistive states.

In fault pruning, fault factors are estimated for each memristor i during training using the ideal and achieved resistance changes — $\Delta R_i^{\text{ideal},(k)}$ and $\Delta R_i^{(k)}$ —

of the N most recent updates of the memristor. A zero-intercept linear regression model is then fitted to these data points to obtain the estimated fault factor

$$\hat{f}_i = \frac{\sum_l \Delta R_i^{\text{ideal},(l)} \Delta R_i^{(l)}}{\sum_l \left(\Delta R_i^{\text{ideal},(l)}\right)^2}. \tag{4}$$

A derivation of this estimator is given in Sect. 3.3. Upon the estimation of the fault factor $\hat{f}_i$, the algorithm decides whether or not to prune the weight in the following way: Assuming that memristors with estimated $\hat{f}_i < 0.1$ have stuck or discordant switching faults, the weight w_i is pruned (i.e., set to zero) in both the full-precision and memristive network. Otherwise, $\hat{f}_i \geq 0.1$ indicates a memristor with a concordant switching fault. Such memristors are still useful for training as their weight change goes in the desired direction, thus, further used. The estimated fault factor $\hat{f}_i$ is easily interpretable – it represents the slope of the linear fit, and in principle, any value greater than 0 means that requested and achieved resistance updates have the same trend. For the threshold, we chose the value of 0.1 since for the estimation of $\hat{f}_i$ we used only a few points data points ($N = 10$) that included the switching noise.

As an alternative, we also considered freezing faulty memristors instead of pruning them. In this case, the algorithm keeps the achieved weight in the high-precision network and does not update the faulty memristor anymore.

Fault Pruning for Feed-Forward Memristive Neural Networks. We next tested fault pruning in the feed-forward neural network setup on the MNIST data set as described above. During the in-the-loop training, the pruning algorithm estimated fault factor $\hat{f}_i$ for each memristor based on the history of the $N = 10$ most recent requested and achieved resistance updates in the memristive network. Figure 2C shows a linear fit to the data points $(\Delta R_i^{\text{ideal},(k)}, \Delta R_i^{(k)})$ for three example memristors. Figure 2C (left) illustrates a memristor with a discordant switching fault assigned at the beginning of the training, $f = -1.6$, that the pruning algorithm discarded ($\hat{f} = -1.54 < 0.1$). Similarly, the example memristor in Fig. 2C (middle) with a stuck fault ($f = 0$) was discarded. The memristor illustrated in the right panel of Fig. 2C, although overestimating the resistance change ($f = 1.43$) was kept for further training.

The pruning algorithm detects faulty memristors and prunes the network connections in an online fashion (during training). This makes it possible to adaptively adjust the network connectivity and avoid the detrimental effects that faulty memristors have on training. We trained feed-forward networks with different proportions of memristor fault types and measured the test accuracy at the end of the training. The fault pruning algorithm preserved the test accuracy even in cases when the proportion of the stuck and discordant switching faults was very significant (see Fig. 3A, middle), whereas the test accuracy degraded drastically when there was no pruning (see Fig. 3A, left). Note that the memristors that did not have stuck or discordant switching faults had concordant switching faults. The pruning algorithm performed marginally better when the

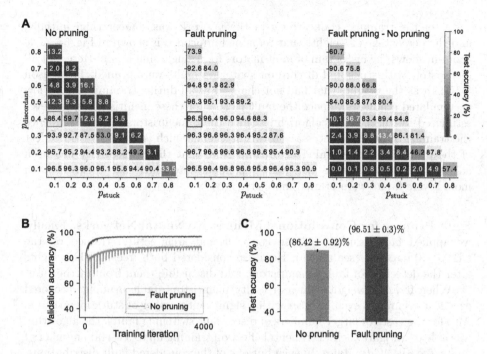

Fig. 3. Performances of feed-forward memristive neural networks trained on the MNIST data set. (A) Test accuracies for different proportions of memristor faults without fault pruning (left), with fault pruning (middle), and the difference in the accuracies of these scenarios (right). (B) Validation accuracy during training with (blue) and without (red) fault pruning (shading indicates STD over 10 training runs) for the cases indicated by colored boxes in A. (C) Final test accuracy for these training runs (means ± STD over 10 training runs). (Color figure online)

number of memristors with stuck and discordant switching faults was small. As the number of memristors with these fault types increased, the use of fault pruning became essential. This is illustrated in Fig. 3A (right), where the differences in test accuracies achieved in both scenarios are shown.

The validation accuracy over memristor updates for the simulations indicated by the blue and red rectangular boxes in Fig. 3A are shown in Fig. 3B (shaded area indicates STD over 10 simulations with different initial weights). Note that training without pruning was rather unstable, showing repeated performance decreases due to faulty memristor behavior. The regular negative peaks in the non-pruned case appear since the in-the-loop training setup forces resistance updates for all weights every 100 training batches. Training with pruning on the other hand was stable and reached a much better final accuracy. The final test accuracies for these cases are plotted in Fig. 3C. The low standard deviations show that the achieved accuracy (both on validation during training and on the test set) over multiple runs was very consistent.

After the training, connectivity in the network was sparser than initially, and the percentage of weights that remained unpruned is shown in Fig. 5A. The zoom-in shows the histogram of fault factors for a single simulation. Here, not all memristors with stuck and discordant switching faults were pruned. The reason for this was the weights that had not changed at all during training (due to low accumulated gradients), hence the fault factors for these memristors were never estimated by the pruning algorithm. Since these memristors did not influence the training, it was not necessary to prune them, which is a positive side effect of the proposed fault pruning algorithm. Note that the connectivity has been adapted by the algorithm in a fault-dependent way, such that networks with more severe faults were pruned more strongly.

Fault Pruning for Convolutional Memristive Neural Networks. Finally, we applied fault pruning on the convolutional architecture, trained on the CIFAR-10 data set (see above). Here, we considered both freezing the weights after the detection of faulty memristors, and discarding them from further use.

When freezing weight values of faulty memristors, fault pruning recovered excellent accuracies even in cases with a significant number of stuck memristors. Also for the cases of larger numbers of discordant switching faults, the algorithm was able to mitigate their detrimental effect on training up to a certain number of faults, see Fig. 4C (middle). In each but one of the considered fault distributions, fault pruning was able to improve network performance over plain training, see Fig. 4C (right). We examined the single instance (cell $(0.2, 0.1)$) where the fault pruning performed slightly worse. There, some connections for which memristors had concordant switching faults f slightly above the threshold value were pruned. When running ten simulations with different initial conditions for this case, pruning performed better on average (pruning $(60.87 \pm 2.48)\%$, no pruning $(58.71 \pm 2.53)\%$ test accuracy). The percentage of unpruned weights/memristors after training (connectivity percentage) is illustrated in Fig. 5B. The zoom-in shows a histogram of fault factors assigned to memristors at the beginning of training, with pruned connections shown in yellow and unpruned ones shown in gray.

We also tested performance when faulty memristors were discarded as in the previous section, see Fig. 4D. In this case, fault pruning achieved better accuracies for intermediate values of $p_{\text{discordant}}$. Simulation details are given in Sect. 3.4.

3   Methods

3.1   Memristor Model

In our simulations, we used the following memristor model for all memristive weights. The memristor model defined the resistance range $[R_{\text{min}}, R_{\text{max}}]$ that the state variable R could take. We used $R_{\text{min}} = 6843.97\,\Omega$, and $R_{\text{max}} = 14109.06\,\Omega$ – the values calculated for a single device-under-test whose more detailed version of

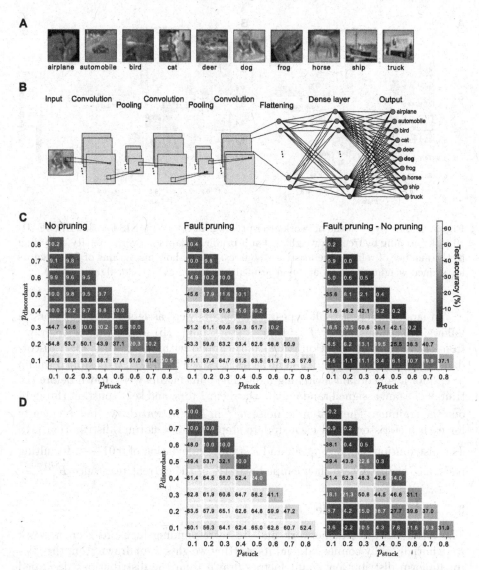

Fig. 4. Performances of memristive CNNs on CIFAR-10. (A) Example CIFAR-10 images. (B) Convolutional neural network architecture. (C, D) Test accuracies for different proportions of memristor faults without fault pruning (left), with fault pruning (middle), and the difference in the accuracies of these scenarios (right). In (C), pruning was done by freezing weights, in (D), by setting them to zero.

a memristor model is described in [17]. Given the maximum value for the weights, w_{max}, for a symmetric range of weights $[-w_{max}, w_{max}]$, the bias resistance R_C and the scaling parameter α were calculated as $R_C = 2R_{min}R_{max}/(R_{min} + R_{max})$, and $\alpha = \frac{w_{max}}{1/R_{min} - 1/R_C}$, respectively. We used $w_{max} = 0.5$ in all our simulations.

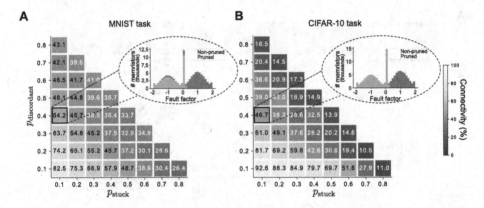

Fig. 5. Connectivity in the network after pruning (in %). (A) MNIST task. (B) CIFAR-10 task (pruning by freezing weights). Fault pruning adapts network sparsity according to the number of reliable memristive resources. Insets show histograms of fault factors for pruned weights (yellow) and non-pruned weights (gray). (Color figure online)

To model different fault types, fault factors were assigned to memristors as follows: (a) a fault factor $f_i = 0$ for a stuck fault, (b) a fault factor f_i drawn from the normal distribution $\mathcal{N}(-1, 0.5)$ capped within $[-2, -0.1]$ for a discordant switching fault, and (c) a fault factor f_i drawn from $\mathcal{N}(1, 0.5)$ capped within $[0.1, 2]$ for a concordant switching fault. The fault factors were drawn before the training began, assigned randomly to the memristors, and kept constant throughout the training. The switching noise $\eta_i^{(k)}$ in Eq. (3) was drawn independently for each memristor i and each update step k from a normal distribution [21]. The distribution had zero mean and a standard deviation of $0.01 \frac{R_i^{(k)}}{3}$. Resulting resistance changes were then capped at $\pm 1\%$ of the current resistance $R_i^{(k)}$.

3.2   Training Schedule

The memristive neural network and its corresponding high-precision network were initially fully connected, and its starting weights were drawn from the Glorot uniform distribution. Fault factors drawn from the distributions described in the previous section were assigned randomly to memristors in the memristive network, simulating in that way the faulty behaviors of memristors. In each training iteration t, weight updates were computed in the high-precision network using the Adam optimizer [12] on one batch of input data (batch size b depended on the task, see below), and the weights in the high-precision network were updated. Since memristance updates are noisy, one usually does not program each individual update in the memristive array, but rather accumulates weight changes until significant updates are available [24]. Hence, memristors were updated typically only when a significant resistance change was available. Therefore, we have to distinguish between training iteration t and update k. To formalize this, denote the achieved resistance for connection i after the most recent update as R_i^{prev} and the proposed resistance after the current training iteration t as R_i^{cur}. Memristor i was updated if $R_i^{\mathrm{cur}} - R_i^{\mathrm{prev}}$ was at least 2% of the current resistance R_i^{prev}. After the update, the achieved resistance value was used to synchronize the corresponding weight w_i in the high-precision network.

In addition to these asynchronous updates, all memristors were updated every 100 training iterations and in the last training iteration. The updates for which the magnitude of the requested change was below the noise level (in our simulations, 1% of R_i^{prev}) were enlarged to $\pm 1\%$ of R_i^{prev}, depending on the sign of the originally requested $\Delta R_i^{\mathrm{ideal},(k)}$. Note that for the memristors with $\Delta R_i^{\mathrm{ideal},(k)} = 0$, the updates were not enforced since the programming of the memristive device was not required. Also here, weights in the high-precision network were synchronized according to the achieved memristance values.

Estimation of the fault factors was implemented as follows: Let $\Delta R_i^{\mathrm{ideal},(k)}$ and $\Delta R_i^{(k)}$ denote the proposed and the achieved resistance change of connection i at the k-th memristor update respectively. The most recent $N = 10$ update pairs $(\Delta R_i^{\mathrm{ideal},(k)}, \Delta R_i^{(k)})$ for memristor i were used to estimate the fault factor $\hat{f}_i$. The connections for which $\hat{f}$ was below the threshold of 0.1 were pruned. We implemented two versions of pruning – setting weights to 0 (being equivalent to removing the weight in the high-precision network, and not using at all memristors in the memristive networks), and keeping the weights/memristors in the network, but without further training. The minimum allowed connectivity was 10%, i.e., at least 10% of the weights had to be used between any two layers. After estimating fault factors, it was possible to prune up to 20% connections for the MNIST task, and up to 50% of connections for the CIFAR-10 task. Hence the candidate weights for pruning, i.e., the weights for which the estimated fault factor $\hat{f}_i$ was smaller than the threshold value 0.1, were first sorted in the ascending order according to their fault factors, and pruned. This prevented removing many connections at once, and also prioritized removing memristors with discordant switching fault type over stuck faults.

3.3   Estimation of the Fault Factors $\hat{f}_i$

For the estimation of the fault factor $\hat{f}_i$, we used a zero-intercept linear regression model

$$\Delta R_i = \hat{f}_i \cdot \Delta R_i^{\mathrm{ideal}} + \epsilon \tag{5}$$

that models the linear relation between requested ($\Delta R_i^{\mathrm{ideal}}$) and achieved ($\Delta R_i$) resistance updates under Gaussian noise. It was estimated from $N = 10$ data points $(\Delta R_i^{\mathrm{ideal},(l)}, \Delta R_i^{(l)})$, $l \in \{k - N + 1, k - N + 2, ..., k - 1, k\}$ representing the N most recent updates of memristor R_i. The least-squares estimator of $\hat{f}_i$ minimizes the squared error $\mathcal{L}(\hat{f}_i)$,

$$\mathcal{L}(\hat{f}_i) := \sum_l \left(\Delta R_i^{(l)} - \hat{f}_i \cdot \Delta R_i^{\mathrm{ideal},(l)} \right)^2, \tag{6}$$

and a closed-form analytical solution can be found as

$$\frac{\partial \mathcal{L}}{\partial \hat{f}_i} = 2 \sum_l \left(\Delta R_i^{(l)} - \hat{f}_i \cdot \Delta R_i^{\text{ideal},(l)} \right) \left(-\Delta R_i^{\text{ideal},(l)} \right) \overset{!}{=} 0$$

$$\hat{f}_i \sum_l \left(\Delta R_i^{\text{ideal},(l)} \right)^2 = \sum_l \Delta R_i^{(l)} \Delta R_i^{\text{ideal},(l)}$$

(7)

Hence, $\hat{f}_i = \frac{\sum_l \Delta R_i^{(l)} \Delta R_i^{\text{ideal},(l)}}{\sum_l \left(\Delta R_i^{\text{ideal},(l)} \right)^2}$ follows. The condition $\sum_l \left(\Delta R_i^{\text{ideal},(l)} \right)^2 \neq 0$ was ensured because the pruning algorithm always enforced updates with magnitudes different than zero.

3.4   Details to Computer Simulations

Details to Feed-forward Networks Trained on the MNIST Task. We trained memristive feed-forward networks on the MNIST task consisting of 50000, 10000, and 10000 training, validation, and test images, respectively. The architecture used was $784 - 128 - 10$ neurons per layer. Over training, the connections both in high-precision and memristive networks were pruned. For pruned connections, memristors were discarded from the memristive network, while the weights in the high-precision network were set to zero. In the high-precision network, all neurons in the hidden and output layer had a trainable bias term. For the optimization of the weights and biases of the (high-precision) feed-forward network, the Adam optimizer with an initial learning rate of 0.01 was used. The learning rate was decayed exponentially every 1000 iteration by a factor of 0.99. The optimizer used batches of $b = 128$ training images to minimize the cross-entropy error function. The network was trained for 10 epochs (forward and backward propagations of the whole dataset), resulting in a total of 3910 training iterations. The performance numbers reported in Fig. 3A represent the test accuracies achieved for a single training run with $p_{\text{discordant}}$ discordant switching and p_{stuck} stuck faults, except for the highlighted ones (the blue and red rectangular boxes) where they are the mean over 10 runs.

Details to Convolutional Networks Trained on the CIFAR-10 Task. We trained memristive convolutional neural networks on the CIFAR-10 task, consisting of 50000 training and 10000 test images.

The architecture that we trained consisted of: (1) an input layer, (2) a $2D$-convolutional layer with 32 output filters, kernels of size (3×3), valid padding, stride $(1, 1)$, with ReLU activation function, (3) a max-pooling layer with a pool size (2×2), (4) a $2D$-convolutional layer with 64 output filters, kernels of size (3×3), valid padding, stride $(1, 1)$, with ReLU activation function, (5) a max-pooling layer with a pool size (2×2), (6) a $2D$-convolutional layer with 64 output filters, kernels of size (3×3), valid padding, stride $(1, 1)$, with ReLU activation function, then flattened which resulted in a layer of 1024 neurons, (7) a densely connected layer (64 neurons), with ReLU activation function, and (8) an output layer of 10 neurons (one per class), with softmax activation function.

Initially fully connected, the connections in the high-precision and memristive networks were pruned during training. Here we used two approaches for pruning. For pruned connections, either both resistance in the memristive network and weight in the high-precision network were frozen, or the weight was set to 0, and the corresponding memristor discarded. In the high-precision network, all neurons had biases that were optimized along the weights using the Adam optimizer. The learning rate was set to 0.005, batch size to $b = 256$ training images, and the cross-entropy error function was minimized for 30 epochs. This resulted in a total of 5880 training iterations. The performance numbers in Fig. 4C, D report the test accuracies representing a single training run.

4   Conclusions

We have proposed fault pruning, a novel training algorithm for robust training of neural networks with memristive weights. We applied this algorithm to both feed-forward and convolutional neural networks. The approach is general, independent of the network structure and the trained task.

Most previously proposed robust-training schemes (e.g., [3,11,23]) are agnostic to the exact location of memristor faults. The objective is to alleviate the impact of faults when memristors are programmed only once at the end of training. In [15], a re-training scheme, as well as a re-mapping of weights to memristors, was proposed. Xia et al. [25] proposed an on-line fault detection method combined with a re-mapping method, but not in the in-the-loop training setup considered here. In contrast to these works, we do not propose re-mapping but assume that arbitrary memristive connections can be pruned.

Our proposed fault pruning algorithm takes advantage of the communication exchange between the two networks in the in-the-loop training scheme. Requested and achieved resistance changes are used to estimate the type of a memristor's fault $\hat{f}_i$, and act accordingly. For the estimation of the faulty behavior, we used a simple linear regression. This can, however, be substituted by more advanced approaches if necessary. In our simulations, the fault type assigned to a memristor was kept constant during training; in practice, the memristor's fault type could change over time. Such a case would not be a problem for fault pruning, because, for the estimation of the fault factor and the fault type, it uses a certain number of most recent memristor updates from which the change could be detected. Our simulations showed that even with a very large percentage of faulty memristors, and in particular with memristors with discordant switching faults, fault pruning managed to preserve very good performance. Another option for handling memristors with discordant fault types not considered in this article could be to adapt the requested update, e.g., by inverting its sign. Advantages of this approach could be investigated in future work.

In summary, we showed in simulations that pruning faulty memristive connections provides a viable strategy for robust training of memristive neural networks. The fault type can be estimated on-line during in-the-loop training, allowing for efficient robust training of performant networks.

Acknowledgements. This research was partially supported by SYNCH project funded by the European Commission under the H2020 FET Proactive programme (Grant agreement ID: 824162) and by the CHIST-ERA grant CHIST-ERA-18-ACAI-004, by the Austrian Science Fund (FWF) project number I 4670-N (project SMALL).

References

1. Bayat, F.M., Prezioso, M., Chakrabarti, B., Nili, H., Kataeva, I., Strukov, D.: Implementation of multilayer perceptron network with highly uniform passive memristive crossbar circuits. Nat. Commun. **9**(1), 1–7 (2018)
2. Bellec, G., Kappel, D., Maass, W., Legenstein, R.: Deep rewiring: training very sparse deep networks. In: International Conference on Learning Representations (2018)
3. Chen, C.Y., Chakrabarty, K.: Pruning of deep neural networks for fault-tolerant memristor-based accelerators. In: 2021 58th ACM/IEEE Design Automation Conference (DAC), pp. 889–894. IEEE (2021)
4. Chen, S., et al.: Wafer-scale integration of two-dimensional materials in high-density memristive crossbar arrays for artificial neural networks. Nat. Electron. **3**(10), 638–645 (2020)
5. Esser, S.K., et al.: Convolutional networks for fast, energy-efficient neuromorphic computing. Proc. Natl. Acad. Sci. **113**(41), 11441–11446 (2016)
6. Han, S., Pool, J., Tran, J., Dally, W.: Learning both weights and connections for efficient neural network. In: Cortes, C., Lawrence, N., Lee, D., Sugiyama, M., Garnett, R. (eds.) Advances in Neural Information Processing Systems, vol. 28. Curran Associates, Inc. (2015)
7. Ielmini, D.: Resistive switching memories based on metal oxides: mechanisms, reliability and scaling. Semicond. Sci. Technol. **31**(6), 063002 (2016)
8. Indiveri, G., Linares-Barranco, B., Legenstein, R., Deligeorgis, G., Prodromakis, T.: Integration of nanoscale memristor synapses in neuromorphic computing architectures. Nanotechnology **24**(38), 384010 (2013)
9. Jeong, H., Shi, L.: Memristor devices for neural networks. J. Phys. D Appl. Phys. **52**(2), 023003 (2018)
10. John, R.A., et al.: Halide perovskite memristors as flexible and reconfigurable physical unclonable functions. Nat. Commun. **12**(1) (2021)
11. Joksas, D., et al.: Committee machines - a universal method to deal with non-idealities in memristor-based neural networks. Nat. Commun. **11**(1), 1–10 (2020)
12. Kingma, D.P., Ba, J.: Adam: a method for stochastic optimization. arXiv preprint arXiv:1412.6980 (2014)
13. Krizhevsky, A.: Learning multiple layers of features from tiny images. Technical report (2009)
14. LeCun, Y., Cortes, C., Burges, C.: MNIST handwritten digit database. ATT Labs. **2** (2010). http://yann.lecun.com/exdb/mnist
15. Liu, C., Hu, M., Strachan, J.P., Li, H.: Rescuing memristor-based neuromorphic design with high defects. In: 2017 54th ACM/EDAC/IEEE Design Automation Conference (DAC), pp. 1–6. IEEE (2017)

16. Liu, Z., Sun, M., Zhou, T., Huang, G., Darrell, T.: Rethinking the value of network pruning. In: International Conference on Learning Representations (2019)
17. Messaris, I., Serb, A., Stathopoulos, S., Khiat, A., Nikolaidis, S., Prodromakis, T.: A data-driven Verilog-A ReRAM model. IEEE Trans. Comput. Aided Des. Integr. Circuits Syst. **37**(12), 3151–3162 (2018)
18. Schmitt, S., et al.: Neuromorphic hardware in the loop: training a deep spiking network on the brainscales wafer-scale system. In: 2017 International Joint Conference on Neural Networks, pp. 2227–2234. IEEE (2017)
19. Srinivas, S., Babu, R.V.: Data-free parameter pruning for deep neural networks. In: Proceedings of the British Machine Vision Conference, pp. 31.1-31.12. BMVA Press (2015)
20. Stathopoulos, S., et al.: Multibit memory operation of metal-oxide bi-layer memristors. Sci. Rep. **7**(1) (2017)
21. Stathopoulos, S., Serb, A., Khiat, A., Ogorzałek, M., Prodromakis, T.: A memristive switching uncertainty model. IEEE Trans. Electron. Devices **66**(7), 2946–2953 (2019)
22. Valov, I., Kozicki, M.: Organic memristors come of age. Nat. Mater. **16**(12), 1170–1172 (2017)
23. Wang, J., Xu, Q., Yuan, B., Chen, S., Yu, B., Wu, F.: Reliability-driven neural network training for memristive crossbar-based neuromorphic computing systems. In: 2020 IEEE International Symposium on Circuits and Systems (ISCAS), pp. 1–4. IEEE (2020)
24. Woźniak, S., Pantazi, A., Bohnstingl, T., Eleftheriou, E.: Deep learning incorporating biologically inspired neural dynamics and in-memory computing. Nat. Mach. Intell. **2**(6), 325–336 (2020)
25. Xia, L., Liu, M., Ning, X., Chakrabarty, K., Wang, Y.: Fault-tolerant training with on-line fault detection for RRAM-based neural computing systems. In: Proceedings of the 54th Annual Design Automation Conference 2017, pp. 1–6 (2017)
26. Xia, Q., Yang, J.J.: Memristive crossbar arrays for brain-inspired computing. Nat. Mater. **18**(4), 309–323 (2019)
27. Yao, P., et al.: Fully hardware-implemented memristor convolutional neural network. Nature **577**(7792), 641–646 (2020)

Spatial Correlations in the Qubit Properties of D-Wave 2000Q Measured and Simulated Qubit Networks

Jessica Park[1,2($\boxtimes$)], Susan Stepney[1], and Irene D'Amico[2]

[1] Department of Computer Science, University of York, York, UK
{jlp567,susan.stepney}@york.ac.uk
[2] Department of Physics, University of York, York, UK
irene.damico@york.ac.uk

Abstract. We show strong positive spatial correlations in the qubits of a D-Wave 2000Q quantum annealing chip that are connected to qubits outside their own unit cell. By simulating the dynamics of spin networks, we then show that correlation between nodes is affected by a number of factors. The different connectivity of qubits within the network means that information transfer is not straightforward even when all the qubit-qubit couplings have equal weighting. The similarity between connected nodes is further changed when the couplings' strength is scaled according to the physical length of the connections (here to simulate dipole-dipole interactions). This highlights the importance of understanding the architectural features and potentially unprogrammed interactions/connections that can divert the performance of a quantum system away from the idealised model of identical qubits and couplings across the chip.

Keywords: Quantum computing · D-Wave · correlations · spin networks

1 Introduction

Quantum computation is currently being advanced on multiple fronts, including: algorithm development, qubit realisation, device manufacturing, and error correction [1,5,9,15]. Due to the relative infancy and challenging scalability of the technology, the hardware is often hard to control precisely, and the individual qubits can be subject to significant heterogeneity. Algorithms will need to be optimised based on the constraints and properties of the hardware, and the hardware will need to be chosen, modified or built based on requirements of the software task. These processes need to be done in parallel such that one the software is not being optimised based on non-optimal hardware and vice versa [3].

Different physical realisations of qubits have different levels of robustness to different errors, and so different realisations may be optimal for different functions [13,14]. It seems likely that fabrication inhomogeneities will result in a

D. Genova and J. Kari (Eds.): UCNC 2023, LNCS 14003, pp. 140–154, 2023.
https://doi.org/10.1007/978-3-031-34034-5_10

device where different individual qubits may be optimal for different functions, potentially allowing improved performance by careful allocation of qubits. Before considering how to exploit heterogeneity in the system, it is crucial to understand its sources and effects. Here we examine how heterogeneity presents itself on a quantum chip, and how this affects the performance when running certain problems.

Section 2 gives an overview of quantum annealing and some specifics about the particular architecture that is considered in the remainder of the paper. Section 3 presents an investigation in the analysis of spatial correlation that we performed on a dataset provided by Los Alamos National Laboratory [11]. The results from this investigation led us to develop and perform tests on a spin network simulator with realistic architectures and dynamics (Sect. 4). Finally, Sect. 5 considers the implications of this work and proposes potentially valuable areas of further study.

2 Quantum Annealing and D-Wave Chimera Architecture

Quantum annealing is a non-universal type of quantum computing most commonly used to find the optimal solution to a problem. It can do this by finding the global minimum of an energy landscape that encodes the problem. Quantum fluctuation and quantum tunnelling allow the annealer to escape certain local minimal in energy landscapes.

In order to solve such optimisation problems, the cost function (to be minimised) and any associated constraints are formulated into an *Ising Hamiltonian* (modelling the energy of coupled qubits). This is an equation that describes the energy landscape of the system. The desired result of the annealing process is that the system reaches the ground state of this Hamiltonian, which corresponds to the optimal solution of the problem.

The Hamiltonian that describes quantum annealing is

$$H(x,s) = \frac{A(s)}{2}\left(\sum_i \hat{\sigma}_X^{(i)}\right) + \frac{B(s)}{2}\left(\sum_i h_i\hat{\sigma}_Z^{(i)} + \sum_{i>j} J_{ij}\hat{\sigma}_Z^{(i)}\hat{\sigma}_Z^{(j)}\right), \quad (1)$$

where $x = \{x_0, x_1, x_i...x_N\}$ is the state of the N-qubit system; s is normalised time; $\hat{\sigma}_X^{(i)}$, $\hat{\sigma}_Z^{(i)}$ are the Pauli matrices acting on qubit x_i; h_i and J_{ij} encode the problem as qubit biases and coupling weights, and, in practice, are limited by the physical hardware graph (qubit-coupling connectivity) of the annealing device.

Annealing occurs between physical times $t = 0$ and $t = t_f$, normalised into an annealing fraction: $s = t/t_f$, so $0 \le s \le 1$. A and B are functions of s and their relative magnitudes describe the state of the system as it moves from a general superposition state (the first term) to the solution state (the second term, the Ising Hamiltonian).

At $t = 0$ ($s = 0$), the system has $A(0) \gg B(0)$: the state starts as a general superposition of states. The system is slowly annealed by increasing B and decreasing A, until at $t = t_f$ ($s = 1$) we have $A(1) \ll B(1)$. This is often referred to as freezing out the quantum fluctuations. At this point the qubits, in an ideal system, are in the ground state of the second term, that is, they are in the state representing the solution to the optimisation problem. The annealing process needs to happen slowly enough such that the system does finish in the ground state and not in an excited state of the Ising Hamiltonian [19]. The point at which $A(s) = B(s)$ is known as the quantum critical point (QCP), by analogy to the theory of phase transitions.

Equation 1 describes an ideal system of perfect qubits and perfect coupling. Physical devices have limitations, imperfections and inhomogenities, however. One major limitation of quantum annealers is qubit connectivity: not all qubit couplings can be realised; indeed most of the J_{ij} are zero (uncoupled). Another relevant limitation is that even potential couplings can be realised only within a certain range of values and only up to a certain precision. The first restricts the coupling range, and the second is a source of unwanted noise and decoherence. Similar issues affect the qubit biases h_i.

Consider the D-Wave 2000Q, which is the annealer we consider here. It is designed with 2048 qubits in the 'Chimera' architecture, which has 256 unit cells of 8 qubits, arranged in a 16×16 grid. There are connections between qubits inside unit cells and between qubits belonging to different unit cells. Figure 1 shows qubit connections in a 2×2 grid of unit cells. The yellow dots in the figure represent the qubits; in reality each qubit is an elongated superconducting loop oriented either horizontally or vertically. This and the differences highlighted before may be a source of inhomogeneity in the qubit performances. The full 2000Q chip creates the 16×16 unit cells by repeating the pattern shown in Fig. 1 eight times in either dimension and connecting them in the obvious way.

How a given problem is embedded into this (and other) fixed topologies is the subject of much research. There is often a requirement to use techniques such as chaining (achieving connections via intermediate qubits) to overcome the limitations [4,6,16,20]. This is typically done with an awareness of the overall chip error rate and how that affects the probability of success in practice [2]. Better characterisation of the individual qubits on the chip would allow for more intelligent and potentially real-time re-configuring embedding algorithms.

3   Exploring Spatial Correlations in the Los Alamos Data

In order to exploit maximum performance from a given quantum device, it is necessary to measure the performance of individual qubits and couplings in that device. Nelson *et al.* [12] perform repeated sampling of each qubit in their D-Wave 2000Q device through a range of input fields, in a process they refer to as QASA (Quantum Annealing Single-qubit Assessment). They extract values for four parameters: inverse temperature β, bias b, transverse field gain λ, and noise η.

When this QASA protocol is performed for all the qubits within a chip in parallel, the variations and correlations across the chip (a 16×16 grid of unit cells) can be analysed. The authors found that the orientation of the qubits

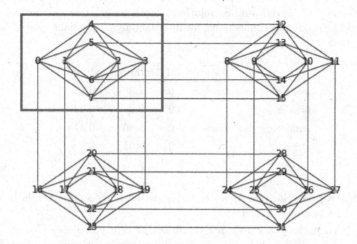

Fig. 1. A graph representation of the D-Wave Chimera architecture as present on the 2000Q quantum annealer. The red box shows the 8 qubits that make up a unit cell. (Diagram created using D-Wave NetworkX Python language package [7] (Color figure online).)

(horizontally or vertically aligned superconducting loops) is correlated with both the inverse temperature and transverse field gain parameters. They hypothesise that this could be due to "asymmetry in the chip's hardware layout or to the details of how global annealing control signals are delivered to the qubits" [12].

The Los Alamos National Laboratory (LANL) research group that performed this experiment have made the raw data available, which we use to perform further investigation into the presence of *spatial correlations* in the four parameters measured for each qubit in the chip, as described in this section.

To measure spatial correlations we use Geary's C, a number which determines whether adjacent measurements are correlated [8]. By adjacent here, we mean qubits that have connections between them, either internal and external to unit cells. C is defined as:

$$C = \frac{(n-1)\sum_i \sum_j w_{ij}(x_i - x_j)^2}{2\sum_i (x_i - \bar{x})^2 \sum_i \sum_j w_{ij}}, \tag{2}$$

where n is the number of qubits, x_i is the parameter value of qubit i, $\bar{x}$ is the mean value of parameter x, and w_{ij} is the connection weight between qubits i and j. We take $w_{ij} = 1$ for connected qubits, zero otherwise [21].

$C = 1$ represents no correlation, $C = 0$ a perfect positive correlation, and $C > 1$ an increasingly negative correlation (there is no fixed maximum values for negative correlation). Positive correlation refers to two variables that tend to move in the same direction. For example, in this case, it would mean that a node with a low bias value tends to be connected to other nodes with low bias

Table 1. Geary's C spatial auto-correlation of four parameters on the Los Alamos D-Wave 2000Q chip, for all connections, for internal only connections, and for external only connections.

	all	internal	external
inverse temperature, β	1.08	1.30	0.58
bias, b	0.93	0.93	0.92
transverse field gain, λ	1.06	1.40	0.32
noise, η	0.91	0.91	0.89

values. Negative correlations mean that the value of one node tends to oppose the value of its connected nodes.

The PySAL package includes a Python script that calculates Geary's C, but this could not be used in this case as it requires consecutively numbered nodes [17]. This data has a number of 'dead' qubits in the chip which are not included in the dictionaries of nodes and edges, so their indices are missing.

We calculate Geary's C for the entire dataset (Table 1, column titled "all"). The values are very close to 1, indicating little correlation between connected qubits in any of the parameters. This is maybe to be expected if the qubits are well isolated from one another.

We also calculate C for two subsets of the data: involving either just the connections internal to unit cells, or just between unit cells (external). The "all" column represents a weighted average of the "internal" and "external" columns; it was calculated using all the connections on the chip, of which there are more internal than external.

Table 1 shows that qubits that are connected *between* unit cells show a strong positive correlation in the inverse temperature and transverse field gain parameters, and still rather strong but negative correlations for internal connections within unit cells. Here we label correlations as 'strong' when there is more than 10% difference from the global value found in the "all" column.

We might expect that internal connections would correspond to physically closer qubits, and therefore more positively correlated properties, but this does not seem to be the case for these parameters. We do not actually know the physical distances between qubits in the D-Wave system: the graphical representation in Fig. 1 is just a schematic, and does not show the real lengths of the different connections. When more details on the physical hardware realisation become available, it will be important to confirm if physical separation distance is responsible for the observed correlation between qubits.

4 Investigating Different Connection Strengths on Dynamics

In the LANL QASA experiment, all the connection weights are set to zero, in order to isolate the qubits from any coupling effects. Nevertheless, differences are seen in correlations between internal (to the unit cell) and externally coupled qubits, implying some holdover effect.

Here we investigate correlations explicitly due to coupling strengths that vary due to different coupling lengths. Due to the planar architecture of the chip, links must be of different physical lengths in order to connect qubits both within and between unit cells. Such physical differences could contribute to differing behaviours of qubits.

The spins in a spin network can represent any type of qubit, including the superconducting qubits used in the D-Wave chip. A spin network is a mathematically general model for this purpose. We have developed a spin network simulator in Python that takes as input a network (based on the Chimera qubit layout shown in Fig. 1) and emulates the natural state dynamics of this is network when one qubit is set to $|1\rangle$ and all other to state $|0\rangle$ at $t = 0$. The connection weights can be scaled based on relative ratios of their representative lengths in the diagram. We test a small simulated network with and without the spin-spin coupling weights having been scaled to their respective lengths.

4.1   Methodology

The qubits in the D-Wave chip are physically implemented by rf-SQUIDs (radio frequency Superconducting Quantum-Interference Devices) and the couplings are implemented by Compound Josephson-junction rf-SQUIDs [9]. The way the physical length of a coupling affects its performance is based on the underlying physical processes. We chose to investigate repulsive dipole-dipole interactions, which scale with distance as

$$J \propto \frac{1}{r^3} \tag{3}$$

to represent the physical interactions taking place within the system. Equation (3) describes well the dominant qubit-qubit interaction for various qubits' physical realisations. Other types of interaction are possible, including interactions beyond nearest neighbours, and will be subject of future investigations. We compare against a control case where all coupling weights are equal (corresponding to an N-d hypercube layout).

All the coupling strengths are scaled based on the shortest connection having a weight of 1. This value is chosen because when the D-Wave chip is operated under normal conditions, all the given coupling weights are rescaled to lie between -1 and 1. We expect the same behaviour for both attractive and repulsive connections so we restrict the experiment to coupling weights between 0 and 1.

The procedure for defining the Hamiltonian matrix of the simulation is given in Algorithm 1. The required inputs define the spin network model as a list of nodes and edges numbered according to Fig. 1. The positions (relative coordinates) of the nodes are hard coded into the simulator based on the graphical representation of the chip shown in Fig. 1. This section of the code produces an $N \times N$ matrix (the Hamiltonian) where the diagonal terms represent the qubit biases (the h_i values in Eq. 1) and the other terms are the coupling weights (J_{ij}).

Algorithm 1. Create Hamiltonian Matrix(*NodeList, EdgeList, ScalingType*)

1: ds := EucLengths(EdgeList)   ▷ Distances; Edge lengths are Euclidean distance
   between the nodes
2: NodeList, EdgeList := Remap(NodeList, EdgeList)   ▷ Remap from native qubit
   indices to ordered range (0,N)
3: M := 2D array of size (N, N)   ▷ Initialise the Hamiltonian matrix
4: **for** idx, item in *EdgeList* **do**
5:     **if** ScalingFactor = Constant **then**
6:         $J := J0$
7:     **else if** ScalingFactor = Dipole **then**
8:         $J := J0 \cdot (min(ds)/ds[idx])^3$
9:     **end if**
10:     M[item[0], item[1]] := J
11:     M[item[1], item[0]] := J
12: **end for**
13: **return** M

If there is an edge connecting nodes i and j, then $0 < J_{ij} \leq 1$ otherwise $J_{ij} = 0$. The resulting matrix is symmetric: $J_{ij} = J_{ji}$. In this simulation, we assume all the qubit biases to have the same value, and hence, as the total energy is defined up to a constant, they can be set to zero: $h_i = 0$.

The Hamiltonian matrix is used to simulate the time evolution dynamics using a method described e.g. in Mortimer *et al.* [10]. This involves solving Schrödinger's equation by expanding $|\Psi(t)\rangle$, the state of the system at any time, in terms of the eigenvectors of the Hamiltonian. This is the preferred method over time step iterations as it doesn't accumulate errors due to the state at each time being calculated directly from the initial state. From the result of this algorithm, the probability of the excitation being measured at each node at each time step can be derived as $|\langle i|\Psi(t)\rangle|^2$, with $|i\rangle$ a shorthand for the state describing the excitation being localised at node i. This is referred to as the fidelity of measuring an excitation at a particular node at a particular time.

A small network with 8 qubits spread over 4 units cells was used for the investigation, this is shown in Fig. 2.

4.2   Results and Discussion

In order to consider how the node coupling affects the system dynamics and therefore the spatial correlations in the system, we define a time window within which to consider the information (excitation) transfer through the network. The time window goes from $t = 0$ to $t = 1/J_{min}$, where J_{min} refers to the smallest coupling weight in the system. This time window was chosen because in real quantum devices, the relevant time scales over which operations can be performed is dependent on the strength of the couplings between the qubits. The gating time between nearby qubits can be estimated as the inverse of their coupling strength $\sim 1/J$, so $t = 1/J_{min}$ corresponds roughly to the longest gating time in the system, and we can expect the excitation to have propagated

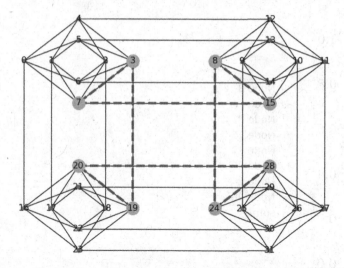

Fig. 2. Model coded for simulations. The blue connections and the yellow nodes are those used in the simulation. The remaining nodes and connections are shown in black and have been included for completeness. (Color figure online)

through the network by that time. Also, within this time, it is reasonable to expect that, in hardware designed for quantum computation, decoherence effects are still extremely low and hence the probability of errors due to additional (and unwanted) interactions remains negligible. Effects of fabrication errors can be taken into consideration within the proposed model, e.g. following Ronke *et. al* [18], however before doing this more information on the hardware details would be desirable. Within this time window, we consider the excitation fidelity at two specific times: The time at which the first peak in the time window occurs; and the time at which the maximum peak (excluding the initial node) occurs. At these times, the excitation fidelity of all nodes in the system can be measured and compared to infer the correlation between connected nodes.

In the 8 node network (Fig. 2), each node has one internal and one external connection. All the internal connections are the same length and the external connections are either vertical or horizontal with different lengths. The excitation begins on node 3 at time $t = 0$. This node is connected to nodes 7 and 19 with the couplings either weighted equally, or with a dipole-dipole interaction according to their length.

With constant (length independent) couplings we expect the fidelities of nodes 7 and 19 to have the same dynamics; this is shown in Fig. 3(a) with the behaviour for node 7 being exactly overlaid by that of node 19.

With dipole-dipole couplings, we expect nodes 7 and 19 to behave differently: the longer external connection here has a coupling strength of only 11% of that of the shorter internal connection. So the shorter connection (to node 7) gives rise to larger fidelity peak, and the longer (to node 19) gives a smaller peak within the considered time-window. This is a weak enough connection to prevent

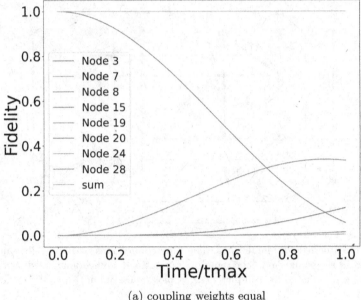

(a) coupling weights equal

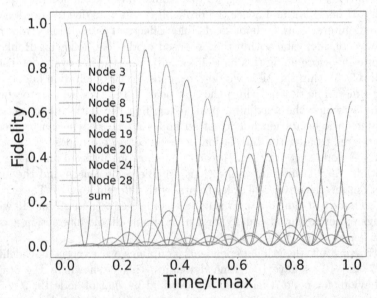

(b) coupling weights scaled like dipole-dipole interactions

Fig. 3. System dynamics of the 8 node network.

noticeable peaks in node 19 until approximately $t = 0.2t_{max}$ allowing for a near perfect state transfer between nodes 3 and 7.

The networks have a high degree of symmetry and a cyclic nature which means any excitation transfer to a node could have come via a number of different routes. The 8-node case is topologically equivalent to a single loop. The excitation could travel around the network both clockwise and anticlockwise passing through each connection once, as well as in any combination of "backwards" and "forwards" steps. More exactly, since this is a quantum system, the fidelities correspond to the probability of the excitation being measured at the node in question at each time step. The fidelity for each node at each time step includes all the possible routes that the excitation could have taken to be measured at that node.

To investigate potential spatial correlations, we show the results for the 8N node network, at $t = maxPeak$ and $t = firstPeak$ in Fig. 4. The red node indicates the location of the initial excitation. In the first peak dynamics, it is clear that when the nodes have constant coupling, the edges (3,7) and (3,19) behave identically. When there are dipole-dipole interactions, there is large difference in excitation transfer across these connections with the short connection producing the highest excitation transfer within the observed time window.

In the constant coupling case, the maximum peak in the time window is also the first peak seen but in the dipole-dipole coupling case the first peak occurs at node 19 whilst the maximum peak is in node 7. At the time of the first peak, node 7 has higher fidelity than node 19 but is still building up and has not yet peaked. This implies that at both peaks, the probability of measuring the excitation at node 7 is higher than at node 19.

As well as considering the overall dynamics, to better compare this simulation to the LANL experiments, we also compared the fidelities of all connected nodes. These results are shown in Fig. 5, where each square represents the edge connecting the nodes labelled at its x and y positions. These squares are then coloured by the similarity in the fidelities of the nodes at either end of this edge and are labelled with the normalised connection lengths for reference. The similarity is defined here as,

$$sim = 1 - |f_i - f_j| \tag{4}$$

where f_i and f_j represent the fidelities of the ith and j^{th} node respectively. Therefore if two nodes have similar fidelities, the similarity value is maximum.

At $t = firstPeak$ it is only relevant to consider the top left of the charts as the fidelity of all but the closest 5 nodes from node 3 are all still very close to 0 which means that the similarity between connected nodes is very close to 1.

In the constant case, we expect the length of the connection to have no effect on the similarity between the connect nodes. Although this is the case in the first row of Fig. 5, in the other rows, this is not the case. We suggest that this is an effect of the fidelity being comprised of the probability of all the different paths that the excitation could have taken from one node to the other. This is a direct effect of the connectivity of the network.

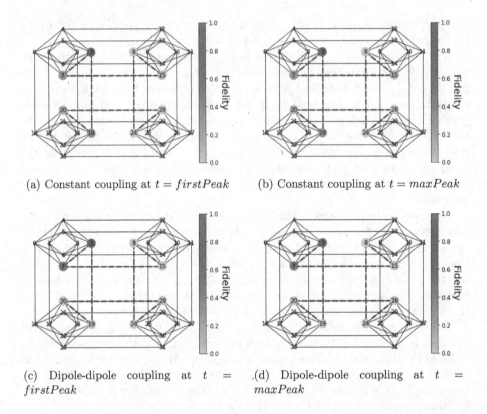

(a) Constant coupling at $t = firstPeak$ (b) Constant coupling at $t = maxPeak$

(c) Dipole-dipole coupling at $t = firstPeak$ (d) Dipole-dipole coupling at $t = maxPeak$

Fig. 4. Node fidelities at two different times with two different coupling.

In the dipole-dipole case, the results are further complicated by the changing connection strengths between the nodes. Intuitively we would expect that a shorter connection length would cause a higher degree of similarity between the nodes. This is not seen at either of the time steps chosen for evaluation here. The charts from the dipole-dipole simulation are noticeably different from the constant case showing that couplings that are affected by physical length will affect the spatial correlations in the system. Because the connectivity is the same in both simulations, the differences must be due to the couplings.

The difference between the constant and dipole-dipole couplings at $t = maxPeak$ is that in the dipole-dipole case, the excitation fidelity is much more concentrated at a small number of nodes meaning that the similarity of these nodes with the others is particularly low. In the constant coupling case, the excitation fidelity is more evenly spread (as seen in Fig. 4) which means that neighbouring nodes have higher spatial correlation.

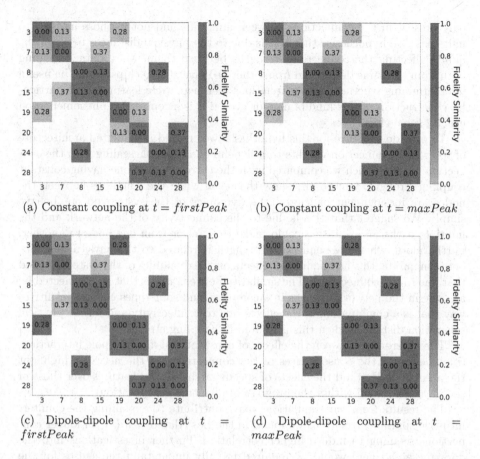

(a) Constant coupling at $t = firstPeak$

(b) Constant coupling at $t = maxPeak$

(c) Dipole-dipole coupling at $t = firstPeak$

(d) Dipole-dipole coupling at $t = maxPeak$

Fig. 5. The similarity in the fidelity of connected nodes in the 8 node Chimera architecture. A square at (i,j) is labelled with the relative length of the connection between the nodes i and j and is colourised by the similarity as defined by Eq. 4.

The similarity between connected nodes is affected both by the connectivity of the network as well as the coupling between nodes. This combination gives rise to complex phenomena. This complexity might explain why in the Los Alamos data the longer connections give rise to strong positive correlation. This simulated network only contains 8 nodes, the full D-Wave 2000Q chip contains 2048 qubits (including some 'dead' ones). The connectivity in the full chip means that the effects seen in the constant coupling case here would be even more pronounced.

5 Conclusions and Future Work

We have shown that there are strong positive spatial correlations in the qubits measured as part of the LANL study on single qubit fidelity beyond the horizontal/vertical delineation shown in the original paper [12]. These correlations are only present in the connections between unit cells and not in those internal to unit cells. We hypothesise that this is due to the physical distances between the qubits affecting the connection strengths between them. More data, including both from the same device and from other D-Wave 2000Q chips, would be useful in determining whether these correlations seen here are a feature of the particular construction of this kind of chip or even if it is a repeatable phenomenon on exactly same chip.

To provide evidence for this hypothesis, we created a simulated architecture of spins with connection weights that depend on a variable scaling with the connection length, which we compared with the corresponding one having constant coupling strength. Our results show that even when the couplings between the nodes are independent of length, the dynamics of the system do not behave simply. We suggest that this is due to the connectivity of the network and the multiple paths an excitation could make to transfer from one node to another. Furthermore, when the connection strength is related to the physical distance between qubits, this has significant effects on the dynamics of the system beyond that due to the connectivity. The similarity between nodes that are connected by an edge in the network behaves in a complex (and sometimes counter-intuitive) way that is a combination of the effects due to connectivity and due to physical separation distance (when this is related to coupling strength).

The differences between the effects of constant and dipole-dipole interaction, combined with the consequences of the connectivity of the network, highlight the need to understand the effects of specific architectural features over those of the idealised model within the progress of quantum computation.

The results from our simulations may contribute to explaining the counter-intuitive spatial correlations we found in the Los Alamos data, with longer connections seeming to induce higher correlation. Further investigations into the data presented here would be required to fully understand the causes for the spatial correlation seen in the D-Wave 2000Q chip. It would also be beneficial to see how the effects seen here scale up with larger simulated networks, different coupling interactions and longer time periods. These results are to be presented in an upcoming paper.

Further analysis of a real quantum annealing chip would be able to confirm how closely the effects displayed here affect the dynamics during a quantum annealing cycle.

Acknowledgements. The authors wish to acknowledge Defence Science Technical Laboratory (Dstl) who are funding this research. We thank Carleton Coffrin and his colleagues at the Los Alamos National Laboratory for sharing the data from their Single Qubit Fidelity Assessment.

References

1. Ahn, C., Doherty, A.C., Landahl, A.J.: Continuous quantum error correction via quantum feedback control. Phys. Rev. A **65**(4), 042301 (2002)
2. Albash, T., Martin-Mayor, V., Hen, I.: Analog errors in Ising machines. Quant. Sci. Technol. **4**(2), 02LT03 (2019)
3. Bandic, M., Feld, S., Almudever, C.G.: Full-stack quantum computing systems in the NISQ era: algorithm-driven and hardware-aware compilation techniques. In: 2022 Design, Automation and Test in Europe Conference and Exhibition (DATE), pp. 1–6. IEEE (2022)
4. Barbosa, A., Pelofske, E., Hahn, G., Djidjev, H.N.: Optimizing embedding-related quantum annealing parameters for reducing hardware bias. In: Ning, L., Chau, V., Lau, F. (eds.) PAAP 2020. CCIS, vol. 1362, pp. 162–173. Springer, Singapore (2021). https://doi.org/10.1007/978-981-16-0010-4_15
5. Bharti, K., Cervera-Lierta, A., Kyaw, T.H., Haug, T., Alperin-Lea, S., Anand, A., Degroote, M., Heimonen, H., Kottmann, J.S., Menke, T., Mok, W.K., Sim, S., Kwek, L.C., Aspuru-Guzik, A.: Noisy intermediate-scale quantum algorithms. Rev. Mod. Phys. **94**(1), 015004 (2022)
6. Chancellor, N., Zohren, S., Warburton, P.A.: Circuit design for multi-body interactions in superconducting quantum annealing systems with applications to a scalable architecture. NPJ Quant. Inf. **3**(1), 1–7 (2017)
7. D-Wave Systems: D-Wave NetworkX (2021)
8. Geary, R.C.: The contiguity ratio and statistical mapping. Incorp. Stat. **5**(3), 115–146 (1954)
9. Harris, R., et al.: Compound Josephson-junction coupler for flux qubits with minimal crosstalk. Phys. Rev. B: Condens. Matter **80**(5), 052506 (2009)
10. Mortimer, L., Estarellas, M.P., Spiller, T.P., D'Amico, I.: Evolutionary computation for adaptive quantum device design. Adv. Quantum Technol. **4**(8) (2021)
11. Nelson, J., Vuffray, M., Lokhov, A.Y., Albash, T., Coffrin, C.: High-quality thermal Gibbs sampling with quantum annealing hardware. Phys. Rev. Appl. **17**(4), 044046 (2022)
12. Nelson, J., Vuffray, M., Lokhov, A.Y., Coffrin, C.: Single-qubit fidelity assessment of quantum annealing hardware. IEEE Trans. Quantum Eng. **2**, 1–10 (2021)
13. Noiri, A., et al.: A fast quantum interface between different spin qubit encodings. Nat. Commun. **9**(1), 5066 (2018)
14. Osada, A., Taniguchi, K., Shigefuji, M., Noguchi, A.: Feasibility study on ground-state cooling and single-phonon readout of trapped electrons using hybrid quantum systems. Phys. Rev. Res. **4**(3), 033245 (2022)
15. Pudenz, K.L., Albash, T., Lidar, D.A.: Error-corrected quantum annealing with hundreds of qubits. Nat. Commun. **5**, 3243 (2014)
16. Raymond, J., Ndiaye, N., Rayaprolu, G., King, A.D.: Improving performance of logical qubits by parameter tuning and topology compensation. In: 2020 IEEE International Conference on Quantum Computing and Engineering (QCE), pp. 295–305 (2020)
17. Rey, S.J., Anselin, L.: PySAL: a Python library of spatial analytical methods. In: Fischer, M.M., Getis, A. (eds.) Handbook of Applied Spatial Analysis: Software Tools, Methods and Applications, pp. 175–193. Springer, Heidelberg (2010). https://doi.org/10.1007/978-3-642-03647-7_11
18. Ronke, R., Spiller, T.P., D'Amico, I.: Effect of perturbations on information transfer in spin chains. Phys. Rev. A **83**(1), 012325 (2011)

19. Venegas-Andraca, S.E., Cruz-Santos, W., McGeoch, C., Lanzagorta, M.: A cross-disciplinary introduction to quantum annealing-based algorithms. Contemp. Phys. **59**(02), 174–196 (2018)
20. Zbinden, S., Bärtschi, A., Djidjev, H., Eidenbenz, S.: Embedding algorithms for quantum annealers with Chimera and Pegasus connection topologies. In: Sadayappan, P., Chamberlain, B., Juckeland, G., Ltaief, H. (eds.) ISC High Performance 2020, vol. 12151, pp. 187–206. Springer, Cham (2020). https://doi.org/10.1007/978-3-030-50743-5_10
21. Zhou, X., Lin, H.: Geary's C. In: Shekhar, S., Xiong, H. (eds.) Encyclopedia of GIS, pp. 329–330. Springer, Boston (2008). https://doi.org/10.1007/978-0-387-35973-1_446

Simulation of Multiple Stages in Single Bin Active Tile Self-assembly

Sonya C. Cirlos[1], Timothy Gomez[2](✉), Elise Grizzell[1], Andrew Rodriguez[1], Robert Schweller[1], and Tim Wylie[1]

[1] University of Texas Rio Grande Valley, Edinburg, TX 78539, USA
{sonya.cirlos01,elise.grizzell01,andrew.rodriguez09,robert.schweller,
timothy.wylie}@utrgv.edu
[2] Massachusetts Institute of Technology, Cambridge, MA 02139, USA
tagomez7@mit.edu

Abstract. Two significant and often competing goals within the field of self-assembly are minimizing tile types and minimizing human-mediated experimental operations. The introduction of the Staged Assembly and Single Staged Assembly models, while successful in the former aim, necessitate an increase in mixing operations later. In this paper, we investigate building optimal lines as a standard benchmark shape and building primitive. We show that a restricted version of the 1D Staged Assembly Model can be simulated by the 1D Freezing Tile Automata model with the added benefits of the complete automation of stages and completion in a single bin while maintaining bin parallelism and a competitive number of states for lines, patterned lines, and context-free grammars.

1 Introduction

Many molecular programmers dream of designing single-pot reactions in which system molecules do the entirety of the computational work without any necessary intervention by the experimenter. This is arguably *true* self-assembly. Yet the power of experimenter intervention, in the form of mixing and splitting pots over a sequence of stages, yields power and efficiency in both theory and practice [16] that is currently unmatched even with some of the most powerful models of active self-assembly. This paper aims to address this gap in the case of 1-dimensional (1D) assembly by showing how an abstract modeling of operations of experimental stages, termed the Staged Assembly Model (SAM) [12], can be efficiently simulated by an abstract model of single-pot *active* self-assembly, termed Tile Automata (TA) [9].

Tile Automata generalizes *passive* tile assembly models (such as the two-handed tile assembly model [7]) by giving tiles dynamic states that update based on local pair-wise rules, thus making it a model of *active* self-assembly. The Staged Assembly Model (SAM) generalizes tile assembly models by the modeling of experimenter-mediated operations, including the ability to store different

This research was supported in part by National Science Foundation Grant CCF-1817602.

portions of the system particles in separate containers or *bins*, and the ability to combine separate bins, or split the contents of a bin among multiple bins, over a sequence of distinct *stages*. Previous results show that both models have substantially increased power over the basic tile self-assembly models they generalize. In particular, by offloading some of the computation onto an experimenter responsible for performing the required mixing operations of the system between stages, SAM can build complex shapes and patterns in near-optimal complexity with respect to tile types, bin counts, and stage counts [10–13,18].

In answer to the long-standing open question of whether the substantial power of the SAM could be efficiently encoded into the reaction rules of an active single-pot system, this paper shows that in the case of 1-dimensional systems, any staged system can be encoded into a single-pot TA system with a comparable state and rule space to the tiles, bins, and stages of the SAM system it simulates. This result provides a corresponding corollary in TA for any results in 1D staged self-assembly. Further, this provides a new approach for programming 1D TA systems since designing staged systems is relatively simple with strong timing guarantees based on separate bins and stages, whereas programming complex TA systems from scratch can be daunting as the single-pot nature of the system requires careful attention to race conditions. As evidence of the power of this new result, we show how several previous results in TA now become simple corollaries of this new result. Further, we show how a general linear pattern can be constructed in TA using a number of states linear in the size of the smallest context-free grammar that produces the target pattern.

1.1   Staged Self-assembly and Tile Automata

Algorithmic self-assembly emerged from a formalization of Wang Tiles to explore self-assembling structures. Defined by Winfree in [17], this was partially motivated by new DNA techniques that allow for the creation of DNA-based 'tiles' that can assemble into lattice structures at the nanoscale [19]. Further experimental work has investigated active DNA-based components capable of complex tasks such as sorting molecules attached to a DNA origami surface [15].

The Staged Tile Assembly Model [12] generalizes the 2-Handed Assembly Model to allow growth to occur in multiple bins, mixing in a sequence described as stages, creating the capability to model experimental techniques, such as in [16] where 2D patterns are built with DNA origami tiles in multiple stages.

Tile Automata was introduced in [9] as a combination of hierarchical passive self-assembly systems and the active self-assembly of Cellular Automata systems where all *tiles* have a transitionable *state*. Affinity rules define which tiles can bond with each other based on their states and with how much strength. Starting from singleton tiles with states, any two producibles in the system may combine if there is enough affinity between adjacent tiles. Transition rules define state changes that may occur between two tiles once they are neighbors in an assembly.

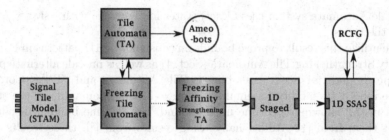

Fig. 1. Informal map of relations between models. Dotted line arrows indicate model is a special case of the previous. Solid lines indicate simulation results.

1.2   Related Work

Shape building was the first problem explored when the staged model was introduced [12]. In the staged model, a constant-sized set of glue types is sufficient to build any shape by encoding the description in the mix graph. The trade-off between the number of glues, bins, and stages was further investigated in later work with $1 \times n$, $\mathcal{O}(1) \times n$ [11], and general assemblies [10]. The complexity of verifying whether an assembly is uniquely produced is PSPACE-complete [6,14].

A restricted class of systems in SAM, called Single Staged Assembly Systems (SSAS) in [13], requires each bin to only contain one terminal assembly built from two input assemblies. This restriction eliminates having multiple assemblies built in the same bin (*bin parallelism*). The size of the smallest SSAS that builds a 1D pattern $\mathcal{P}$ is equivalent (up to constant factors) to the size of the smallest Context-Free Grammar (CFG) that defines only $\mathcal{P}$. However, when bin parallelism is allowed, staged is more efficient than CFGs for a specific family of strings.

In [18], they built on previous results and define Polyomino Context-Free Grammars (PCFG), which generalize CFGs to 2D. The size of the smallest staged system that uniquely produces a patterned assembly is within a log factor of the smallest PCFG. In some cases, staged is much better.

One strength of Tile Automata is the possibility of being a "unifying" model, where multiple models can be connected through simulation results. The work that introduced the model [9] showed that the freezing model, where a tile may never repeat a state, simulates the non-freezing version of the model. Tile Automata was shown to simulate a model of programmable matter called Amoebots [2]. The chain of simulation was further extended in [8] where the Signal-Passing Tile Assembly Model (STAM) was shown to simulate Tile Automata. Work done in [3] shows how the 1D STAM can simulate a s stage 1D SSAS system using a single tile with $\mathcal{O}(s^4)$ glues types (Fig. 1).

1.3   Our Contributions

We show that the 1D version of Freezing Affinity Strengthening Tile Automata can simulate the 1D staged assembly model, even with flexible glues (Sect. 3).

The Tile Automata system uses $\mathcal{O}(sbt)$ states for a system with s stages, b bins, and t tile types.

We utilize this result to prove bounds on constructing 1D patterns in Freezing Affinity Strengthening Tile Automata (Sect. 4) as well as provide alternate proofs of upper bounds for linear assemblies in Tile Automata and STAM (Corollary 1). We inherit the ability to simulate Context-Free Grammars from the staged model in [13] showing the same upper bound. For the line building results we inherit them from [12] Additionally using results from [8], these results carry over to the STAM as well.

2   Model and Definitions

We provide simplified definitions for 1D Tile Automata, then define 1D Staged Assembly as a generalization. Refer to previous work [1,12] for full definitions of the models.

2.1   The 1D Tile Automata Model (TA)

In this dimensionally restricted version of the model, a *Tile Automata system*[1] is a triple (Σ, Π, Δ) where Σ is an alphabet of state types, Π is an affinity function, and Δ is a set of transition rules for states in Σ. An example 1D Tile Automata system is shown in Fig. 2.

Tile. Let Σ be a set of *states* or symbols. A tile $t = (\sigma, p)$ is a non-rotatable unit square placed at point $p \in \mathbb{Z}^1$ and has a state of $\sigma \in \Sigma$.

Assembly. An assembly A is a sequence of tiles $\{t_1, t_2, t_3, \ldots, t_{|A|}\}$. Let $A(i)$ and $A_\Sigma(i)$ represent the ith tile and its state in assembly A, respectively. For a tile t in assembly A let $\rho_A(t)$ be the position of t in A.

Affinity Function. An *affinity function* Π takes an ordered pair in Σ^2 as input and outputs either 0 or 1. The *affinity strength* between two states for the ordered orientation is the binary output of the corresponding function. An assembly A is *stable* if, for every pair of tiles, $\Pi(A_\Sigma(i), A_\Sigma(i+1)) = 1$. Informally, if all adjacent tiles in assembly A have an affinity, A is stable. Two assembles, A and B are *combinable* if the concatenation of the two assemblies $AB = C$ is also a stable assembly.

Transition Rules. Transition rules allow states to change based on their neighbors. A *transition rule* is denoted $(\sigma_{1a}, \sigma_{2a}) \rightarrow (\sigma_{1b}, \sigma_{2b})$ with $\sigma_{1a}, \sigma_{2a}, \sigma_{1b}, \sigma_{2b} \in \Sigma$. If states σ_{1a} and σ_{2a} are adjacent to each other, they can transition to states σ_{1b} and σ_{2b}, respectively. An assembly A is *transitionable* to an assembly B if there exists two adjacent tiles $A(i), A(i+1) \in A$, two adjacent tiles

---

[1] Typical TA models are defined with a temperature parameter τ however, with consideration of solely 1D, eliminating the possibility of cooperative binding, we assume $\tau = 1$.

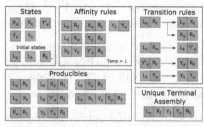

(a) A Tile Automata System

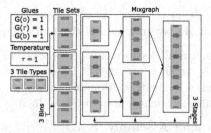

(b) Staged Self-Assembly Example

Fig. 2. (a) An example of a Tile Automata system Γ. Recursively applying the transition rules and affinity functions to the initial assemblies of a system yields a set of producible assemblies. Any producibles that cannot combine with, break into, or transition to another assembly are considered terminal. Note that none of the transition rules allow states to change color. (b) A simple staged self-assembly example. The system has 3 bins, 3 stages, and 3 tile types, assigned to bins, as shown in the mix graph. Only terminal assemblies can pass to a successive stage. The result of this system is the assembly shown in the bin in stage 3.

$B(i), B(i+1) \in B$, a transition rule $(A_\Sigma(i), A_\Sigma(i+1)) \to (B_\Sigma(i), B_\Sigma(i+1)) \in \Delta$, and $A(j) = B(j)$ for all $j \neq i, i+1$.

Affinity Strengthening. *Affinity Strengthening* requires that any transition preserves affinities between tiles within assemblies. For each transition rule $(\sigma_a, \sigma_b) \to (\sigma_c, \sigma_d)$, $\Pi(\sigma_c, \sigma_d) = 1$. By limiting our focus to affinity strengthening systems, we do not need to consider the scenario where a stable assembly becomes unstable (and would fall apart).

Freezing. In a freezing system, a tile may not transition to any state more than once. Thus, if a tile with state σ_a transitions into another state σ_b, it is not allowed to transition back to σ_a.

Producibility. We define the set of producible assemblies starting from a set of initial assemblies Λ. For a given 1D Tile Automata system $\Gamma = (\Sigma, \Pi, \Delta)$ and initial assembly set Λ, the set of *producible assemblies* of Γ, denoted $\text{PROD}_\Gamma(\Lambda)$, is defined recursively:

- (Base) $\Lambda \subseteq \text{PROD}_\Gamma(\Lambda)$
- (Combinations) For any $A, B \in \text{PROD}_\Gamma(\Lambda)$ s.t. A and B are combinable into C, then $C \in \text{PROD}_\Gamma(\Lambda)$.
- (Transitions) For any $A \in \text{PROD}_\Gamma(\Lambda)$ s.t. A is transitionable into B using $\delta \in \Delta$, then $B \in \text{PROD}_\Gamma(\Lambda)$.

For a system Γ, we say $A \to_1^\Gamma B$ for assemblies A and B if A is combinable with some producible assembly to form B, if A is transitionable into B, or if $A = B$. Intuitively, this means that A may grow into assembly B through one or fewer combinations or transitions.

We define the relation $\to^{\Gamma}$ to be the transitive closure of $\to_1^{\Gamma}$, i.e., $A \to^{\Gamma} B$ means that A may grow into B through a sequence of combinations and transitions.

Terminal Assemblies. A producible assembly A of a Tile Automata system Γ is *terminal* provided A is not combinable with any producible assembly of Γ, and A is not transitionable to any producible assembly of Γ. Let $\text{TERM}_{\Gamma}(\Lambda) \subseteq \text{PROD}_{\Gamma}(\Lambda)$ denote the set of producible assemblies of Γ that are terminal.

Unique Assembly. A 1D TA system Γ, starting from initial assemblies Λ, *uniquely produces* a set of assemblies $\mathcal{A}$ if

- $\mathcal{A} = \text{TERM}_{\Gamma}(\Lambda)$,
- for all $B \in \text{PROD}_{\Gamma}(\Lambda)$, $B \to^{\Gamma} A$ for some $A \in \mathcal{A}$

2.2 Staged Assembly Model

Here, we define the Staged Assembly model using the definitions from above.

Tile Types and Glues. In the staged assembly model, tiles are defined by their glues. Let G be a set of glues. A *tile type* is an ordered pair of glues $(w, e) \in G^2$ where tile $t = (w, e)$ has west glue w and east glue e. The affinity function Π for the staged assembly model takes as input two tile types $t_1 = (a, b)$, $t_2 = (c, d)$ and outputs 1 if $b = c$ and 0 otherwise.

When allowing *Flexible Glues* we remove the restriction that Π outputs 0 when $b \neq c$ allowing for a general glue function. *Note this is equivalent to the affinity function of Tile Automata.*

Assembly. An assembly A in a staged assembly system is a sequence of tile types $\{t_1, t_2, t_3, \ldots, t_{|A|}\}$. Let $A(i)$ be the ith tile type in assembly A.

Staged Assembly Systems. An *r-stage, b-bin mix-graph* $M_{r,b}$, is an acyclic r-partite digraph consisting of rb vertices $m_{i,j}$ for $1 \leq i \leq r$ and $1 \leq j \leq b$, and edges of the form $(m_{i,j}, m_{i+1,j'})$ for some i, j, j'. A *staged assembly system* is a duple $\Upsilon = (M_{r,b}, T)$ where $M_{r,b}$ is an r-stage, b-bin mix-graph, $T \subset G^2$ is a set of tiles types labeled from the set of pairs of glues G.

Two-Handed Assembly and Bins. We define the assembly process in terms of bins[2]. Each bin can be considered an instance of a Tile Automata system without transition rules where $\Delta = \emptyset$. However, each bin has a different set of initial assemblies denoted as $\Lambda_{i,j}$ where i is the stage and j is the bin. Let T_j be the set of initial tile types in bin j.

1. $\Lambda_{1,j} = \{T_j\}$ (this is a bin in the first stage);
2. For $i \geq 2$, $\Lambda_{i,j} = \left(\bigcup_{k:\ (m_{i-1,k}, m_{i,j}) \in M_{r,b}} \text{TERM}_{\Upsilon}(\Lambda_{i-1,k}) \right)$.

Thus, the jth bin in stage 1 is provided with the initial tile set T_j. Each bin in any later stage receives an initial set of assemblies consisting of the terminally

---

[2] Each bin may be seen as an instance of the 2-Handed Assembly Model.

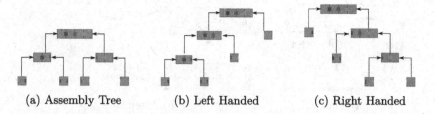

| (a) Assembly Tree | (b) Left Handed | (c) Right Handed |

Fig. 3. Examples of assembly trees for the same assembly. (a) A balanced tree. (b) A left-handed assembly tree. (c) A right-handed assembly tree.

produced assemblies' bins in the previous stage indicated by the edges of the mix-graph. The *output* of the staged system is the union of all terminal assemblies from each bin in the final stage. We say this set of output assemblies is *uniquely produced* if each bin in the staged system uniquely produces its respective set of terminal assemblies.

2.3 Assembly Trees

We may represent the assembly process in a single bin as an assembly tree in the staged model. An example tree can be seen in Fig. 3a.

Definition 1 (Assembly Tree). *An assembly tree T_A^b, for a producible assembly A in a bin b, is a binary tree where each node represents a subassembly of A. The root represents assembly A, and each leaf represents an initial assembly of b. Each node can be formed by combining the assemblies represented by the children.*

An assembly tree is a *Left-Handed* Assembly Tree if every assembly that attaches on the right side is an initial assembly. A *Right-Handed* Assembly Tree is the inverse where every left assembly is an initial assembly. Examples of these two types of trees are in Figs. 3b and 3c.

3 Simulation of General 1D Staged

In this section, we show how to simulate all 1D staged systems with TA systems. First, we define what simulate means for these systems, followed by a high-level overview of our simulation, and then the details.

3.1 Simulation

Here, we utilize a simplified definition of simulation in which the set of final terminal assemblies, from the *target* staged system to be simulated, is exactly the same, under a mapping function, as the final terminal assemblies of the *source* TA system that is simulating it. This is a standard type of simulation

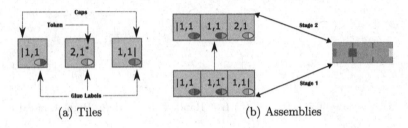

(a) Tiles   (b) Assemblies

Fig. 4. (a) Each of our Tile Automata states conceptually represents two glue labels that say which tile type they map to (a glue may be null, as in the leftmost state). They may also contain features such as the left/right cap or the active state token. (b) Assemblies map based on the glue labels on the Tile Automata states. Multiple Tile Automata assemblies represent the same Staged assembly, but sometimes in different stages.

used, and we omit technical definitions in this version. A stronger definition of simulation incorporates *dynamics*, in which assemblies may attach in the target system if and only if they attach in the source system. However, our approach focuses on simulating a restricted set of dynamics that are sufficient to ensure the production of all final (and partial) assemblies. We leave the problem of fully simulating the dynamics of a staged system as future work (Fig. 4).

3.2 Overview

We create a Tile Automata system with initial tiles representing the initial tile types of the staged system. Each assembly in our Tile Automata system represents an assembly in a specific stage and bin. Each state is a pair consisting of a tile type t and a stage-bin label representing t in that specific stage and bin. Some states will have an *active state token*(*) used to track the progress of the Tile Automata assembly in the assembly tree. We simulate only left- or right-handed assembly trees based on the parity of the stage number. The logic for the transition rules is described in Algorithm 1 using a *Glue-Terminal Table*. Each Tile Automata assembly builds according to the assembly trees of the staged system by having the token "read" the glues to decide if an assembly is terminal in a bin and needs to transition to the next stage.

3.3 Glue-Terminal Table

For the simulation to work, we need to know the glues used in each bin of the target system because we cannot "read" the absence of a glue/assembly in self-assembly. However, we can use the Glue-Terminal Table to construct the transition rules. This table stores which glues correspond with each bin.

Definition 2 (Glue-Terminal Table). *For a staged system $\Upsilon = (M_{r,b}, T)$, the Glue-Terminal table $GT((s,b),g)$ is a binary $|M_{r,b}| \times G$ table with rows labeled with stage-bin pairs and columns labeled with glues. The entry $GT((s,b),g)$ is*

Algorithm 1: Algorithm to create transition rules for each pair of states in a Tile Automata system.

Data: Left state a and right state b, and glue-terminal table GT.
Result: Transition rule $(a, b) \rightarrow (a', b')$ if such a rule exists.
1 Let $L(\sigma)/R(\sigma)$ be the left/right glue label of the tile type σ maps to.
2 Let $\text{STAGE}(\sigma)$ be the stage σ is in. Let $\text{BIN}(\sigma)$ be the bin σ is in.
3 Let $\text{NEXT\_BIN}(\sigma)$ be the bin σ will be in the next stage.
4 Let $\text{HAS\_TOKEN}(\sigma)$ be *true* if σ contains a token, *false* otherwise.
5 **if** $R(a) \neq L(b)$ **then**
6   Return null;
7 **if** $\text{HAS\_TOKEN}(a) \wedge \text{STAGE}(a)$ is odd **then**
8   **if** b has a right cap **then**
9   **if** $GT((\text{STAGE}(b), \text{BIN}(b)), R(b)) = Used$ **then**
10          $a' \leftarrow a - *; b' \leftarrow b + *; b' \leftarrow b' - |$;
11   **else if** $GT((\text{STAGE}(b) + 1, \text{NEXT\_BIN}(b)), R(b)) = Used$ **then**
12          $a' \leftarrow a - *; b' \leftarrow b - |$;
13          $\text{STAGE}(b') \leftarrow \text{STAGE}(b') + 1; \text{BIN}(b') \leftarrow \text{NEXT\_BIN}(b')$;
14   **else**
15          $a' \leftarrow a; b' \leftarrow b$;
16          $\text{STAGE}(a') \leftarrow \text{STAGE}(a') + 1; \text{BIN}(a') \leftarrow \text{NEXT\_BIN}(a')$;
17          $\text{STAGE}(b') \leftarrow \text{STAGE}(b') + 1; \text{BIN}(b') \leftarrow \text{NEXT\_BIN}(b')$;
18   **else**
19        $a' \leftarrow a - *; b' \leftarrow b + *$;
20        $\text{STAGE}(b') \leftarrow \text{STAGE}(b') + 1; \text{BIN}(b') \leftarrow \text{NEXT\_BIN}(b')$;
21   Return $(a, b) \rightarrow (a', b')$;
22 **if** $\text{HAS\_TOKEN}(b) \wedge \text{STAGE}(b)$ is even **then**
23   **if** a has a left cap **then**
24   **if** $GT((\text{STAGE}(a), \text{BIN}(a)), L(a)) = Used$ **then**
25          $b' \leftarrow b - *; a' \leftarrow a + *; a' \leftarrow a' - |$;
26   **else if** $GT((\text{STAGE}(a) + 1, \text{NEXT\_BIN}(a)), L(a)) = Used$ **then**
27          $b' \leftarrow b - *; a' \leftarrow a - |$;
28          $\text{STAGE}(a') \leftarrow \text{STAGE}(a') + 1; \text{BIN}(a') \leftarrow \text{NEXT\_BIN}(a')$;
29   **else**
30          $b' \leftarrow b; a' \leftarrow a$;
31          $\text{STAGE}(b') \leftarrow \text{STAGE}(b') + 1; \text{BIN}(b') \leftarrow \text{NEXT\_BIN}(b')$;
32          $\text{STAGE}(a') \leftarrow \text{STAGE}(a') + 1; \text{BIN}(a') \leftarrow \text{NEXT\_BIN}(a')$;
33   **else**
34        $b' \leftarrow b - *; a' \leftarrow a + *$;
35        $\text{STAGE}(a') \leftarrow \text{STAGE}(a') + 1; \text{BIN}(a') \leftarrow \text{NEXT\_BIN}(a')$;
36   Return $(a, b) \rightarrow (a', b')$;

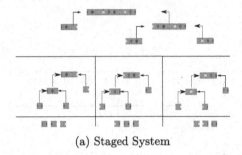

(s, b)	Red	Blue	Green	Yellow
(1, 1)	Term	Used	Used	Term
(1, 2)	Used	Used	Term	Term
(1, 3)	Used	Term	Term	Used
(2, 1)	Term	Term	Used	Used

(a) Staged System   (b) Glue-Terminal Table

Fig. 5. (a) Example Staged system to be simulated. (b) Glue-Terminal Table for shown staged system. In the table, s is the stage and b is the bin.

true (Used) if there exists at least two producible assemblies in bin b that attach using glue g in stage s. If it is false (Term.), the glue is never used in bin b for stage s.

This table can be computed recursively by checking the glues of the that are assemblies in the previous bin. Computing terminal assemblies can be done much easier since it's 1D (Fig. 5).

3.4   States and Initial Tiles

A state in our Tile Automata system has the following properties: each state has the first two properties and the second two properties are optional. The first label has sb possible options, the second has t, and the rest only increase the state space by a constant factor. This results in an upper bound on the states used of $\mathcal{O}(sbt)$.

- **Stage-Bin Label.** Each state $(s, i)_t$ is labeled with a pair of integers (s, i) saying the state represents the ith bin in stage s.
- **Glue Labels.** Each state $(s, i)_t$ represents a tile t from the staged system. We say this state has the glue labels of t when defining our affinity rules in Tile Automata. This label also defines our mapping from TA states to staged tiles in both directions.
- **Active State Token.** A state $(s, i)_t^*$ may have an Active State Token $*$. The token is used to enforce the left/right handed assembly trees by starting on one side of an assembly, and allowing attachment to other states with matching glue and stage-bin labels.
- **Caps.** A state may have a cap on one side, denoted $|s, i)_t$ or $(s, i|_t$. This means that on the side of the cap $|$, there are no affinity rules for that state. Until an assembly is ready to attach, it will have caps on its left and right most tiles.

We create an initial state for each pair $b_{1,i}, t$ where $b_{1,i}$ is the ith bin of the first stage and t is a tile input to that bin. If the left glue of the t is used in the

$b_{1,i}$, then we include the state $(1, i_t|$, i.e., the right cap state. If the left glue is open, but the right glue is used, the tile is the first in a left-handed assembly tree. In this case, we include the token left cap state $|1, i_t^*)$.

If a tile is terminal in the first bin, we instead include an initial state representing the first bin where the state is consumed. For example, if a tile t is input to bin $(1, i)$ and is terminal, but its right glue is used in an attachment in bin $(2, j)$ (where there's an edge between $(1, i)$ and $(2, j)$), then we instead include an initial state $|2, j_t)$.

3.5   Bin Simulation

In any odd stage, we construct every terminal using a sequence of attachments representing a left-handed assembly tree. For even stages, we use a right-handed assembly tree. We control this with the token by defining our affinity rules such that every attachment occurs between one state with the token and one without a cap. We switch between the left and right handed trees to reduce the amount of times the token must walk back and forth on the assembly since the token ends on the opposite side each time.

We walk through an example of a bin in the first stage in Fig. 6a. The token left cap state $|1, 1_t^*)$ attaches to the right cap state $(1, 1_{t'}|$ if t' attaches to the right of t. These two states then transition. If the right glue of t' is used in the bin, the token moves to that state and removes the cap. This process can then repeat in the bin. Looking at the next tile t'', the right glue is unused, and thus, the assembly is terminal, and the transition should move it to the next stage, now changing directions as outlined in Fig. 6b. The process for defining transitions is described in Algorithm 1; when given two states and the Glue-Transition table, a transition rule is returned if one would exist in the system. Note that this algorithm is non-deterministic as one bin may output to multiple bins in the next stage, so a pair of states may have multiple transition rules.

Theorem 1. *For any 1D staged system Υ with flexible glues, s stages, b bins, and t tile types, there exists a 1D Freezing Affinity-Strengthening Tile Automata system Γ with $\mathcal{O}(sbt)$ states that simulates Υ.*

Proof. Consider a staged system $\Upsilon = (M_{r,b}, T)$ with s stages, b bins and t tiles types. Tile Automata system $\Gamma = (\Sigma, \Pi, \Delta)$ which simulates Υ is defined and discussed below.

State Complexity $\mathcal{O}(sbt)$. Each tile type in Υ requires a unique state in Γ for every bin in every stage, resulting in $s \cdot b \cdot t$ states. The additional state increase for the token and caps of each state is constant for a total of $\mathcal{O}(sbt)$ states.

Flexible Glues, Freezing and Affinity Strengthening. A state $\sigma_t \in \Sigma$ with tile type $t \in T$ has affinity with a state $\sigma_t' \in \Sigma$ with tile type $t' \in T$ if t attaches to t' in Υ. With the affinity function we can encode general glues so we can simulate flexible glues. For every transition rule $\delta \in \Delta$, δ does not alter the tile type a state represents since only the stage, bin, token, or cap are affected.

Every transition rule is freezing and either removes a cap, moves the token forward, or advances to the next stage. Once a state with a tile type t has lost

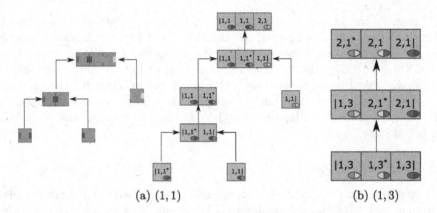

Fig. 6. (a) Example simulation of an assembly in stage 1. Notice the token moves leftward through the assembly as it builds to enforce a left handed assembly tree. (b) Transition for terminal assembly in bin $(1,3)$. Since the rightmost glue is terminal in bin $(1,3)$ the token changes the stage to 2 and starts moving left to remove the cap.

its cap it can never regain it. In a single stage, the token may walk over each tile a maximum of 2 times as both sides of the assembly must be checked to decide if the assembly is terminal. Note that this token walk involves adding an additional distinct state so the tiles do not visit the same state twice.

Simulation. We prove this is a correct simulation by induction on the size of the assemblies. The initial assemblies cover our base case for single tiles in Λ. The tile input in the first stage in Υ ensures each included assembly is in Λ. For the recursive case, assume every assembly $A \in \text{PROD}_\Upsilon$ with $|A| < x$ is simulated. Let b be the bin in which A is produced. A must be produced using two assemblies B and C, each of size $< x$, which are also in bin b. From our assumption, B and C have assemblies representing them- $B', C' \in \text{PROD}_\Gamma(\Lambda)$. Since B and C are produced in the same bin and have matching assemblies B' and C' with matching tokens, they may combine into an assembly A'. A will represent A since it has the same labels.   □

3.6   Lines

Using Theorem 1, we provide an alternate proof from [5] of length-n lines with $\mathcal{O}(\log n)$ states.

Corollary 1. *For all $n \in \mathbb{N}$, there exists a freezing Tile Automata system that uniquely assembles a $1 \times n$ line in $\mathcal{O}(\log n)$ states.*

Proof. In [12], it is shown that there exists a staged assembly system that uniquely produces a $1 \times n$ line with 6 tile types, 7 bins, and $\mathcal{O}(\log n)$ stages. From Theorem 1, there exists a Freezing Affinity-Strengthening Tile Automata system Γ with $\mathcal{O}(sbt)$ states that simulates any staged system Υ with s stages,

b bins and t tile types. Therefore, simulating the staged assembly system from [12] can be done with $\mathcal{O}(\log n)$ states.   □

4   Patterns

4.1   Colors and Patterns

In this section, we augment the Tile Automata model with the concept of a tile's color being based on the current state. For a set of color labels C, this is a partition of the states into $|C|$ sets. We only consider constant-sized C. Thus, the *color* of a tile t is the partition of the tile's state, denoted as $c(t)$.

Definition 3 (Pattern). *A pattern P over a set of colors C is a partial mapping of $\mathbb{Z}$ to elements in C. Let $P(z)$ be the color at $z \in \mathbb{Z}$. A scaled pattern P^{hw} is a pattern replacing each pixel within a $1 \times w$ line of pixels.*

Definition 4 (Patterned Assemblies). *We say a positioned assembly A' represents a pattern P if for each tile $t \in A'$, $c(t) = P(\rho_{A'}(t))$ and $dom(A') = dom(P)$. We say a positioned assembly B' represents a pattern P at scale $h \times w$ if it represents the scaled pattern P^{hw}.*

A system Γ uniquely assembles a pattern P if it uniquely assembles an assembly A, such that A contains a positioned assembly that represents P.

Definition 5 (Color-Locked). *A Tile Automata system is Color-Locked if for every transition rule $\delta = (S_{1a}, S_{2a}, S_{1b}, S_{2b}, d) \in \Delta$, $c(S_{1a}) = c(S_{1b})$ and $c(S_{2a}) = c(S_{2b})$, i.e., tiles are not allowed to change their color.*

4.2   Context-Free Grammars

A **context-free grammar (CFG)** is a set of recursive rules used to generate patterns of strings that define a given language. A CFG is a quadruple $G = (V, \Upsilon, R, S)$ where V is a finite set of nonterminal symbols (variables), Υ is a finite set of terminal symbols, R is the set of production rules, and $S \in V$ is the start symbol. Assuming the CFG is in Chomsky Normal Form (CNF), the production rules of the CFGs are in the form $A \to BC$ or $A \to a$, where $A, B, C \in V$ and $a \in \Upsilon$. A CFG derives a string by recursively replacing nonterminal symbols with terminal and nonterminal symbols based on its production rules.

Definition 6 (Minimum Context Free Grammars). *We define the size of a grammar G as the total number of symbols in the right-hand side of the rules. Let CF_P be the size of the smallest CNF CFG that produces the singleton language $\{P\}$.*

Restricted Context-Free Grammars (RCFG). In this work, we focus on the CFG class used in [13], which they name Restricted CFGs. These restricted grammars produce a singleton language, $|L(G)| = 1$, and thus are deterministic. This is the same concept of Context-Free Straight Line grammars from [4]. Note

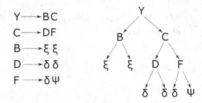

Fig. 7. A restricted context-free grammar (RCFG) G and its corresponding parse tree that produces a pattern P, $\xi\xi\delta\delta\delta\psi$. This is a deterministic grammar, producing only pattern P.

a Restricted CFG is not necessarily in CNF but any RCFG can be transformed into CNF with only a constant factor increase in rule size. Figure 7 presents an example RCFG G and its parse tree that derives a pattern of symbols P, $\xi\xi\delta\delta\delta\psi$. The parse tree shows how internal nodes are nonterminal symbols, and leaf nodes contain a terminal symbol whose in-order traversal derives the output string. Notice that since RCFG G is deterministic, each nonterminal symbol $N \in V$ has a unique subpattern $g(N)$ that is defined by taking N as the start symbol S and applying the production rules. Here, the language or output pattern P of G can be denoted by $L(G) = g(S)$.

4.3 Tile Automata Upper Bounds

In [13], the authors define the size of a staged assembly system Υ (denoted $|\Upsilon|$) to be the number of edges in its mix graph.

Corollary 2. *For any pattern P, there exists a Freezing Tile Automata system Γ that uniquely assembles P with $\mathcal{O}(CF_P)$ states and 1×1 scale. This system is cycle-free, and transition rules do not change the color of tiles.*

Proof. In [13], the authors show that, given a RCFG G deriving a pattern P, there exists a 1D SSAS Υ that assembles pattern P with B total bins, t tile types, and at 1×1 scale with $|\Upsilon| = \mathcal{O}(CF_P)$. Theorem 1 gives an upper bound based on the number of stages times the number of bins. However, the construction also gives an upper bound of $\mathcal{O}(Bt)$ as each state stores the bin and tile it maps to. It follows that there exists a Freezing TA system Γ that uniquely assembles P with $\mathcal{O}(CF_P)$ states and 1×1 scale if Γ simulates Υ.   □

5   Conclusion

In this paper we show how to convert any 1D staged assembly system to an equivalent 1D freezing Tile Automata system. We then show how this generalizes some previous results. We then show the immediate connection to context-free grammars and patterns. There are many interesting directions for future work.

– What is the most efficient method to compute the glue-terminal table?

- Can we improve the number of states needed in the TA simulation? Could it be reduced to $\mathcal{O}(st + bt)$ or even $\mathcal{O}(sg + bg)$ where g is the number of glues in the system? What is the lower bound?
- Does allowing for 1D scaling help achieve better bounds?
- Can 1D staged simulate 1D freezing Affinity-Strengthening Tile Automata? I.e., are they equivalent? If so, how many tiles, bins, and stages are needed?
- What challenges arise when attempting to generalize this to 2D? The glue-terminal table must not only store whether or not an assembly is terminal based on its glues, but also its geometry.
- What is the lower bound for building patterns in 1D freezing Affinity-Strengthening Tile Automata? Are there languages that Tile Automata can assemble more efficiently than staged?

References

1. Alaniz, R.M., et al.: Building squares with optimal state complexity in restricted active self-assembly. In: Proceedings of the Symposium on Algorithmic Foundations of Dynamic Networks, SAND 2022, vol. 221, pp. 6:1–6:18 (2022)
2. Alumbaugh, J.C., Daymude, J.J., Demaine, E.D., Patitz, M.J., Richa, A.W.: Simulation of programmable matter systems using active tile-based self-assembly. In: Thachuk, C., Liu, Y. (eds.) DNA 2019. LNCS, vol. 11648, pp. 140–158. Springer, Cham (2019). https://doi.org/10.1007/978-3-030-26807-7_8
3. Barad, G., et al.: Simulation of one dimensional staged dna tile assembly by the signal-passing hierarchical tam. Procedia Comput. Sci. **159**, 1918–1927 (2019)
4. Benz, F., Kötzing, T.: An effective heuristic for the smallest grammar problem. In: Proceedings of the 15th Annual Conference on Genetic and Evolutionary Computation, pp. 487–494 (2013)
5. Caballero, D., Gomez, T., Schweller, R., Wylie, T.: Verification and computation in restricted tile automata. In: 26th International Conference on DNA Computing and Molecular Programming, DNA 2020, vol. 174, pp. 10:1–10:18 (2020)
6. Caballero, D., Gomez, T., Schweller, R., Wylie, T.: Covert computation in staged self-assembly: verification is pspace-complete. In: 29th Annual European Symposium on Algorithms, ESA 2021, pp. 23:1–23:18 (2021)
7. Cannon, S., et al.: Two hands are better than one (up to constant factors): self-assembly in the 2HAM vs. aTAM. In: 30th Inter. Sym. on Theoretical Aspects of Computer Science, STACS 2013, vol. 20, pp. 172–184 (2013)
8. Cantu, A.A., Luchsinger, A., Schweller, R., Wylie, T.: Signal passing self-assembly simulates tile automata. In: 31st International Symposium on Algorithms and Computation, ISAAC 2020, pp. 53:1–53:17 (2020)
9. Chalk, C., Luchsinger, A., Martinez, E., Schweller, R., Winslow, A., Wylie, T.: Freezing simulates non-freezing tile automata. In: Doty, D., Dietz, H. (eds.) DNA 2018. LNCS, vol. 11145, pp. 155–172. Springer, Cham (2018). https://doi.org/10.1007/978-3-030-00030-1_10
10. Chalk, C., Martinez, E., Schweller, R., Vega, L., Winslow, A., Wylie, T.: Optimal staged self-assembly of general shapes. Algorithmica **80**(4), 1383–1409 (2018)
11. Chalk, C., Martinez, E., Schweller, R., Vega, L., Winslow, A., Wylie, T.: Optimal staged self-assembly of linear assemblies. Nat. Comput. **18**(3), 527–548 (2019). https://doi.org/10.1007/s11047-019-09740-y

12. Demaine, E.D., et al.: Staged self-assembly: nanomanufacture of arbitrary shapes with o (1) glues. Nat. Comput. **7**(3), 347–370 (2008)
13. Demaine, E.D., Eisenstat, S., Ishaque, M., Winslow, A.: One-dimensional staged self-assembly. In: Proceedings of the 17th International Conference on DNA Computing and Molecular Programming, DNA 2011, pp. 100–114 (2011)
14. Schweller, R., Winslow, A., Wylie, T.: Verification in staged tile self-assembly. Nat. Comput. **18**(1), 107–117 (2019)
15. Thubagere, A.J., et al.: A cargo-sorting DNA robot. Science **357**(6356), eaan6558 (2017)
16. Tikhomirov, G., Petersen, P., Qian, L.: Fractal assembly of micrometre-scale dna origami arrays with arbitrary patterns. Nature **552**(7683), 67–71 (2017)
17. Winfree, E.: Algorithmic Self-Assembly of DNA. Ph.D. thesis, California Institute of Technology (June 1998)
18. Winslow, A.: Staged self-assembly and polyomino context-free grammars. Nat. Comput. **14**(2), 293–302 (2015)
19. Woods, D., Doty, D., Myhrvold, C., Hui, J., Zhou, F., Yin, P., Winfree, E.: Diverse and robust molecular algorithms using reprogrammable dna self-assembly. Nature **567**(7748), 366–372 (2019)

Single-Shuffle Card-Based Protocol with Eight Cards per Gate

Kazunari Tozawa[1]([✉]), Hiraku Morita[2], and Takaaki Mizuki[3]

[1] The University of Tokyo, Tokyo, Japan
`tozawaka@g.ecc.u-tokyo.ac.jp`
[2] University of St. Gallen, St. Gallen, Switzerland
[3] Tohoku University, Miyagi, Japan

Abstract. Card-based cryptography allows us to securely compute arbitrary functions using a deck of physical cards. Its performance is mainly measured by the number of used cards and shuffles, and there is a line of work that aims to reduce either of them. One of the seminal work is by Shinagawa and Nuida (Discrete Applied Mathematics 2021) that shows any Boolean function can be constructed by shuffling only once based on the garbling scheme. Their construction requires $2n + 24g$ cards for an n-input Boolean function that is represented by g logical gates. In this paper, we reduce the number of cards to $2n + 8g$ for arbitrary functions while keeping it working with only one shuffle.

Keywords: Card-based cryptography · Garbled circuit · XOR shuffle

1 Introduction

Card-based cryptography is unconventional computing which performs cryptographic tasks such as secure computations, which exploits a deck of physical cards [8,14,15,20]. A card-based cryptographic protocol typically uses a two-color deck consisting of [♡] and [♣] whose backs are all identical [?], and the following encoding rule is usually used to represent Boolean values:

$$[♣][♡] = 0, \quad [♡][♣] = 1.$$

The complexity of a card-based protocol is measured in terms of the number of cards and shuffles, which correspond to the space and time complexities of the protocol, respectively.

As for minimizing the number of required cards, the currently known best result is that $2n+6$ cards are sufficient to construct any n-variable Boolean function [19]. However, it needs an exponential number of shuffles. As for minimizing the number of shuffles, Shinagawa and Nuida [24] proved that only one shuffle is enough to design a protocol securely computing any Boolean function (although it needs a relatively large number of cards as mentioned below). This paper mainly focuses on the latter, i.e., improving the Shinagawa–Nuida single-shuffle construction.

D. Genova and J. Kari (Eds.): UCNC 2023, LNCS 14003, pp. 171–185, 2023.
https://doi.org/10.1007/978-3-031-34034-5_12

More specifically, Shinagawa and Nuida [24] have investigated the relation between card-based cryptography and garbled circuit techniques. They have proposed a card-based variant of a garbled circuit, called *Card-based Garbled Circuit*. The protocol enables us to compute any Boolean function with the optimal number of shuffles, namely exactly one shuffle. Regarding the number of cards, the protocol for an n-input Boolean function requires $2n + 24g$ cards, where g is the number of gates (when describing the function as a circuit).

Technical Overview of Our Scheme. Our goal is to minimize the number of cards required to represent a card-based garbled circuit. To address this, we propose a new method to represent garbled gates with a small number of cards, that is, 8 cards per gate. Our method helps to reduce the primitive cost of card-based garbled circuits which can be seen as reducing the size of the garbled tables, allowing the number of cards to be reduced proportionally to the number of gates.

The basic idea of garbled circuit techniques is to consider each gate as an encryption of the corresponding truth table. A truth table of a logic gate consists of 12 cells, so the most straightforward way to represent it in card-based cryptography is to use 24 cards with standard encoding, as shown in Fig. 1a. The Shinagawa-Nuida single-shuffle construction shows that this representation allows privacy-preserving computations of any binary gate. The garbling stage of their scheme aims to encrypt the truth table of each gate by turning down the cards and randomly permuting the rows of the table. The resulting truth table looks as shown in Fig. 1b. Since the positions of the result values are uniformly random, the evaluation stage of the gate can make all values in the operand cells public.

On the other hand, our scheme uses only 8 cards to represent a truth table as shown in Fig. 1c. This reduction comes from the observation that the operand cell values are only positional information for each result cell. In other words, we can omit the cards required for the operand cells, as long as the positional information is recoverable. A similar optimization has already been proposed in the context of garbled circuits, called the *point-and-permute* technique [2]. We propose a variant of the point-and-permute technique in card-based cryptography.

Our Contributions. We propose a protocol for any Boolean circuit with a single shuffle. Compared to the existing protocol [24], we reduce the number of cards from $2n + 24g$ to $2n + 8g$, where g is the number of gates.

Related Work. As mentioned above, the goal of this paper is to provide a generic construction for securely computing any Boolean functions using only one shuffle. The Shinagawa-Nuida's single-shuffle construction [24] has been the only one that achieves the goal. There are several single-shuffle protocols for specific elementary functions such as the AND [4,16,18], XOR [18], 3-input equality [6, 23], 3-input majority [25], n-input AND [13], and n-input XOR [13] functions. Another aspect of previous work is to reduce the number of cards; especially, designing card-minimal protocols has attracted attention [5,9–12,21,25].

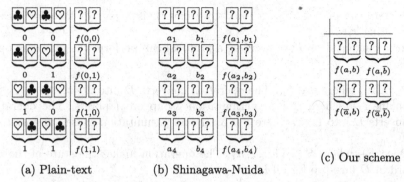

(a) Plain-text   (b) Shinagawa-Nuida

(c) Our scheme

Fig. 1. Card-based representations of the truth table for gate f

Bellare *et al.* [3] proposed garbling schemes, an abstraction of garbled circuit methods, and formalized security properties of garbled circuits: privacy and obliviousness.

2 Preliminaries

2.1 Notation

We use a bold symbol to represent a vector (or an ordered set). Let v_i denote the i-th (starting from 1) element of v. We write $v \parallel w$ for the concatenation of v and w.

Let S_n denote the symmetric group on n elements. For a vector v of degree n, we define a place-permutation action of S_n as $(v \cdot \pi)_i = v_{\pi(i)}$, where $\pi \in S_n$. For two permutations π, ρ, we use the notation $\pi\rho$ to represent the product of permutations such that $v \cdot (\pi\rho) = (v \cdot \pi) \cdot \rho$ for any vector v. We use the notation $(a, b) \in S_n$ to denote the transposition (*i.e.*, a cycle with two elements) that swaps a and b.

For $b, c \in \mathbb{Z}_2$, we will write $\bar{b}$, $b \oplus c$, $b \vee c$ and $b \wedge c$ for the negation of b, the XOR, OR and AND of b and c, respectively.

2.2 Card-Based Cryptographic Protocol

In this paper, we follow the computation model proposed in [17]. There are two kinds of cards: The face side of a card is either ♣ or ♡, and the back side is indistinguishable from the other cards, denoted by ?. Each card during the protocol execution can be in one of the two states: face-top or face-down. A deck is a finite vector on $\{♡, ♣\} \times \{\text{face-top, face-down}\}$.

As mentioned before, a bit $x \in \mathbb{Z}_2$ is represented by a single pair of cards as follows:

$$0 = ♣♡ \qquad\qquad 1 = ♡♣$$

A *commitment* of $x \in \mathbb{Z}_2$, denoted by $\mathsf{Com}(x)$, is a pair of face-down cards representing x.

For a current deck D of n cards, a protocol can perform the following operations:

- (Perm, π), where $\pi \in S_n$. The operation converts D into $D \cdot \pi$.
- $(\mathsf{Shuffle}, G)$, where G is a permutation group on n points. The operation converts D into $D \cdot \pi$, where π is a random permutation chosen uniformly on G.
- (Open, S), where $S \subseteq \{1, \ldots, n\}$. The operation makes the state of the i-th card in D face-top for all $i \in S$.

In particular, when G is isomorphic to some symmetric group S_k for $k \leq n$, $(\mathsf{Shuffle}, G)$ is called a pile-scramble shuffle [7]. Let $\boldsymbol{I}^{(1)}, \ldots, \boldsymbol{I}^{(k)}$ be the disjoint ordered subsets of $\{1, \ldots, n\}$ of the same size s. We define G as the permutation group generated by the products of parallel transpositions $(\boldsymbol{I}_1^{(i)}, \boldsymbol{I}_1^{(j)})(\boldsymbol{I}_2^{(i)}, \boldsymbol{I}_2^{(j)}) \cdots (\boldsymbol{I}_s^{(i)}, \boldsymbol{I}_s^{(j)})$ for all $i < j$. In this case, we use the syntactic sugar $(\mathsf{PileShuffle}, \boldsymbol{I}^{(1)}, \ldots, \boldsymbol{I}^{(k)})$ for $(\mathsf{Shuffle}, G)$.

The protocol is in a committed format if the output is also encoded in the same manner as input; $0 = \boxed{\clubsuit}\boxed{\heartsuit}, 1 = \boxed{\heartsuit}\boxed{\clubsuit}$. Our construction in this paper focuses on a committed format so that it will be easy to use the committed output of our protocol as an input of some other protocols.

2.3 Garbled Circuit

Let $f = (n, m, g, \mathsf{Wires}, A, B, G)$ be a Boolean circuit. Here, n, m and g denote the numbers of inputs, outputs and gates, respectively. All input wires and gates in f are assigned unique numbers belonging to $\mathsf{Inputs} = \{1, \ldots, n\}$ and $\mathsf{Gates} = \{n+1, \ldots, n+g\}$, respectively. The wire coming out of gate i is also assigned i, so the wires correspond to $\mathsf{Wires} = \{1, \ldots, n+g\}$. The functions $A, B : \mathsf{Gates} \to \mathsf{Wires} \setminus \mathsf{Outputs}$ respectively specify the first and second input wires of a gate, and $G : \mathsf{Gates} \times \{0,1\} \times \{0,1\} \to \{0,1\}$ specifies the functionality of each gate. We simply write A_i, B_i and G_i for $A(i)$, $B(i)$ and $G(i, \cdot, \cdot)$, and write A_i^{-1} and B_i^{-1} for $A^{-1}(i)$ and $B^{-1}(i)$, respectively. We assume that $A_i < B_i < i$ holds for all i. Then all output wires in f belong to $\mathsf{Outputs} = \{n+g-m+1, \ldots, n+g\}$.

Garbling scheme [3] consists of the following algorithms:

- $(F, e, d) \leftarrow \mathsf{Gb}(1^k, f)$: Given a security parameter $k \in \mathbb{N}$ and a function $f : \{0,1\}^n \to \{0,1\}^m$, it outputs a garbled circuit F, encoding information e, and decoding information d
- $X \leftarrow \mathsf{Enc}(e, x)$: Given encoding information e and an input $x \in \{0,1\}^n$, it outputs a garbled input X
- $Y \leftarrow \mathsf{Eval}(F, X)$: Given a garbled function F and a garbled input X, it outputs a garbled output Y
- $y \leftarrow \mathsf{Dec}(d, Y)$: Given decoding information d and a garbled output Y, it outputs a plain output y

· The security properties we focus on are described as follows:

- Privacy: The tuple (F, X, d) should not reveal any information on the input x except the output $f(x)$. Here, there must exist a simulator $\mathcal{S}$ that takes input $(1^k, f, f(x))$ and outputs (F', X', d') that is indistinguishable from (F, X, d) that would be generated by the protocol.
- Obliviousness: The tuple (F, X) should not reveal any information on x. Here, there must exist a simulator $\mathcal{S}$ that takes input $(1^k, f)$ and outputs (F', X') that is indistinguishable from (F, X) that would be generated by the protocol.

Note that in this paper we do not use the security parameter k and only consider the security properties in the information-theoretical sense.

2.4 Card-Based Garbling Scheme

Our card-based garbling protocol (Protocol 2) realizes the standard garbling and encoding algorithms at once, as in Shinagawa and Nuida [24]. In addition, when considering a protocol in a committed form, the decoding phase is omitted. In summary, the functionalities of a card-based garbling scheme are described as follows:

- $I \leftarrow \mathsf{Init}(x, f)$: Given an input x and a function $f : \{0, 1\}^n \rightarrow \{0, 1\}^m$, it outputs a committed initial state I
- $(F, X) \leftarrow \mathsf{CardGb}(I)$: Given a security parameter $k \in \mathbb{N}$ and an initial state regarding an input x and a function f, it outputs a garbled circuit F, decoding information d, and a garbled input X
- $Y \leftarrow \mathsf{CardEval}(F, X)$: Given a garbled function F and a garbled input X, it outputs a garbled output Y

3 Main Protocol

In this section, we propose an efficient protocol for card-based garbled circuits. The main idea of our scheme is to use an elaborate shuffling technique for randomization. We show that the XOR shuffle technique for the secret-sharing-based scheme of [1] is also applicable to card-based cryptography. As a result, the XOR shuffle provides an analog of the point-and-permute technique in the field of garbled circuits, reducing the number of cards required to represent the circuit.

3.1 Example: For a Circuit with One Gate

To grasp the intuition of our idea, let us consider the simplest case with a single binary logic gate. In this case, the Boolean circuit is described as $(2, 1, 1, \{1, 2, 3\}, \{3 \mapsto 1\}, \{3 \mapsto 2\}, f)$, where f is the functionality of the logic gate. The procedure has three phases: initialization, garbling, and evaluation.

Initialization. Let x_1 and x_2 be distinct inputs, and f be the binary Boolean function we want to evaluate at the gate. Given the commitments of x_1 and x_2, the initial state is set as follows:

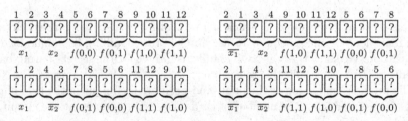

Here, the first four cards are the commitments of x_1 and x_2, and the latter eight cards are the commitments of the values of $f(0,0)$, $f(0,1)$, $f(1,0)$, and $f(1,1)$, *i.e.*, an encryption of the truth table for f. See Sect. 3.2 for the detail.

Garbling. In order to obliviously select the desired output from the encrypted truth table while keeping the input values secret, we apply an XOR shuffle to the initial state[1]. An XOR Shuffle consists of two consecutive pile-scramble shuffles as follows:

1. (PileShuffle, $\{1,5,6,7,8\}$, $\{2,9,10,11,12\}$)

2. (PileShuffle, $\{3,5,6,9,10\}$, $\{4,7,8,11,12\}$)

A pile scramble shuffle allows us to swap the positions of the white- and black-marked cards with equal probability while maintaining the order of the cards marked each color. After the XOR shuffle, the final state can be one of the following four cases:

where $\overline{x}$ denotes the negation of x. The key property of the XOR shuffle is that each case has an equal probability thanks to the randomness given by pile-scramble shuffles. Accordingly, the distribution of the two values committed on the first four cards is uniform on $\{0,1\}^2$ regardless of the input values x_1 and x_2. See Sect. 3.3 for the details.

---

[1] Note that a similar procedure was used for changing an integer encoding into two commitments [22].

Evaluation. The evaluation phase of our protocol proceeds as follows. The players first reveal the first four cards to obtain the two randomized values, denoted by b_1 and b_2. Then, depending on the values of b_1 and b_2, the players choose two of the latter eight cards according to the following rule:

- If $b_1 = 0$ and $b_2 = 0$, take 5 and 6
- If $b_1 = 0$ and $b_2 = 1$, take 7 and 8
- If $b_1 = 1$ and $b_2 = 0$, take 9 and 10
- If $b_1 = 1$ and $b_2 = 1$, take 11 and 12

The correctness of the protocol comes from the definition of XOR shuffle. When $b_1 = x_1 \oplus r_1$ and $b_2 = x_2 \oplus r_2$ for some $r_1, r_2 \in \mathbb{Z}_2$, the latter part are the commitments of the values of $f(r_1, r_2)$, $f(r_1, \overline{r_2})$, $f(\overline{r_1}, r_2)$ and $f(\overline{r_1}, \overline{r_2})$. Therefore, the two chosen cards are the commitment of the desired output value. See Sect. 3.4 for the details.

3.2 Initialization Phase

We first define the initial state of the protocol. Let $f = (n, m, g, \text{Wires}, A, B, G)$ be a Boolean circuit. For $i \in$ Gates, we define an eight-card representation of the truth table of gate i as follows:

$$\text{Com}(f, i) := \text{Com}(G_i(0,0)) \parallel \text{Com}(G_i(0,1)) \parallel \text{Com}(G_i(1,0)) \parallel \text{Com}(G_i(1,1)).$$

We now describe a protocol for Init below. The protocol requires $2n + 8g$ cards.

Protocol 1. Init

Input: $(\boldsymbol{x}, f)$, where $\boldsymbol{x}$ is a vector of input values, and f is a Boolean circuit.
Output: I, where I is an initial state consisting of $2n + 8g$ face-down cards.

1. Set $I = (\text{Com}(\boldsymbol{x}_1) \parallel \cdots \parallel \text{Com}(\boldsymbol{x}_n) \parallel \text{Com}(f, n+1) \parallel \cdots \parallel \text{Com}(f, n+g))$.
2. Output I.

For simplicity, we define the offset a : Wires $\rightarrow \{1, \ldots, 2n+8g\}$, which assigns the first position in the deck to the wire number of the circuit, as follows:

$$\mathsf{a}(i) = \begin{cases} 2i - 1 & i \in \text{Inputs} \\ 8i - 6n - 7 & i \in \text{Gates} \end{cases}$$

Example. As an example, we consider the Boolean circuit in Fig. 2. Note that this example is the same as the Appendix example in [24]. Formally, the circuit is defined as $f = (3, 1, 3, A, B, G)$ where $A(4) = 1, A(5) = 3, A(6) = 4$, $B(4) = 2, B(5) = 4, B(6) = 5$, G_4, G_5 and G_6 are AND, XOR, and OR gates, respectively. In this case, the initial state of the protocol is set as 30 face-down cards arranged as follows:

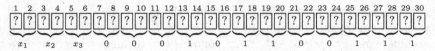

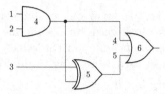

Fig. 2. Boolean Circuit f

3.3 Garbling Phase

Next, the protocol proceeds to the garbling phase. The players perform a series of pile-scramble shuffles according to the circuit. This ensures that the input values are uniformly random after the garbling phase without changing the semantics of the circuit.

Our scheme requires a total of $n + g - m$ pile-scramble shuffles. Each pile-scramble shuffle is defined for each $i \in \mathsf{Wires} \setminus \mathsf{Outputs}$, and runs consecutively in this index order. Unlike the single-gate circuit, a pile-scramble shuffle requires many different positions to be shuffled simultaneously according to the circuit topology. To specify the positions to be exchanged in each pile-scramble shuffle, we define the ordered subsets $\boldsymbol{P}^{(i,1)}, \boldsymbol{P}^{(i,2)} \subseteq \{1, \ldots, 2n + 8g\}$ for $i \in \mathsf{Wires} \setminus \mathsf{Outputs}$ as follows:

$$\boldsymbol{P}^{(i,1)} = \boldsymbol{I}^{(i,1)} \parallel (\parallel_{j \in A_i^{-1}} \boldsymbol{L}^{(j,1)}) \parallel (\parallel_{j \in B_i^{-1}} \boldsymbol{R}^{(j,1)})$$

$$\boldsymbol{P}^{(i,2)} = \boldsymbol{I}^{(i,2)} \parallel (\parallel_{j \in A_i^{-1}} \boldsymbol{L}^{(j,2)}) \parallel (\parallel_{j \in B_i^{-1}} \boldsymbol{R}^{(j,2)})$$

where $\boldsymbol{I}^{(i,1)}, \boldsymbol{I}^{(i,2)}, \boldsymbol{L}^{(j,1)}, \boldsymbol{L}^{(j,2)}, \boldsymbol{R}^{(j,1)}, \boldsymbol{R}^{(j,2)}$ are given as:

$$\boldsymbol{I}^{(i,1)} = \begin{cases} \{\mathsf{a}(i) + 0\} & i \in \mathsf{Inputs} \\ \{\mathsf{a}(i) + 0, \mathsf{a}(i) + 2, \mathsf{a}(i) + 4, \mathsf{a}(i) + 6\} & i \in \mathsf{Gates} \end{cases}$$

$$\boldsymbol{I}^{(i,2)} = \begin{cases} \{\mathsf{a}(i) + 1\} & i \in \mathsf{Inputs} \\ \{\mathsf{a}(i) + 1, \mathsf{a}(i) + 3, \mathsf{a}(i) + 5, \mathsf{a}(i) + 7\} & i \in \mathsf{Gates} \end{cases}$$

$$\boldsymbol{L}^{(j,1)} = \{\mathsf{a}(j) + 0, \mathsf{a}(j) + 1, \mathsf{a}(j) + 2, \mathsf{a}(j) + 3\}$$

$$\boldsymbol{L}^{(j,2)} = \{\mathsf{a}(j) + 4, \mathsf{a}(j) + 5, \mathsf{a}(j) + 6, \mathsf{a}(j) + 7\}$$

$$\boldsymbol{R}^{(j,1)} = \{\mathsf{a}(j) + 0, \mathsf{a}(j) + 1, \mathsf{a}(j) + 4, \mathsf{a}(j) + 5\}$$

$$\boldsymbol{R}^{(j,2)} = \{\mathsf{a}(j) + 2, \mathsf{a}(j) + 3, \mathsf{a}(j) + 6, \mathsf{a}(j) + 7\}$$

The pile-scramble shuffle determined by $\boldsymbol{P}^{(i,1)}$ and $\boldsymbol{P}^{(i,2)}$ results in an XOR shuffling, as discussed in Sect. 3.1. Here we point out the difference between this definition and the single gate case. In a general circuit, there can be non-input wires and branching wires. When $j \notin \mathsf{Inputs}$, the players must randomize all 4 possible commitments for input to j, defined as $\boldsymbol{I}^{(i,1)}$ and $\boldsymbol{I}^{(i,2)}$. When j is a branching wire, *i.e.*, when $A_j^{-1} \cup B_j^{-1}$ contains two or more wires, the players must randomize all the truth tables on the output side of wire j, defined as $L^{(j,1)}$, $L^{(j,2)}$, $R^{(j,1)}$ and $R^{(j,2)}$.

Protocol 2. CardGb

Input: I, where I is an initial state.
Output: (F, X), where F and X are decks with $8g$ and $2n$ face-down cards, respectively.

1. For $i \in$ Wires $\setminus$ Outputs do:
   (a) Compute (PileShuffle, $\boldsymbol{P}^{(i,1)}$, $\boldsymbol{P}^{(i,2)}$).
2. Parse the resulting deck as $X \parallel F$ and output it.

The garbling phase randomizes the circuit semantics as follows. In X and F, the Boolean value assigned to each non-output wire is randomized by a single pile-scramble shuffle. Note that each pile-scramble shuffle can be viewed as a group action by a random element in $S_2 \cong \mathbb{Z}_2$. Let r_i denote a random element in $\mathbb{Z}_2$ resulting from the i-th pile-scramble shuffle, except that we set $r_i = 0$ if $i \in$ Outputs. For each $i \in$ Inputs, the input value x_i is randomized to $x_i \oplus r_i$ and stored in X. For each $j \in$ Gates, the four outcome values are randomized and rearranged to be $G_j(r_{A_j}, r_{B_j}) \oplus r_j$, $G_j(r_{A_j}, \overline{r_{B_j}}) \oplus r_j$, $G_j(\overline{r_{A_j}}, r_{B_j}) \oplus r_j$, and $G_j(\overline{r_{A_j}}, \overline{r_{B_j}}) \oplus r_j$ in order.

Furthermore, we can make a more critical observation that the resulting circuit semantics is determined independently of the order of the $n + g - m$ pile-scramble shuffles. Due to the successive pile-scramble shuffles, the truth table of each gate j is randomized by three kinds of group actions, defined as $\boldsymbol{I}$, $\boldsymbol{L}$, and $\boldsymbol{R}$, by the distinct random elements r_j, r_{A_j}, and r_{B_j}. The key fact here is that, by definition, these group actions are all commutative. This is because they form the group $S_2 \times S_2 \times S_2$ and its natural action on 8 points. Accordingly, the players can apply the pile-scramble shuffles in any order.

From the above observation, we can define a variant of the CardGb protocol that only requires a single shuffle. Let G_i be the permutation group determined by $\boldsymbol{P}^{(i,1)}$ and $\boldsymbol{P}^{(i,2)}$, and let $G_f := \{g_1 g_2 \cdots g_{n+g-m} \in S_{2n+8g} \mid g_j \in G_j\}$. Note that G_f is also a permutation group, since any two of G_j are commutative. Thus, we can combine the $n + g - m$ pile-scramble shuffles into one shuffle as follows.

Protocol 3. CardGb (with a single shuffle)

Input: I, where I is an initial state.
Output: (F, X), where F and X are decks with $8g$ and $2n$ face-down cards, respectively.

1. Compute (Shuffle, G_f).
2. Parse the resulting deck as $X \parallel F$ and output it.

Example. Consider the garbling phase of the example given by Fig. 2. In this case, $n + g - m = 5$, so the garbling phase contains 5 consecutive pile-scramble shuffles. Since wire 1 is the first input of gate 4, the first pile-scramble shuffle is described as $(\mathsf{PileShuffle}, \{1, 7, 8, 9, 10\}, \{2, 11, 12, 13, 14\})$:

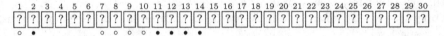

Similarly, wires 2 and 3 respectively determine the second pile-scramble shuffle $(\mathsf{PileShuffle}, \{3, 7, 8, 11, 12\}, \{4, 9, 10, 13, 14\})$ and the third pile-scramble shuffle $(\mathsf{PileShuffle}, \{5, 15, 16, 17, 18\}, \{6, 19, 20, 21, 22\})$:

Next, consider the pile-scramble shuffle given by wire 4. This wire comes out of gate 4 and goes into the second input of gate 5 and the first input of gate 6. Accordingly, all the cards corresponding to gates 4, 5, and 6 are shuffled in a way that preserves the circuit semantics. Such a shuffle is given as the pile-scramble shuffle $(\mathsf{PileShuffle}, \boldsymbol{P}^{(4,1)}, \boldsymbol{P}^{(4,2)})$, where $\boldsymbol{P}^{(4,1)} = \boldsymbol{I}^{(4,1)} \parallel \boldsymbol{R}^{(5,1)} \parallel \boldsymbol{L}^{(6,1)}$ and $\boldsymbol{P}^{(4,2)} = \boldsymbol{I}^{(4,2)} \parallel \boldsymbol{R}^{(5,2)} \parallel \boldsymbol{L}^{(6,2)}$:

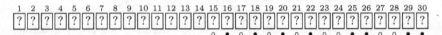

Likewise, the fifth pile-scramble shuffle is defined as $(\mathsf{PileShuffle}, \boldsymbol{P}^{(5,1)}, \boldsymbol{P}^{(5,2)})$, where $\boldsymbol{P}^{(5,1)} = \boldsymbol{I}^{(5,1)} \parallel \boldsymbol{R}^{(6,1)}$ and $\boldsymbol{P}^{(5,2)} = \boldsymbol{I}^{(5,2)} \parallel \boldsymbol{R}^{(6,2)}$.

Finally, let us review the circuit semantics after successive pile-scramble shuffles. Let r_i denote the bit corresponding to the i-th pile-scramble shuffle. Then the following holds:

$$x_1 \oplus r_1 \quad x_2 \oplus r_2 \quad x_3 \oplus r_3 \quad g_0^4 \oplus r_4 \quad g_1^4 \oplus r_4 \quad g_2^4 \oplus r_4 \quad g_3^4 \oplus r_4 \quad g_0^5 \oplus r_5 \quad g_1^5 \oplus r_5 \quad g_2^5 \oplus r_5 \quad g_3^5 \oplus r_5 \quad r_4 \vee r_5 \quad r_4 \vee \overline{r_5} \quad \overline{r_4} \vee r_5 \quad \overline{r_4} \vee \overline{r_5}$$

where

$$g_0^4 = r_1 \wedge r_2, \qquad g_1^4 = r_1 \wedge \overline{r_2}, \qquad g_2^4 = \overline{r_1} \wedge r_2, \qquad g_3^4 = \overline{r_1} \wedge \overline{r_2},$$
$$g_0^5 = r_3 \oplus r_4, \qquad g_1^5 = r_3 \oplus \overline{r_4}, \qquad g_2^5 = \overline{r_3} \oplus r_4, \qquad g_3^5 = \overline{r_3} \oplus \overline{r_4}.$$

Protocol 4. CardEval

Input: (F, X), where F and X are decks consisting of $8g$ and $2n$ face-down cards, respectively.

Output: Y, where Y is a deck consisting of $2m$ face-down cards.

1. Set $D = X \parallel F$.
2. Compute (Open, $\{1, \ldots, 2n\}$).
3. Set $\mathsf{Out}(i)$ to the Boolean value represented by $(2i - 1)$-th and $2i$-th cards for all $i \in$ Inputs.
4. For $i \in$ Gates \ Outputs do:
   - If $\mathsf{Out}(A_i) = 0$ and $\mathsf{Out}(B_i) = 0$, compute (Open, $\{\mathsf{a}(i), \mathsf{a}(i) + 1\}$) and set $\mathsf{Out}(i)$ to the value.
   - If $\mathsf{Out}(A_i) = 0$ and $\mathsf{Out}(B_i) = 1$, compute (Open, $\{\mathsf{a}(i) + 2, \mathsf{a}(i) + 3\}$) and set $\mathsf{Out}(i)$ to the value.
   - If $\mathsf{Out}(A_i) = 1$ and $\mathsf{Out}(B_i) = 0$, compute (Open, $\{\mathsf{a}(i) + 4, \mathsf{a}(i) + 5\}$) and set $\mathsf{Out}(i)$ to the value.
   - If $\mathsf{Out}(A_i) = 1$ and $\mathsf{Out}(B_i) = 1$, compute (Open, $\{\mathsf{a}(i) + 6, \mathsf{a}(i) + 7\}$) and set $\mathsf{Out}(i)$ to the value.
5. Set Y to an empty deck.
6. For $i \in$ Outputs do:
   - If $\mathsf{Out}(A_i) = 0$ and $\mathsf{Out}(B_i) = 0$, append the face-down cards at $\{\mathsf{a}(i), \mathsf{a}(i) + 1\}$ to Y.
   - If $\mathsf{Out}(A_i) = 0$ and $\mathsf{Out}(B_i) = 1$, append the face-down cards at $\{\mathsf{a}(i) + 2, \mathsf{a}(i) + 3\}$ to Y.
   - If $\mathsf{Out}(A_i) = 1$ and $\mathsf{Out}(B_i) = 0$, append the face-down cards at $\{\mathsf{a}(i) + 4, \mathsf{a}(i) + 5\}$ to Y.
   - If $\mathsf{Out}(A_i) = 1$ and $\mathsf{Out}(B_i) = 1$, append the face-down cards at $\{\mathsf{a}(i) + 6, \mathsf{a}(i) + 7\}$ to Y.
7. Output Y.

3.4 Evaluation Phase

The evaluation phase is an iterative process to obtain a commitment of the desired Boolean value as output. At each step, the players open two designated cards. The first step starts with opening the cards corresponding to the input wires. Then, if a gate takes the values at the two input wires, the players refer to the values to determine the following card positions and open only two out of the eight cards corresponding to the gate.

Let us consider the correctness of our scheme. To prove this, we show that the circuit randomized by the garbling phase provides the same output as the plain-text circuit evaluation when computed through the evaluation phase of our scheme. Let v_j be the output value of gate j in the circuit f when x is input. Then, it suffices to show that the evaluation phase of our scheme gives the output value of gate j as $v_j \oplus r_j$, where r_j is the same as introduced in Sect. 3.3.

The proof is shown by induction on the circuit structure. The base case follows from the fact that each $i \in$ Inputs is assigned $x_i \oplus r_i$ in X. Assume that the statement holds up to $j-1$. Then $\mathsf{Out}(A_j) = v_{A_j} \oplus r_{A_j}$ and $\mathsf{Out}(B_j) = v_{B_j} \oplus r_{B_j}$. On the other hand, by the definition of CardGb, the four secret values represented by the eight cards starting from $\mathsf{a}(j)$ in F is $G_j(r_{A_j}, r_{B_j}) \oplus r_j$, $G_j(r_{A_j}, \overline{r_{B_j}}) \oplus r_j$, $G_j(\overline{r_{A_j}}, r_{B_j}) \oplus r_j$, and $G_j(\overline{r_{A_j}}, \overline{r_{B_j}}) \oplus r_j$. Hence, according to the definition of the evaluation phase, the players specify the two cards representing $G_j(v_{A_i}, v_{B_j}) \oplus r_j$, which is the desired conclusion.

Remark that the evaluation phase leaks no information about the initial state I. During the evaluation phase, $2(n + g - m)$ cards become open in total, so the players know $n + g - m$ Boolean values. However, due to $n + g - m$ pile-scramble shuffles in the garbling phase, there is enough randomness in F and X to hide the secret values. This property can be viewed as the counterpart of the obliviousness property in garbled schemes.

Example. Here we demonstrate the evaluation phase for the example given by the circuit in Fig. 2. First, the players open all cards in X. Suppose the result is:

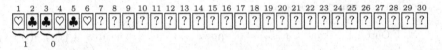

The next step is evaluating gate 4 with inputs 1 and 0. The evaluation protocol picks the third committed value from $\mathsf{a}(4)$ and opens it.

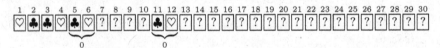

Similarly, gate 5 is evaluated with inputs 0 and 0, opening the first committed value from $\mathsf{a}(5)$.

In the final step of evaluating gate 6 with inputs 0 and 1, the players choose the second committed value from $\mathsf{a}(6)$ and output it as $Y := \boxed{?}^{25}\boxed{?}^{26}$.

Let us check the correctness of this case. As discussed in Sect. 3.3, the garbling phase randomizes the circuit semantics using five random Boolean values r_i. The values revealed during the evaluation phase satisfy the following:

$$x_1 \oplus r_1 = 1, \quad x_2 \oplus r_2 = 0, \quad x_3 \oplus r_3 = 0, \quad (\overline{r_1} \wedge r_2) \oplus r_4 = 0, \quad (r_3 \oplus r_4) \oplus r_5 = 1.$$

In addition, Y is a commitment of $r_4 \vee \overline{r_5}$. Accordingly, we have the following:

$$r_4 \vee \overline{r_5} = r_4 \vee (r_3 \oplus r_4) = (\overline{r_1} \wedge r_2) \vee (r_3 \oplus (\overline{r_1} \wedge r_2)) = (x_1 \wedge x_2) \vee (x_3 \oplus (x_1 \wedge x_2)),$$

which is the desired output.

3.5   Card-Based Protocols for Standard Garbling Scheme

This section introduces card-based protocols for computing the functionalities in Sect. 2.3 to investigate the relation to the standard garbling schemes. By making some modifications to the protocols in the previous sections, we can define a card-based garbled circuit scheme suitable for the original garbling scheme definition. In this case, our scheme requires $4n + 8g + 2m$ cards in total and one shuffle each in Gb, Enc and Dec, respectively. On the other hand, this scheme allows us to split the computational procedure into two parts that depend only on f or x, respectively. Hereafter, let XOR denote the functionality for computing the element-wise XOR of two decks in a committed form. Using the protocol proposed in [18], XOR can be computed with only one shuffle.

First, we define a protocol for the garbling phase Gb. The initial state consists of $4n+8g+2m$ face-down cards and is defined as the output of $\mathsf{Init}(\mathbf{0}, f)$ followed by m commitments of 0, where $\mathbf{0}$ denotes the $2n$ cards consisting of n commitments of 0. The protocol computes CardGb on the first $2n + 8g$ cards. Then, executes additional m pile-scramble shuffles for each $i \in$ Outputs as follows.

$$(\mathsf{PileShuffle}, \boldsymbol{I}^{(i,1)} \parallel \{6g + 2m + 2i - 1\}, \boldsymbol{I}^{(i,2)} \parallel \{6g + 2m + 2i\})$$

Finally, the protocol outputs the first $2n$ cards as e, the next $8g$ cards as F, and the last $2m$ cards as f. Note that the additional m pile-scramble shuffles are commutative with each other and also with the other $n + g - m$ shuffles, so all the required pile-scramble shuffles can be combined into one shuffle.

The rest part is straightforward. We can define a protocol for the encoding phase $\mathsf{Enc}(e, x)$ as simply computing XOR of e and the commitment of x. Similarly, our protocol for the decoding phase $\mathsf{Dec}(d, Y)$ simply computes XOR of d and Y, opens the results and outputs the Boolean values. The evaluation phase Eval is the same as CardEval.

It is easy to verify the correctness and obliviousness of this scheme. The proof is similar to the case of the CardGb and CardEval protocols. In addition, this protocol provides the counterpart of the privacy property in garbling schemes. This follows from the fact that the obliviousness proof in Sect. 3.4 leaks no information on x in an information-theoretic sense.

4   Conclusion

Shinagawa and Nuida [24] showed a surprising result that any Boolean function can be securely computed using only one shuffle by combining card-based cryptography with Yao's garbled circuit technique. Their protocol requires $2n + 24g$ cards, where g is the number of gates and n is the number of function inputs. This paper improved upon this existing approach by introducing an XOR shuffle technique that helps to reduce the number of required cards. Consequently, we showed that, instead of having $2n + 24g$ cards, only $2n + 8g$ cards are sufficient for constructing a single-shuffle protocol.

Acknowledgements. This work was supported by JSPS KAKENHI Grant Numbers JP21H05052, JP21K11881, and JST, CREST Grant Number JPMJCR22M1, Japan.

References

1. Attrapadung, N., et al.: Oblivious linear group actions and applications. In: Vigna, G., Shi, E. (eds.) ACM CCS 2021, pp. 630–650. ACM Press (2021). https://doi.org/10.1145/3460120.3484584
2. Beaver, D., Micali, S., Rogaway, P.: The round complexity of secure protocols (extended abstract). In: 22nd ACM STOC, pp. 503–513. ACM Press (1990). https://doi.org/10.1145/100216.100287
3. Bellare, M., Hoang, V.T., Rogaway, P.: Foundations of garbled circuits. In: Yu, T., Danezis, G., Gligor, V.D. (eds.) ACM CCS 2012, pp. 784–796. ACM Press (2012). https://doi.org/10.1145/2382196.2382279
4. Boer, B.: More efficient match-making and satisfiability *The Five Card Trick*. In: Quisquater, J.-J., Vandewalle, J. (eds.) EUROCRYPT 1989. LNCS, vol. 434, pp. 208–217. Springer, Heidelberg (1990). https://doi.org/10.1007/3-540-46885-4_23
5. Haga, R., Hayashi, Y., Miyahara, D., Mizuki, T.: Card-minimal protocols for three-input functions with standard playing cards. In: AFRICACRYPT 2022. LNCS, vol. 13503, pp. 448–468. Springer, Cham (2022)
6. Heather, J., Schneider, S., Teague, V.: Cryptographic protocols with everyday objects. Formal Aspects Comput. **26**(1), 37–62 (2014). https://doi.org/10.1007/s00165-013-0274-7
7. Ishikawa, R., Chida, E., Mizuki, T.: Efficient card-based protocols for generating a hidden random permutation without fixed points. In: Calude, C.S., Dinneen, M.J. (eds.) UCNC 2015. LNCS, vol. 9252, pp. 215–226. Springer, Cham (2015). https://doi.org/10.1007/978-3-319-21819-9_16
8. Isuzugawa, R., Miyahara, D., Mizuki, T.: Zero-knowledge proof protocol for Cryptarithmetic using dihedral cards. In: Kostitsyna, I., Orponen, P. (eds.) UCNC 2021. LNCS, vol. 12984, pp. 51–67. Springer, Cham (2021). https://doi.org/10.1007/978-3-030-87993-8_4
9. Kastner, J., Koch, A., Walzer, S., Miyahara, D., Hayashi, Y., Mizuki, T., Sone, H.: The minimum number of cards in practical card-based protocols. In: Takagi, T., Peyrin, T. (eds.) ASIACRYPT 2017. LNCS, vol. 10626, pp. 126–155. Springer, Cham (2017). https://doi.org/10.1007/978-3-319-70700-6_5
10. Koch, A., Schrempp, M., Kirsten, M.: Card-based cryptography meets formal verification. New Gener. Comput. **39**(1), 115–158 (2021). https://doi.org/10.1007/s00354-020-00120-0
11. Koch, A., Walzer, S., Härtel, K.: Card-based cryptographic protocols using a minimal number of cards. In: Iwata, T., Cheon, J.H. (eds.) ASIACRYPT 2015. LNCS, vol. 9452, pp. 783–807. Springer, Heidelberg (2015). https://doi.org/10.1007/978-3-662-48797-6_32
12. Koyama, H., Miyahara, D., Mizuki, T., Sone, H.: A secure three-input AND protocol with a standard deck of minimal cards. In: Santhanam, R., Musatov, D. (eds.) CSR 2021. LNCS, vol. 12730, pp. 242–256. Springer, Cham (2021). https://doi.org/10.1007/978-3-030-79416-3_14
13. Kuzuma, T., Toyoda, K., Miyahara, D., Mizuki, T.: Card-based single-shuffle protocols for secure multiple-input AND and XOR computations. In: ASIA Public-Key Cryptography, pp. 51–58. ACM, NY (2022). https://doi.org/10.1145/3494105.3526236
14. Miyahara, D., Ueda, I., Hayashi, Y., Mizuki, T., Sone, H.: Analyzing execution time of card-based protocols. In: Stepney, S., Verlan, S. (eds.) UCNC 2018. LNCS, vol. 10867, pp. 145–158. Springer, Cham (2018). https://doi.org/10.1007/978-3-319-92435-9_11

15. Mizuki, T., Asiedu, I.K., Sone, H.: Voting with a logarithmic number of cards. In: Mauri, G., Dennunzio, A., Manzoni, L., Porreca, A.E. (eds.) UCNC 2013. LNCS, vol. 7956, pp. 162–173. Springer, Heidelberg (2013). https://doi.org/10.1007/978-3-642-39074-6_16
16. Mizuki, T., Kumamoto, M., Sone, H.: The five-card trick can be done with four cards. In: Wang, X., Sako, K. (eds.) ASIACRYPT 2012. LNCS, vol. 7658, pp. 598–606. Springer, Heidelberg (2012). https://doi.org/10.1007/978-3-642-34961-4_36
17. Mizuki, T., Shizuya, H.: A formalization of card-based cryptographic protocols via abstract machine. Int. J. Inf. Secur. 13(1), 15–23 (2013). https://doi.org/10.1007/s10207-013-0219-4
18. Mizuki, T., Sone, H.: Six-card secure AND and four-card secure XOR. In: Deng, X., Hopcroft, J.E., Xue, J. (eds.) FAW 2009. LNCS, vol. 5598, pp. 358–369. Springer, Heidelberg (2009). https://doi.org/10.1007/978-3-642-02270-8_36
19. Nishida, T., Hayashi, Y., Mizuki, T., Sone, H.: Card-based protocols for any boolean function. In: Jain, R., Jain, S., Stephan, F. (eds.) TAMC 2015. LNCS, vol. 9076, pp. 110–121. Springer, Cham (2015). https://doi.org/10.1007/978-3-319-17142-5_11
20. Ruangwises, S., Itoh, T.: Physical ZKP for connected spanning subgraph: applications to bridges puzzle and other problems. In: Kostitsyna, I., Orponen, P. (eds.) UCNC 2021. LNCS, vol. 12984, pp. 149–163. Springer, Cham (2021). https://doi.org/10.1007/978-3-030-87993-8_10
21. Ruangwises, S., Itoh, T.: Securely computing the n-variable equality function with 2n cards. Theor. Comput. Sci. 887, 99–110 (2021). https://doi.org/10.1016/j.tcs.2021.07.007
22. Shikata, H., Toyoda, K., Miyahara, D., Mizuki, T.: Card-minimal protocols for symmetric boolean functions of more than seven inputs. In: ICTAC 2022. LNCS, vol. 13572, pp. 388–406. Springer, Cham (2022). https://doi.org/10.1007/978-3-031-17715-6_25
23. Shinagawa, K., Mizuki, T.: The six-card trick: secure computation of three-input equality. In: Lee, K. (ed.) ICISC 2018. LNCS, vol. 11396, pp. 123–131. Springer, Cham (2019). https://doi.org/10.1007/978-3-030-12146-4_8
24. Shinagawa, K., Nuida, K.: A single shuffle is enough for secure card-based computation of any boolean circuit. Discret. Appl. Math. 289, 248–261 (2021). https://doi.org/10.1016/j.dam.2020.10.013
25. Toyoda, K., Miyahara, D., Mizuki, T.: Another use of the five-card trick: card-minimal secure three-input majority function evaluation. In: Adhikari, A., Küsters, R., Preneel, B. (eds.) INDOCRYPT 2021. LNCS, vol. 13143, pp. 536–555. Springer, Cham (2021). https://doi.org/10.1007/978-3-030-92518-5_24

Modelling and Evaluating Restricted ESNs

Chester Wringe[1], Susan Stepney[1]($\boxtimes$), and Martin A. Trefzer[2]

[1] Department of Computer Science, University of York, York, UK
{chester.wringe,susan.stepney}@york.ac.uk
[2] School of Physics, Engineering and Technology, University of York, York, UK
martin.trefzer@york.ac.uk

Abstract. We investigate various methods of combining Echo State Networks (ESNs), including a method that we dub *Restricted ESNs*. We provide a notation for describing Restricted ESNs, and use it to benchmark a standard ESN against restricted ones. We investigate two methods to keep the weight matrix density consistent when comparing a Restricted ESN to a standard one, which we call "overall consistency" and "patch consistency". We benchmark restricted ESNs on NARMA10 and the sunspot prediction benchmark, and find that restricted ESNs perform similarly to standard ones. We present some application scenarios in which restricted ESNs may offer advantages over standard ESNs.

Keywords: Reservoir Computing · Hierarchical ESNs · Reservoir of Reservoirs

1 Introduction

Artificial Neural Networks (ANNs) are an unconventional computational model inspired by the brain. ANNs have non-linear summing nodes connected by weighted edges, where the edge weights are trained to give the desired outputs. While training methods such as backpropagation are used in feed-forward Neural Networks, they are costly to use in recurrent NNs (RNNs).

Reservoir Computing in general [13,15,21], and the Echo State Network (ESN) random RNN model in particular, provides a solution to the RNN training problem: instead of training the recurrent, inner weights, these are randomly initialised, and only the weights of the edges to the output nodes are trained. This provides an efficient training method, and also allows the inner network (or "reservoir") to be treated as a black box. One may use any material or substrate as an *in materio* reservoir, provided it has sufficiently complex dynamics [3,6,9].

Our long term aim is to scale up the capacity of *in materio* reservoirs, by combining several reservoirs together. Combining reservoirs has some potential advantages: it allows us to more fully exploit substrates whose computational capacity does not scale well as the size of the device increases [7], and to exploit heterogeneous substrates with different properties for more complex tasks, particularly using multiple timescales.

D. Genova and J. Kari (Eds.): UCNC 2023, LNCS 14003, pp. 186–201, 2023.
https://doi.org/10.1007/978-3-031-34034-5_13

Here, we introduce a notation for describing a form of reservoir combination. We perform some experiments using the ESN model, to compare performances of multiple connected small reservoirs against a single large one. We hope that this will form a basis to experiment on heterogeneous reservoirs in future work.

2 Background

Two ways of combining multiple reservoir computers emerge in the literature. The first, which we call restricted ESNs (Sect. 2.1) is the subject of our experiments here. The second, which we call modular reservoirs (Sect. 2.2), are models of larger systems that contain within them multiple reservoir computers, each with their own set of inputs and individually trained output weights.

2.1 Restricted ESNs

A *restricted ESN* has the same overall structure as a single ESN, with one input layer and one output layer. Its internal reservoir (a random RNN in the ESN model) has its overall state partitioned into "subreservoirs" with typical RNN connections within a subreservoir, and *restricted* connections between the sub-reservoirs. There are several models in the literature that follow this structure.

The dual-reservoir network (DRN) [20] connects two subreservoirs in the network with an "unsupervised encoder", for which the weights are chosen using Principal Component Analysis (PCA). Triefenbach et al. have a bidirectional dual-reservoir model [28], which consists of two subreservoirs running in parallel, with one of the subreservoirs receiving the inputs in chronological order, and the other receiving its inputs in reverse chronological order.

The Reservoir of Reservoirs (RoR) [5] is a model with dense connections within each subreservoir, and sparse random connections between subreservoirs. Two models are investigated: RoR, where the inputs are sent to only one subreservoir, and RoR-IA, where the inputs are sent to all of the subreservoirs. The multilayered echo state machine (ML-ESM) [22] arranges the subreservoirs sequentially, with each subreservoir fully connected to its neighbouring subreservoirs with fixed weights.

The Reservoir with Random Static Projections (R^{2}SP) [2] and the ϕESN [10] are both models that combine ESNs with an Extreme Learning Machine. There are several deep-ESN models [4,11,12,19], based on deep learning networks. In these, the subreservoirs are arranged sequentially, and the inputs are sent only to the first subreservoir. They are compared to the grouped-ESN, where the subreservoirs are arranged in parallel, and deep-ESN Input-to-All (deep-ESN IA), a deep-ESN with inputs sent to every subreservoir.

The scale-free highly clustered ESN (SHESN) [8] has each subreservoir connected to every other subreservoir by "backbone nodes", of which there is one in every subreservoir. The hierarchically clustered ESN (HESN) [16] builds on the SHESN by allowing several backbone nodes per subreservoir, and by making them randomly connected as opposed to fully connected. the HESN and the modular ESN [24] are the closest models to the ones we study here.

The Decoupled ESN (DESN) [29] is a restricted ESN that tackles multi-timescale tasks by decoupling certain sections of the inner state from each other using a lateral inhibition unit.

2.2   Modular ESNs

A *modular* ESN typically comprises multiple individual reservoirs, each with its own input layer and trained output weights, connected in a variety of ways.

The Dynamic Feature Discoverer (DFD) [14] is a Modular Reservoir based on Deep Belief Networks, with the ESNs being components of a larger system. The ESNs may be replaced by other components, such as Extreme Learning Machines. The ESNs are arranged hierarchically, with each ESN being fed the standard input as well as the outputs of all the ESNs lower in the hierarchy. This hierarchy also allows the DFD to contain separate timescales, such that each ESN in the hierarchy runs more slowly than the one previous.

Modular ESNs are also used in acoustic modelling [27,28]. This model is based on the Hidden Markov Model, with the different ESNs with different timescales arranged linearly and hierarchically, with each reservoir processing dynamics that are slower than the previous ones.

The ConvESN [18] is a modular reservoir model based on Convolutional Neural Networks. The reservoirs are arranged in parallel and analyse dynamics at different timescales. The trained outputs of the ESN are then joined together in a convolutional layer.

3   A Restricted ESN Model

Here we investigate restricted ESNs. This provides a model that should allow for the simulation of *in materio* subreservoirs implemented with different materials, with some physical interconnect between subreservoirs. We introduce a notation that can be used to describe a variety of possible restrictions that may occur in practice. This section is not intended to introduce a new model, but instead to describe all of the models reviewed in Sect. 2.1.

3.1   The Standard ESN Model

The classic ESN model [13,15] is a Random Recurrent Neural Network where only the output weights are trained. A standard ESN can be described by a set of state update equations, three state vectors, and three weight matrices (corresponding to input, internal, and output states and weights).

At time t, the state of the ESN is described by the input vector $\mathbf{u}(t)$, the internal state vector $\mathbf{x}(t)$, and the output vector $\mathbf{v}(t)$. The connections between the nodes represented by the vectors are described by the weight matrices $\mathbf{W}_u$ for the random input weights, $\mathbf{W}$ for the random internal weights, and $\mathbf{W}_v$ for the trained output weights (Fig. 1).

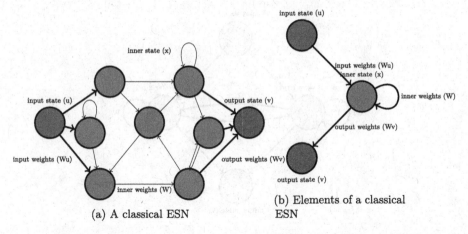

(a) A classical ESN

(b) Elements of a classical ESN

Fig. 1. (a) an example of a standard ESN with 7 nodes; (b) an abstraction of its different elements. The ESN takes one or more inputs **u**, which are sent to the inner state **x** through weighted input edges $\mathbf{W}_u$. The weights within the inner state, **W**, allow recurrent edges and are randomly initialised. The output state **v** receives the inner state through edges with trained weights $\mathbf{W}_v$.

The update equations for the ESN are [26]:

$$\mathbf{x}(t+1) = f(\mathbf{W}_u \mathbf{u}(t) + \mathbf{W}\mathbf{x}(t)) \tag{1}$$
$$\mathbf{v}(t+1) = \mathbf{W}_v \mathbf{x}(t)$$

where f is a nonlinear function, typically the hyperbolic tangent tanh(.).

3.2 Restricting the Standard Model

The restricted ESN is a variant of the standard ESN model that partitions the internal reservoir state into several smaller subreservoirs. This division may be interpreted as restrictions on the connections of the internal state, and thus on the internal weight matrix **W**. The state vector **x** of a restricted ESN with n subreservoirs is the concatenation of the subreservoir state vectors:

$$\mathbf{x} = \begin{pmatrix} \mathbf{x}_1 \\ \mathbf{x}_2 \\ \dots \\ \mathbf{x}_n \end{pmatrix} \tag{2}$$

where $\mathbf{x}_i$ is the state of the subreservoir i. The weight matrix is the concatenation of internal subreservoir weight matrices, and weight matrices describing the connections between subreservoirs:

$$\mathbf{W} = \begin{bmatrix} \mathbf{W}_1 & \mathbf{B}_{1,2} & \dots & \mathbf{B}_{1,n} \\ \mathbf{B}_{2,1} & \mathbf{W}_2 & \dots & \mathbf{B}_{2,n} \\ \dots & & & \\ \mathbf{B}_{n,1} & \mathbf{B}_{n,2} & \dots & \mathbf{W}_n \end{bmatrix} \tag{3}$$

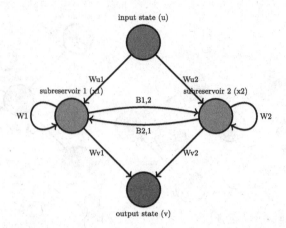

Fig. 2. Elements of a restricted ESN with 2 subreservoirs, 1 and 2, showing the partitioned state and components of the internal weight matrix.

where $\mathbf{W}_i$ is the weight matrix that represents the connections within subreservoir i, and $\mathbf{B}_{i,j}$ represents the connections from subreservoir i to subreservoir j. The output and input weight matrices are unchanged. These elements are illustrated in Fig. 2. Equation 1 still defines the transfer from the overall state at time t to time $t+1$.

These submatrices may each have their own, independent properties such as connection density D, the proportion of non-zero values. Here we consider uniform subreservoirs and connectivities, and denote the average density of the subreservoirs as D_W, and the average density between subreservoirs as D_B. N_i is the number of nodes in subreservoir i; $N = \sum_{i=1}^{n} N_i$ is the number of nodes in the entire state.

4   Benchmarking

We are developing this model in order to provide a means to join *in materio* reservoirs with different properties and timescales. Before investigating such heterogeneous systems, however, we need to investigate homogeneous restricted reservoirs, to determine the effect of restriction alone. Does a restricted ESN (with its N nodes partitioned into subreservoirs) perform significantly differently from a standard ESN of the same dimension (a single reservoir of N nodes)?

In order to test this question, we must determine what constitutes a fair comparison between a restricted and a standard ESN with the same number of nodes. We perform a comparison of the two models over a range of different sizes, on two common benchmark tasks.

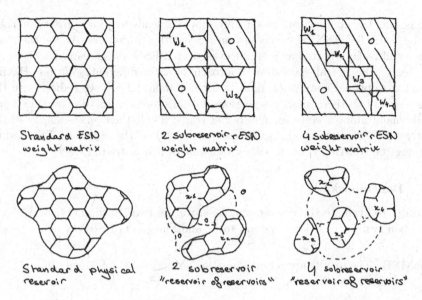

Fig. 3. Illustration of the patch-consistent argument made in the experiments. In this argument, we give each ESN an analogous reservoir made out of a physical substrate. To restrict the reservoir is to split the substrate up into smaller pieces, and connecting them loosely. Therefore, assuming a uniform density D across the standard reservoir, each subreservoir should have that same density $D_W = D$ within the subreservoir, and a lower density D_B between subreservoirs.

4.1 Experimental Setup

We wish to discover whether any difference in performance found is due merely to the architecture, or to some other parameter affected by the restriction.

We further wish to ensure that the standard and restricted ESN can each exhibit their best performance on the given task; however, what this entails is not obvious. In the case of the standard ESN, we may perform a simple search to find some "optimal" weight matrix density for the task. Given this optimised density, two possibilities present themselves for the Restricted ESN:

Patch-consistent Density. To describe this case, we take a physical analogy to describe the structure of the restricted ESN. If we see this restriction as combining multiple physical (material) reservoirs together, then restricting a standard reservoir may be analogous to splitting a material up into different sections, and joining those sections together, in order to use smaller quantities to emulate a larger reservoir. As such, we should keep the density within the subreservoirs consistent with the overall density of the standard ESN, with sparser connections between subreservoirs. This reasoning is illustrated in Fig. 3.

Overall-consistent Density. While the patch-consistent approach follows from a physical material argument, it is not the only way to approach the issue of ensuring fair comparison, as such an approach leads to a lower overall density of the restricted ESN. If we choose an ESN with optimal density for the task, this could be interpreted as giving the restricted ESN a disadvantage.

Hence, the overall-consistent approach offers a different solution: Having found the optimal connection density for a standard ESN, we redistribute the edges so that there are more connections within subreservoirs than outside them, while maintaining a constant number of edges. Thus, the overall density of the restricted ESN remains the same as the density of the standard ESN, while keeping the constraints on topology that makes it a restricted ESN.

4.2 Benchmarks

In order to evaluate the reservoir models, we use two benchmarks, NARMA10 (an open system, or driven system, task) and Sunspots (a closed system task).

NRMSE. The results are reported as the Normalised Root Mean Square Error [17] evaluated over 50 runs.

$$NRMSE(\hat{\mathbf{v}}, \mathbf{v}) = \sqrt{\frac{\langle (\hat{\mathbf{v}} - \mathbf{v})^2 \rangle}{\langle (\hat{\mathbf{v}} - \langle \hat{\mathbf{v}} \rangle)^2 \rangle}} \qquad (4)$$

where $\hat{\mathbf{v}}$ is the desired output; $\mathbf{v}$ is the observed output; $\langle x \rangle$ is the mean $\frac{1}{N} \sum_{i=1}^{N} x_i$.

NARMA10. The Normalised Auto-Regressive Moving Average (NARMA) tasks are a family of benchmark tasks [1] frequently used as a reservoir computing benchmark. Here, we use NARMA10, the system with a memory of 10 timesteps:

$$x(t+1) = 0.3x(t) + 0.05x(t) \sum_{i=0}^{9} x(t-i) + 1.5u(t-9) + 0.1 \qquad (5)$$

The input at time t, $u(t)$, is uniformly sampled between 0 and 0.5. We use a training length of 3000 data points and washout and testing lengths of 1000 data points each.

Sunspots. The Sunspots benchmark is a dynamical systems benchmark task that involves predicting the next output of the dataset based on the previous outputs. This task has a long history of being used in machine learning generally [30], as well as reservoir computing specifically [23, 25, 26].

For this experiment, we use the monthly readings from the Zurich dataset[1], from January 1749 to December 1983. As the existing data limits our input lengths, the training length for this experiment is 1500 data points, with a washout length of 500 data points, and a testing length of 820 data points.

---

[1] https://machinelearningmastery.com/time-series-datasets-for-machine-learning/.

Algorithm 1 Optimal density for standard ESN

```
 1: procedure GRIDSEARCH(start, end, step, N)
 2:     d := start                                            ▷ search over densities
 3:     for d in (start, end, step) do
 4:         create ESN with density d
 5:         testsum := 0
 6:         for j in range N do
 7:             observed output := test ESN on benchmark
 8:             testsum += NRMSE(desired output, observed output)
 9:         means[d] := testsum / N
10:     return means

11: coarse := GRIDSEARCH(0, 1, 0.1, 50)
12: d₁ := density of the smallest value in coarse
13: d₂ := density of the smaller of d₁'s neighbours
14: fine := GRIDSEARCH(d₁, d₂, 0.01, 50)
15: return min(fine)
```

Density. To find the optimal density D_O of the standard ESN, we use a two-level grid search (Algorithm 1).

For the patch-consistent rESN, the density within each subreservoir, D_W, is set equal to D_O, while a further two-level grid search is used to find the optimal density between subreservoirs, D_B. In this case, the algorithm is modified to use a step of 0.025 for the first level, and 0.0025 for the second. A further constraint is placed on D_B that it should be less than $D_W/4$. (If no such constraint is set, then the optimal value for D_B is simply D_W.)

For the overall-consistent rESN, we introduce a parameter $f > 1$, where $D_B = D_W/f$. From this, we can derive D_B and D_W in terms of f, overall density D_O, and number of subreservoirs n (Appendix A). We then bound f using the inequality derived in Appendix B. Given an upper bound for possible f values, we then use a similar two-level grid search[2] to find the best f value for a reservoir of size N, density D_B, for the given benchmark.

Having found the optimal densities and distributions, we then evaluate the standard and restricted reservoirs against the task over 50 runs. The experiments are performed for ESNs of size $N \in [16, 64, 128, 256]$, and with 2 and 4 equal-sized subreservoir restricted ESNs respectively.

The densities used for each size for each task can be found in Tables 1, 2, 2 and 4. In the patch-consistent case, we can have a connection density D_B of 0.00. In this case there are no connections between subreservoirs, and the subreservoirs run unconnected in parallel.

---

[2] The grid search is modified to split the range of f into 10 and use that as the initial step, and then split the range between the optimal value and its neighbour into 10 for the secondary step.

Table 1. Densities used in the NARMA overall-consistent experiment

N	D_O	f (2 subreservoirs)	f (4 subreservoirs)
16	0.30	10.10	2.95
64	0.10	102.40	29.50
128	0.10	188.90	284.90
256	0.10	1310.92	981.60

Table 2. Densities used in the NARMA patch-consistent experiment

N	D_W	D_B (2 subreservoirs)	D_B (4 subreservoirs)
16	0.30	0.00	0.025
64	0.10	0.00	0.00
128	0.10	0.00	0.00
256	0.10	0.00	0.00

Table 3. Densities used in the Sunspots overall-consistent experiment

N	D_O	f (2 subreservoirs)	f (4 subreservoirs)
16	0.20	7.70	5.70
64	0.30	308.70	4.90
128	0.40	265.70	4.38
256	0.40^a	986.70	4.90

^{a} The ideal density, 0.89, is too high to distribute. The best density given these constraints is used instead, which leads to a worse performance of the standard reservoir.

Table 4. Densities used in the Sunspots patch-consistent experiment

	D_W	D_B (2 subreservoirs)	D_B (4 subreservoirs)
16	0.20	0.00	0.05
64	0.30	0.00	0.10
128	0.40	0.025	0.00
256	0.89	0.125	0.00

5 Results

5.1 NARMA10

In this task, the "optimal" density becomes consistent from 64 nodes onward at 0.1 (Tables 1, 2). We note quite a variation in the results across different sizes, as this task is performed better with a larger ESN.

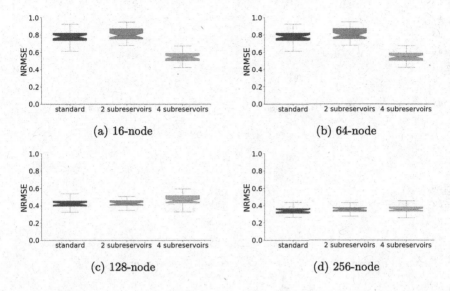

(a) 16-node   (b) 64-node

(c) 128-node   (d) 256-node

Fig. 4. The results for the NARMA overall–consistent experiments.

Overall Consistency. The results as summarised in the boxplots (Fig. 4) show noticeably better behaviour for the 4–subreservoir ESN in the 16 and 64 node case. There are no significant differences in results between the standard and 2–subreservoir ESNs of these sizes, however.

For 128 and 256 nodes, the results are similar across the standard and restricted ESNs.

The significantly better behaviour for the 4-subreservoir ESNs in the smaller cases might be explained through the search for an optimal structure while keeping the optimal density.

This may also explain why this behaviour is not as obvious in larger-sized ESNs. When searching for the optimal configuration of the restricted ESN, we find a maximal f-value, and then perform a two-level grid search between 1 and this maximum. The maximal f-value is smaller with smaller ESNs and with more subreservoirs, meaning that the search in these cases would be finer, and hence more likely to find a good result.

We hypothesise that there is therefore a greater chance of finding a good configuration in these experiments. It may also follow that we could replicate these better results for larger ESNs by performing a more thorough search.

Patch Consistency. In these experiments (Fig. 5) we can observe that, for 16 and 64 nodes, the 4–subreservoir case leads to a worse performance, although the 2–subreservoir case is similar to the standard one. In the 128 and 256 node cases, we observe similar results across standard and restricted ESNs.

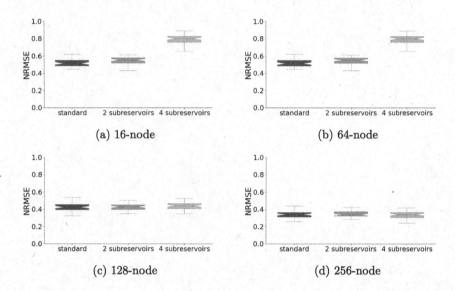

Fig. 5. The results for the NARMA patch–consistent experiments.

Our hypothesis is that the poor results for the 16 and 64 nodes 4–subreservoir cases are due to the low density of these ESNs. In the patch-consistent case, the density goes down as the number of subreservoirs increases. As the density is a probability, the lower the density, the higher chance there is of not having an edge between any two nodes. This means that, for very low numbers of nodes, we may generate nearly (or completely) empty weight matrices. Future work may compare these very-low-connectivity ESNs to Extreme Learning Machines (ELMs).

5.2   Sunspots

Unlike in the NARMA experiments, we observe no consistent optimal density across reservoir sizes; instead the optimal density increases with reservoir size (Tables 3, 4). We also observe that there is much less variation in performance across different ESN sizes (the task is relatively easy). It follows that any effect that restricting the ESN has will also, for the most part, be much smaller.

Both of these facts are likely due to the fact that sunspot prediction is an easier task than NARMA10. Despite less variation, however, the trends appear to be similar to the ones observed in the NARMA experiments.

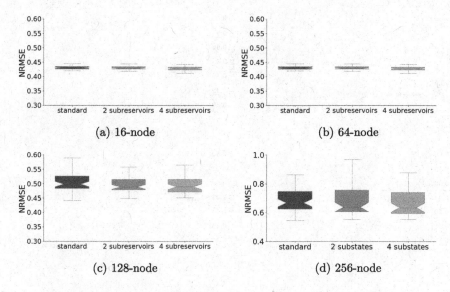

Fig. 6. The results for the sunspots overall–consistent experiments.

Overall Consistency. We observe (Fig. 6) little variation between the results from the standard and restricted ESNs, with the 4-subreservoir case being slightly better in the smaller sizes. However, as noted in Table 3, the ideal density in the 256-node case cannot be redistributed in an overall-consistent manner. Thus, while the restricted reservoirs in this case perform the same as their standard counterpart, this is not the optimal performance of a 256-node reservoir in this task, as observed in Fig. 6d.

Patch Consistency. We observe (Fig. 7) similar results across configurations from 64 nodes onward. We observe poor performance in the 16 node, 4–subreservoir case. This is, once again, likely due to the small size and low density leading to empty weight matrices.

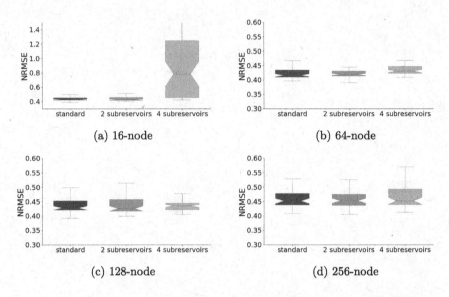

(a) 16-node   (b) 64-node

(c) 128-node   (d) 256-node

Fig. 7. The results for the Sunspots patch–consistent experiments.

6   Discussion and Conclusions

In smaller-sized ESNs, there seems to be significant variation of results incurred from restricting ESNs with overall or patch consistency. However, this difference disappears once each subreservoir is reasonably large (for the NARMA and sunspots tasks, this being 32 nodes.)

The more physically realistic of these models is the patch-consistent density. This model also has the advantage of not placing any constraints on the initial standard reservoir's density. However, it is also the one with the more significant differences in performance in smaller sizes. When modelling these reservoirs, work may be needed to determine what makes a given subreservoir "reasonably large". We will therefore focus on these larger reservoirs in our future work.

Nevertheless, these results indicate that the restricted ESN model, using either overall or patch consistency, does not have a detrimental impact on performance when compared to a single large ESN. Hence restricted ESNs can form a suitable basis for building models of scaled-up reservoirs, heterogeneous reservoirs comprising subreservoirs of different materials, and for working on multiple timescale models.

Acknowledgement. This work was made possible by PhD studentship funding from the Computer Science Department of the University of York.

A   Calculating D_W for the Overall-Consistent Case

Given an ESN with N nodes and an average density $0 \leq D \leq 1$, we wish to restrict that ESN to have n subreservoirs of equal size; we assume n divides N. We set the density within the subreservoirs, D_W, to be greater than the density outside the subreservoirs by a factor of f, that is, $D_W = fD_B$.

In a restricted ESN with n subreservoirs, each of size N/n, there are n regions in the edge matrix $\mathbf{W}$ of size $(N/n)^2$ with density D_W, and a further $n^2 - n$ regions also of size $(N/n)^2$ with density D_B.

Hence the average density D of such a restricted ESN is:

$$D = \frac{nD_W + (n^2 - n)D_B}{n^2} \tag{6}$$

Substituting $D_W = fD_B$, and rearranging to get an expression for D_B in terms of D, we get:

$$D_B = \frac{Dn}{f + n - 1} \tag{7}$$

Once D_B is known, we also have D_W from $D_W = fD_B$.

B   Optimising f

In order to find the best possible restricted ESN within our constraints, we optimise over the parameter f. However, we must somehow limit our search space.

In the restricted ESN, we want D_B to be strictly less than D_W (less dense connections than subreservoirs); therefore, $f > 1$.

To find an upper bound, we assume that every subreservoir is connected to every other subreservoir, that is, every connection weight matrix $\mathbf{B}_{i,j}$ has at least one entry. This requires $D_B \geq (n/N)^2$. (In the experiments, the weight matrices are generated probabilistically, so when close to this density limit, it may be the case that there is not an edge between all subreservoirs.)

Rearranging Eq. 7 gives:

$$f = \frac{Dn}{D_B} - n + 1 \tag{8}$$

The lower limit on D_B gives an upper limit on f:

$$f \leq \frac{N^2 D}{n} - n + 1 \tag{9}$$

We also have an upper limit on the derived density, $D_W \leq 1$ (equality implies there are no zero elements in the relevant weight matrix). Substituting for D_W in Eq. 7 gives:

$$\frac{fDn}{f + n - 1} = D_W \leq 1 \tag{10}$$

Rearranging gives another upper limit on f:

$$f \leq \frac{n-1}{Dn-1} \tag{11}$$

Hence we have the upper and lower bounds on f:

$$1 < f \leq \min\left(\frac{N^2 D}{n} - n + 1, \frac{n-1}{Dn-1}\right) \tag{12}$$

References

1. Atiya, A.F., Parlos, A.G.: New results on recurrent network training: unifying the algorithms and accelerating convergence. IEEE TNN **11**(3), 697–709 (2000)
2. Butcher, J.B., Verstraeten, D., Schrauwen, B., Haycock, P.W.: Extending reservoir computing with random static projections. In: ESANN 2010, pp. 303–308 (2010)
3. Caluwaerts, K., D'Haene, M., Verstraeten, D., Schrauwen, B.: Locomotion without a brain: physical reservoir computing in tensegrity structures. Artif. Life **19**(1), 35–66 (2013)
4. Canaday, D., Pomerance, A., Gauthier, D.J.: Model-free control of dynamical systems with deep reservoir computing. J. Phys. Complex. **2**(3), 035025 (2021)
5. Dale, M.: Neuroevolution of hierarchical reservoir computers. In: GECCO 2018, pp. 410–417. ACM (2018)
6. Dale, M., Miller, J.F., Stepney, S., Trefzer, M.A.: Evolving carbon nanotube reservoir computers. In: Amos, M., Condon, A. (eds.) UCNC 2016. LNCS, vol. 9726, pp. 49–61. Springer, Cham (2016). https://doi.org/10.1007/978-3-319-41312-9_5
7. Dale, M., O'Keefe, S., Sebald, A., Stepney, S., Trefzer, M.A.: Computing with magnetic thin films: using film geometry to improve dynamics. In: Kostitsyna, I., Orponen, P. (eds.) UCNC 2021. LNCS, vol. 12984, pp. 19–34. Springer, Cham (2021). https://doi.org/10.1007/978-3-030-87993-8_2
8. Deng, Z., Zhang, Y.: Collective behavior of a small-world recurrent neural system with scale-free distribution. IEEE TNN **18**(5), 1364–1375 (2007)
9. Fernando, C., Sojakka, S.: Pattern recognition in a bucket. In: Banzhaf, W., Ziegler, J., Christaller, T., Dittrich, P., Kim, J.T. (eds.) ECAL 2003. LNCS (LNAI), vol. 2801, pp. 588–597. Springer, Heidelberg (2003). https://doi.org/10.1007/978-3-540-39432-7_63
10. Gallicchio, C., Micheli, A.: Architectural and Markovian factors of echo state networks. Neural Netw. **24**(5), 440–456 (2011)
11. Gallicchio, C., Micheli, A.: Echo state property of deep reservoir computing networks. Cognit. Comput. **9**(3), 337–350 (2017)
12. Gallicchio, C., Micheli, A., Pedrelli, L.: Deep reservoir computing: a critical experimental analysis. Neurocomputing **268**, 87–99 (2017)
13. Jaeger, H.: The "echo state" approach to analysing and training recurrent neural networks - with an erratum note. Bonn, Germany: German National Research Center for Information Technology GMD Technical Report **148**(34), 13 (2001)
14. Jaeger, H.: Discovering multiscale dynamical features with hierarchical echo state networks. Technical report TR-10, Jacobs University Bremen (2007)
15. Jaeger, H., Maass, W., Principe, J.: Special issue on echo state networks and liquid state machines. Neural Netw. **20**(3), 287–289 (2007)

16. Jarvis, S., Rotter, S., Egert, U.: Extending stability through hierarchical clusters in echo state networks. Front. Neuroinform. 4 (2010)
17. Lukoševičius, M.: A practical guide to applying echo state networks. In: Montavon, G., Orr, G.B., Müller, K.-R. (eds.) Neural Networks: Tricks of the Trade. LNCS, vol. 7700, pp. 659–686. Springer, Heidelberg (2012). https://doi.org/10.1007/978-3-642-35289-8_36
18. Ma, Q., Chen, E., Lin, Z., Yan, J., Yu, Z., Ng, W.W.Y.: Convolutional multi-timescale echo state network. IEEE Trans. Cybern. 51(3), 1613–1625 (2021)
19. Ma, Q., Shen, L., Cottrell, G.W.: Deep-ESN: a multiple projection-encoding hierarchical reservoir computing framework. arXiv:1711.05255 [cs.LG] (2017)
20. Ma, Q., Shen, L., Zhuang, W., Chen, J.: Decouple adversarial capacities with dual-reservoir network. In: Liu, D., Xie, S., Li, Y., Zhao, D., El-Alfy, E.-S.M. (eds.) ICONIP 2017. LNCS, vol. 10638, pp. 475–483. Springer, Cham (2017). https://doi.org/10.1007/978-3-319-70139-4_48
21. Maass, W., Natschläger, T., Markram, H.: Real-time computing without stable states. Neural Comput. 14(11), 2531–2560 (2002)
22. Malik, Z.K., Hussain, A., Wu, Q.J.: Multilayered echo state machine: a novel architecture and algorithm. IEEE Trans. Cybern. 47(4), 946–959 (2017)
23. Rodan, A., Tino, P.: Minimum complexity echo state network. IEEE TNN 22(1), 131–144 (2011)
24. Rodriguez, N., Izquierdo, E., Ahn, Y.Y.: Optimal modularity and memory capacity of neural reservoirs. Netw. Neurosci. 3(2), 551–566 (2019)
25. Schwenker, F., Labib, A.: Echo state networks and neural network ensembles to predict sunspots activity. In: ESANN 2009 (2009)
26. Stepney, S.: Non-instantaneous information transfer in physical reservoir computing. In: Kostitsyna, I., Orponen, P. (eds.) UCNC 2021. LNCS, vol. 12984, pp. 164–176. Springer, Cham (2021). https://doi.org/10.1007/978-3-030-87993-8_11
27. Triefenbach, F., Jalal, A., Schrauwen, B., Martens, J.P.: Phoneme recognition with large hierarchical reservoirs. Adv. Neural. Inf. Process. Syst. 23, 2307–2315 (2010)
28. Triefenbach, F., Jalalvand, A., Demuynck, K., Martens, J.P.: Acoustic modeling with hierarchical reservoirs. IEEE TASLP 21(11), 2439–2450 (2013)
29. Xue, Y., Yang, L., Haykin, S.: Decoupled echo state networks with lateral inhibition. Neural Netw. 20(3), 365–376 (2007)
30. Yule, G.U.: On a method of investigating periodicities in disturbed series, with special reference to Wolfer's sunspot numbers. Phil. Trans. Roy. Soc. A 226(636–646), 267–298 (1927)

Author Index

Printed in the United States
by Baker & Taylor Publisher Services